ANGLICAN CATHEDRALS
OUTSIDE THE BRITISH ISLES

ANGLICAN CATHEDRALS

OUTSIDE THE BRITISH ISLES

By

BASIL F. L. CLARKE

With a Foreword by

JOHN BETJEMAN

LONDON

S·P·C·K

1958

First published in 1958
S.P.C.K.
Holy Trinity Church
Marylebone Road
London, N.W.1

Printed in Great Britain by
William Clowes and Sons, Limited,
London and Beccles

CONTENTS

Figures in italics in the list below refer to the pages between which illustrations of the cathedrals appear.

The name of the diocese is given in brackets where it differs from that of the place.

Part I: General

1. INDIA, PAKISTAN, BURMA, AND CEYLON

vii

5. AFRICA, MISSIONARY DIOCESES

6. CANADA

9. NEW ZEALAND

10. MISSIONARY BISHOPRICS

11. AMERICA

12. EUROPE

13. CHINA

Part II

The Protestant Episcopal Church in the United States of America

22. EIGHTH PROVINCE (The Pacific)

23. OVERSEAS MISSIONARY DISTRICTS

ACKNOWLEDGEMENTS

Acknowledgement is made to the following for photographs used in this book, and the publishers would like to thank the Deans of Cathedrals who have helped by supplying photographs.

Associated Commercial Photographers Ltd.
Australian Department of the Interior
Sir Herbert Baker & Scott
Borneo Mission
J. Boyd Ellis
British Columbia and Yukon Church Aid Society
The Reverend R. Brownrigg
Dr Frank Cash
The Church Missionary Society
Colonial Portrait Studio
Courier Journal & Louisville Times
Del Ankers
Ellis Dudgeon
Editions d'Art Yvon
Galbraith
Gateway Film Productions
Gibbney Studios
Gibraltar Diocesan Office
A. Hansen Studio
E. O. Hoppé
Korean Mission
H. R. Lawley
Jack Lord
F. Maure
Moulin Studios

National Council New York Department of Promotion
National Film Board of Canada
National Publicity Studios, Wellington, N.Z.
High Commissioner for New Zealand
Amador Packer
Basil R. Pugin
C. E. Redman
Roberts Tobacco Co., Havana
Rose Stereograph Co.
Owen H. Sanders
K. R. Sanderson
J. Schick
Dr A. T. Schofield
N. S. Seaward
Singapore Press
Society for the Propagation of the Gospel
Sparrow Industrial Pictures Ltd.
Tasmania House
The Bishop of Taunton
Universities Mission to Central Africa
U.S. Information Service
Hilton Wilkinson
Wolfe Commercial Photo Service
Alan Yates

ACKNOWLEDGEMENTS

Acknowledgement is made to the following for photographs used in this book, and the publishers would like to thank the Deans of Cathedrals who have helped by supplying the photographs.

FOREWORD

I DOUBT if there is such a thing as an average Englishman. One would have to be smug and unenterprising indeed to glory in the adjective "average". But I suspect that the devil suggests to those of us who live in the British Isles and are nominal Anglicans that cathedrals of our communion abroad need not be taken very seriously. There are all too many faint hearts who think of an overseas diocese as a place where a few old colonels keep the flag flying and where the bishop is a glorified vicar with a medicine chest from which he can dispense to natives of the "mission boy" type. This book will come as a shock and encouragement to the faint-hearted. Our communion, as they will see, is far from an extension of the British raj abroad, but consists of flourishing and growing native churches.

All the same, with the best will in the world it is very difficult for those of us in the British Isles at any rate to form an idea of what these native churches are like as buildings. The photographs in missionary magazines and the illustrations in the lives of missionaries rarely show them, or else are so bad, being taken out of focus and on the slant with a box camera, that the building is a vague blur. Holy men are notoriously uninterested in aesthetics. Reading that admirable Quarterly Intercession Paper for the Church's Work Abroad which, if one lives long enough, covers the activity of every Anglican diocese, I have often wondered what "Our beautiful cathedral at Likoma" and "Our cathedral church at Belize" can be like. To one living in England a cathedral suggests an enormous building like Canterbury, Winchester, or York. Yet we know that a cathedral need not be large. It merely has to be the seat of a bishop. And those of us who know Ireland will let our imaginations go to the other extreme and imagine "Our beautiful cathedral at Likoma" or "Our cathedral church at Belize" as no more than a small chancel built of local material and only differing from the smallest country church in that it contains an episcopal throne.

A book which gives all Anglicans, whether Japanese, Chinese, Indian, African, American, or Eskimo, an idea of what the cathedrals other than those in the British Isles are like has been badly needed.

Some of the cathedrals are magnificent as architecture, particularly those of the Protestant Episcopal Church of America. Others are the small beginnings of a growing faith, like St Thomas's pro-cathedral at Car Nicobar, which is built of wood with a thatched roof. Large or small, they will encourage all of us in England by showing us we are members of a vast and increasing Church whose boundaries are neither racial nor political.

No more suitable author than the Reverend B. F. L. Clarke could have been found. He is a well-known authority on nineteenth-century church architecture, and the amazing growth of the Anglican communion has gone on mostly in that and this century. He writes in a learned and laconic style, so that even his accounts of places one has never seen nor is likely to see are interesting and enjoyable reading.

JOHN BETJEMAN

PREFACE

THIS book has had necessarily to be compiled largely with the aid of scissors and paste. But, as it makes no pretension to being a work of scholarship, I have given as few references as possible. Most of the facts have come from magazines, pamphlets, and papers, to which it seemed unnecessary to refer in detail. If I have relied to any extent on a book, I have said so; but it is not a subject about which much has been written. I have done my best to check the facts, but I am sure that there must be some mistakes. It is often difficult enough to piece together the architectural history of a modern church in England; there are gaps and apparent contradictions in the records. But at any rate it is possible to go and see the church for one's self, and come to a conclusion about it: the most ambitious world tour could hardly include all the cathedrals of the Anglican Communion. And I know that there are some omissions. The reason for these is simply that I have not been able to find anything to say. When the trail was cold, I had to send s.o.s.'s overseas: many of them were answered, but some were not—and that has meant several gaps. The section on China is particularly sketchy, for obvious reasons.

My thanks are due to the Missionary Societies who have given information—and particularly to S.P.G. I have spent many hours in the library of S.P.G. House (Sir William Emerson, architect), inspired by the Latin text on the Butterfield fireplace; and no one could have been more unfailingly helpful than the librarian.

I have had to trouble a good many deans and rectors, and some have taken very great trouble to reply as fully as possible. One or two bishops have also helped. To all of them I give my grateful thanks. I wish that there were room to mention them all by name. I should record, too, the help of the R.I.B.A., the National Gallery of Canada, and the National Historic Places Trust of New Zealand.

It was not easy to decide in what order to present these notes. I tried first to arrange the cathedrals in chronological order, so as to give some idea of the progress of Anglican expansion overseas. But it soon became clear that this was impossible: the oldest dioceses do not necessarily have the oldest buildings (e.g. Nova Scotia); and the most recent diocese (Barrackpore) has for its cathedral a church that is, for India, comparatively old. So I have followed the order of *Crockford*. It is not ideal, but it seemed the safest thing to do. The *Episcopal Church Annual* arranges the American dioceses in alphabetical order, but also mentions the provinces to which they belong: I have arranged them by provinces. This is, of course, a geographical grouping—except that five missionary districts (Puerto Rico, Virgin Islands, Haiti, the Dominican Republic, and the Panama Canal Zone) are included in the Province of New York and New Jersey, and three (the Philippines, Honolulu, and Alaska) in the province of the Pacific.

I do not think that I (or my authorities) have been quite consistent in the use of the expression "pro-cathedral": some churches that are called cathedrals ought really, I think, to be pro-cathedrals. But it is not a very important matter. (A full cathedral establishment is, of course, an exception overseas, and a dean is usually a parish priest as well.)

It may be as well to say that not every diocese of the Anglican Communion has a cathedral, so that there are some dioceses that are not mentioned here at all.

It will be obvious that I have, for the most part, avoided criticism, and confined myself to stating facts. Some of the buildings are nothing special; but the wonder is that, in many of the places, there are any buildings at all.

BASIL F. L. CLARKE

Knowl Hill,
Berks.
1957.

PART I

General

Introduction

THE churches that were built in the colonies in the late 17th, 18th, and early 19th centuries were like the less ambitious churches that were being built at home. America has some more sophisticated designs, but the ordinary churches built by Englishmen abroad had simple and straightforward plans and elevations, such as almost anyone could draw. Such designs, made by local workmen, may still be found in diocesan registries in England attached to faculty petitions. They are rather crude, and not at all original, but they resulted in very satisfactory churches.

This simple classical style looks at home anywhere, in hot or in cold countries. It is taken for granted in America and Canada as the colonial style; but, with thickened walls, overhanging cornices, and verandahs, it suits India equally well. It is unreasonable to say, as some do, that English-looking churches are out of place, and that the builders ought to have adopted the native style of each country. What was the native style in Canada, the West Indies, or Australia? The only country that had an architecture of its own was India; but it was obviously impossible to adapt Hindu temple architecture to churches.[1] Englishmen naturally built in the way that they understood. And, whatever the Victorian ecclesiologists might say about it later on, they tried to make their churches look like churches. The simplest wooden church in Canada or Newfoundland had, if possible, a cupola or spire; there were solid Georgian towers in the West Indies; and some of the more ambitious churches in India and elsewhere had a plain variety of the Gibbs steeple. Inside, there were the usual pews, galleries, and pulpit; the royal arms; and the Ten Commandments, Creed, and Lord's Prayer over the altar.

In 1661 a contract was signed between the churchwardens of St Michael's, Bridgetown, Barbados (now the cathedral), and Captain Robert Cullimore, who was to build a new church. It was more or less complete in 1665: but in December 1674 the Governor moved in Vestry that the chancel should be raised according to the rubric of the Church of England, and that there should be a font at the west end. In 1680,

---

[1] I am not denying, of course, that national ways of building can be used for churches; but it must be done at a later stage, and by the people themselves.

wainscot with the Creed, Lord's Prayer, Ten Commandments, and Moses and Aaron, a marble font with white Portland stone for it to stand on, and a table cloth of purple velvet with white silk and a golden fringe, were obtained from England. The church was described as "a building of 100 feet in length, and 60 feet wide within the walls, exclusive of a very large chancel . . . At the west stood a steeple, whose height from the foundation to the top of the spire was 124 feet and large in proportion." It was destroyed in a hurricane in 1780, and rebuilt afterwards by Mr Griffiths.

St Mary's, Fort St George, Madras, was begun in 1678: the design was probably made by Edward Fowle, the master gunner. It was described in 1711 as "a large pile of arched building, adorned with curious carved work, a stately altar, organs, a white copper candlestick, very large windows, which render it inferior to the Churches of London in nothing but bells, there being only one to mind sinners of devotion; though I've heard a contribution for a set was formerly remitted to Company." In 1792 the Governor reported to the Vestry that he had instructed Major Maule to prepare a design and estimate for the rebuilding of the steeple. Maule was killed in 1793, but his successor, Lieutenant-Colonel Gent, prepared a fresh design, and the steeple was built under his superintendence. The plan was obviously adapted from one of the rejected designs for the steeple of St Martin-in-the-Fields, in Gibbs's *Book of Architecture*.

Churches of this kind were still being built in India in the middle of the 19th century, and even later.

Gothic made its appearance in due course—the kind of Gothic that annoyed the serious revivalists more than anything else; which cheerfully mingled E.E. and Perp., and relied for effect chiefly on battlements and pinnacles. It was, of course, not the real thing: the designers had no understanding of the real nature of Gothic, and it had never crossed their minds that one variety of it was any better or worse than any other. They did not realize how serious a subject it was, nor that they were trespassing on holy ground. The truth simply was that this kind of Gothic was easy to draw, and that a church-like effect could be obtained without much difficulty. Many of the architects who worked for the Church Building Commissioners in England produced churches like this: every large town has one, and the type is the same all over the country. Similar churches were designed by some of the early architects in Canada and Australia, and by civil and military engineers in

India, at the same time—and, indeed, much later. They were, of course, condemned by the ecclesiologists; and they are condemned now by enlightened churchmen who are sure that a church ought to be built in the style of the country. But they are treated with respect in the dominions; and recent converts in pagan countries are not always so keen about their native architecture. A missionary once showed me a photograph of the rather poor E.E. church in which he ministered. I said, "Wouldn't your people prefer something more like what they have been used to?" He said, "No. They don't want anything to remind them of their old life." In the 19th century, the Indian Christians in the Diocese of Madras called Gothic arches "praying arches", because they were the shape of the hands put together in prayer. The arches that they had seen were certainly far from correct in their mouldings, but they affected them in a way that the ecclesiologists would have appreciated. Gothic was Christian architecture to them, and they had some appreciation of symbolism.

From 1840 onwards, Ecclesiology[1] became a serious study in England. Naturally, church building at home was the first concern of the ecclesiologists; but from the beginning they were also concerned with the colonies. It was a time of great expansion overseas: what ought the new churches to be like? There was, of course, no doubt that correct arrangement, including chancels, ought to be introduced everywhere. And there was no doubt that Gothic ought to be used, and that it could be adapted to every country. "Christian architecture, various in form, but one in spirit, like the Faith which it embodies, must take root wherever the foot of Christian bishop has trodden, limited no longer to the narrow peculiarities of European nations—on the one hand, on the rich and sultry plains of India, amid the wrecks of two false religions, two mighty civilizations, enforced to do them defiance in grandeur and pomp, as well as truthfulness; and on the other, amid the dreary pine wastes of Newfoundland, commanding ice and snow, frost and cold, to bless the LORD, praise him, and magnify him for ever."

But the difficulty, in the early days of the movement, was to suggest a suitable style. English Gothic had been at its best in the 14th century: but large traceried Middle-Pointed windows would be impossible in hot countries. What ought to be done?

[1] The word means the study of Church building and arrangement. It does *not* mean, as speakers at ecumenical conferences seem to imagine, the theology of the Church.

A writer in the *Ecclesiologist* in 1847 said that the colonists themselves must find out what was wanted: they must learn ecclesiology. At home they were only feeling their way to a successful revival: development in other climates must be a much harder task. The problem was in the tropics. There was no difficulty in temperate climates; in Australia churches could be much the same as in England. But in the tropics the churches built in the Spanish colonies might serve as models.

In 1848 the Reverend J. F. Bourne wrote from Demarara a description of some of the old Spanish churches in Central America, but he did not think that they were models to be followed: they were heathen in style, ill-ventilated, and not adapted to resist earthquakes.

In 1851 a long article gave notes on the Cathedral of Las Palmas, in the Canary Islands, and a Few Thoughts on Tropical Architecture. "The only truly indigenous architecture, so to call it, of the tropics is the speluncar" (cave-like), with thick walls and few windows. Gothic, developed for tropical purposes, must discard tracery. Not much could be done about external appearance: tropical architecture should cultivate the grace of humility, and not try to emulate nature: "that style must be very grandiose indeed which natural scenery will endure as a rival to her tropical throne.... We would ask such of our readers as have seen bananas and plantains grow, or who know what the colour and shape and size of the basaltic cliffs of the Atlantic islands, all extinguished volcanoes, are, how they think a smart white smug 'Early English' church, all natty and nice, with its trim, neat windows, and a cocky little spire, would look under such associations." That was the principle of what Mr Ferrey had done in sending out his church for St Helena. The tropics would stand no mediocrity: unless mountain and precipice, forest and fell, tree and river, could be beaten, an unprofitable contest should not be waged with them. Skill in decoration and construction, ornament and adaptation, should be reserved for the interior. Materials would depend on the locality.

It had not taken long for the ecclesiologists to move away from their earliest, narrowly English point of view. The problem became far simpler when it was admitted that foreign Gothic could be used. And it was soon realized that to build in Gothic was not simply to imitate old models: once the spirit and the principles had been grasped, there was no end to possible developments.

Nevertheless, the actual achievements of this period are rather disappointing. Some churches were built on these principles: but most of the new churches in hot climates were ordinary and English. In Canada, New Zealand, and Australia development was naturally on English lines.

Most of the well-known English architects of the 19th century designed some churches overseas, though they did not personally superintend the building of them. Sometimes a missionary priest went out with working drawings, and built a church himself—such as the Reverend F. H. Cox, who built an ecclesiological model church in Tasmania: St John the Baptist, Buckland, which is a reproduction of Carpenter's church of St John the Baptist, Cookham Dean. The Reverend W. Grey acted as diocesan architect for Newfoundland, and reported in 1853 that he had made designs for eight new churches, and for additions to two older ones. He had also given architectural lectures to the students of Queen's College, and to the clergy—which he hoped had had some influence. For "we must look in the main to the Clergy to be the architects. I see no prospect at present of any really good church architects coming out here; and we want a person *on the spot* to design our wooden churches,—one who is thoroughly acquainted with the wants and resources of the country; it is little use to send home for designs to persons who do not know our manner of building, or the climate of Newfoundland. . . . It is no disgrace to follow such men as William of Wykeham." The Bishop was building the cathedral from Scott's designs, and was waging war on high pews and galleries; but the people's ideas about church building were those of a past age, and they failed to appreciate the cathedral.

There was some tension between such men and the older type of surveyor, who, with no definite ideas in his mind, built churches of an obstinately old-fashioned kind. As in England, the ecclesiologists usually triumphed, and "church-like" came to mean what it meant at home; but the victory was often neither sudden nor complete, and non-ecclesiological churches were built at dates which would be almost unbelievable in England. Missionaries with an Evangelical outlook generally accepted the ecclesiological plan and arrangement after an interval; and, having accepted it, they were apt to cling to it for some time after High Churchmen had begun to make other experiments. But everyone realizes now that English 19th-century ways of worship are not necessarily the best for Christians of all nations—though it should also be added that they are not necessarily the worst.

There were, to begin with, no cathedrals overseas, as there were no
bishops. The earliest bishops used already existing churches: there were
many things to be done in their dioceses before cathedral-building could
be thought of. There is, however, one exception: Holy Trinity, Quebec,
was definitely built as a cathedral. The letters patent issued in 1804 said
that it was "to be an episcopal seat and cathedral church and for ever
hereafter to be called, known, and distinguished by the name of the
cathedral church of the Holy Trinity of the bishopric of Quebec".

But the cathedral-building movement of the 19th century really began
in 1838 with Daniel Wilson of Calcutta. He wrote, "I seem to myself
like Moses surveying from Mount Pisgah the promised land. I figure
to myself my beautiful spire, rising up 220 feet—the fine deeply but-
tressed Gothic nave, chancel, and transepts, marking the massive
grandeur of the Christian religion—the magnificent organ sounding
out, 'Thou art the King of Glory, O Christ'—my native Presbyters in
their snow-white vestures, walking down the aisles—the Christian
neophytes responding in the choir—and Jesus acknowledged as the Lord
of all." This is a remarkable confession to have come from so stalwart
an Evangelical, who considered the Tractarian movement to be an
"egregious drivelling fatuity". The first stone of the cathedral was laid
on 8 October 1839; the consecration was eight years later.

In 1845 the cathedral of Antigua was begun, after the old church
had been destroyed by an earthquake.

In the same year, Bishop Medley sailed for Fredericton with plans
for a cathedral which would be an ecclesiological model. In 1846 the
Bishop of Colombo was contemplating the building of a cathedral, and
sent home for plans, stating what would be required. R. C. Carpenter
made two designs, but they were unfortunately set aside. The plans
that were finally adopted were made by Captain Pickering, and the
building was erected in 1852–4 under Corporal Moore of the 15th Regiment. It is nothing more than an ordinary Victorian E.E. parish church.
Carpenter's design may be seen in the *Ecclesiologist*, and in Beresford
Hope's *English Cathedral of the Nineteenth Century*. It is a pity that
it was not carried out—nor his plans for a cathedral for Jamaica.

The year 1846 was also that in which, after two earlier false starts,
the building of Sydney Cathedral was undertaken. It was also the year
in which Bishop Feild of Newfoundland came to England to procure
plans for his cathedral—which were made by Scott.

In 1849 the old parish church-cathedral of Toronto was burned down, and a more imposing cathedral was begun in the next year. The same thing happened at Montreal in 1856; the old church was burned, and a new building was begun—a real cathedral, said the *Ecclesiologist*, of ample dimensions and imposing architecture.

And cathedral-building has continued from the mid-19th century until the present day. Several entirely new projects have been undertaken; and where a new cathedral has been out of the question, the old building has been adorned and enlarged. In many dioceses it is not possible to have more than a makeshift building; but a worthy cathedral is always the ideal—and where it has been accomplished, as in New Guinea and Borneo, it has had the effect of stimulating the church life of the diocese.

Most English churchmen know very little about the cathedrals of the Anglican Communion; it is hoped that this book will widen their knowledge, and perhaps increase their interest. One thing, perhaps, ought to be said. There may be some who will look at the illustrations and say, "But they don't look like cathedrals to me: they aren't large enough."

There is, of course, no reason why a cathedral should be large. But, to the average Englishman, a cathedral simply means a large church. Have we not all seen picture postcards of Tideswell church, the Cathedral of the Peak, and of Widdecombe church, the Cathedral of the Moor? Neither of these churches has ever been a cathedral; but as they are somewhat larger than the other churches in the neighbourhood, the motorist feels sure that they ought to be.

It will not be necessary to explain to the instructed churchman that a cathedral is, in fact, the church in which a bishop has his *cathedra*, or throne, and that it does not in the least matter whether it is large or small. But it may be as well to say so, lest this book fall into the hands of a reader who is not quite sure about it, and he be tempted to say, "This can't be a cathedral: our church at Anytown isn't one, and it is much larger than that." Size is of no account. The point is that a cathedral implies a bishop, and where there is a bishop, there is the Church. And the extension throughout the world of our branch of the Church—if I may use an expression which has gone out of favour since Victorian times, though I still think that there is something to be said for it—is a fact of which all churchmen should be aware, and of which they should be duly proud.

I

India, Pakistan, Burma, and Ceylon

ST PAUL'S CATHEDRAL, CALCUTTA

The first church to be used as a cathedral was St John's (the New Church), an early and good example of the adaptation of the Georgian church to the Indian climate. It was begun in 1784, and consecrated in 1787. The building committee had previously rejected a proposal to build a church after the model of St Stephen's, Walbrook. Lieutenant Agg of the Engineers designed and built it, and the altar piece of the Last Supper was painted and given by Zoffany.

This is how it struck Bishop Heber, when he arrived in 1823: "A very pretty building, all but the spire, which is short and clumsy. The whole composition, indeed, of the church is full of architectural blunders, but still it is, in other respects, handsome. The inside is elegant, paved with marble, and furnished with very large and handsome glass chandeliers, the gift of Mr M'Clintock, with a light pulpit, with chairs on one side of the chancel for the Governor-General and his family, and on the other for the Bishop and Archdeacon."

A proposal was made in 1818 for building a cathedral of St Paul, but nothing came of it. Bishop Wilson revived the project, when it was decided that St John's could not be enlarged. He proposed to "erect a lofty and spacious airy church, in the Gothic or rather Christian style of architecture, unencumbered with galleries": a spire would "give the whole a becoming customary ecclesiastical aspect". The foundation stone was laid on 8 October 1839; in May 1840 the ground plan was lengthened by 50 feet; by 1843 the walls were completed, and in 1844 the pinnacles were added. The spire was completed in March 1845, and the roofs were finished in 1846. There were several gifts: the Queen gave the Communion plate, and the Dean and Chapter of Windsor presented glass from St George's Chapel. This was one of a series of windows designed by West and painted by Jervais and Forrest; several were erected, including the great east window of the Resurrection; but the Crucifixion window, which was designed for the west end, was never used. The mullions and tracery of the east window at Calcutta were omitted to make room for it. The East India Company gave £15,000 and the site, the Archbishop of Canterbury £200, and the University of Oxford £300 and books to the value of £200. The Reverend John Craig, the architect of All Saints', Leamington, gave the brass eagle lectern, designed by Butterfield. Captain Kittoe gave the handsome stone font.

The architect was Colonel Forbes of the Bengal Engineers, "a man of infinite talent", according to James Fergusson, in his *History of the Modern Styles of Architecture*, "but who, like all his brother officers, fancied that Architecture was the simplest and most easily learned of the Arts, instead of being one of the most difficult, and requiring the longest and most exclusive study". The style is Gothic: it was stated that the tower and spire were copied from Norwich, with improvements suggested by Canterbury, while most of the details, internal and external, were copied from York. Bishop Heber's Life calls it Hindu-Gothic, and Beresford Hope, in his *English Cathedral of the Nineteenth Century*, says that it was "apparently founded on some rude print of the Duomo of Milan". If it had been built twenty years earlier, it would probably have been termed "neat" and "handsome"; but few people could take it very seriously after 1847.

The material is brick covered with chunam,[1] with iron used in the roof. The plan is interesting: it is practically all choir. The naves of English cathedrals were not used for worship at this time; all the congregation were put into the choirs. So the Bishop, as the *Ecclesiologist* observed, had reproduced the general arrangements of a modern English choir. The nave was left out altogether. "The great and crowning defect of the interior is its unreality. The vestibule is made to assume

[1] "Chunam is made from gravelly limestone, or from shells washed out of salt-water marshes, burned with charcoal, and then powdered. The powder is mixed with clean, sharp, river sand, in various proportions, according to the use for which it is intended. For finer works, the powder is very finely ground, and the water used in preparing it for mortar is generally mixed with molasses or coarse sugar." (*Architectural Magazine*, Volume i, p. 272.)

the form of a short nave, and the east end is so arranged as to present the appearance of possessing lateral aisles."

The consecration, on 8 October 1847, was described by the Bishop: "When I entered the great western door, the whole length of the sacred edifice opened before me—248 feet, including the walls; a sea of heads on all hands! the beautiful picture of the Crucifixion rising above them in the great eastern window; the holy table, with Her Majesty's superb service of Communion plate; the stalls for the clergy on the south and north sides of the choir; the governor-general's and bishop's seats; the pews thronged with anxious auditors; all was a magic scene.

"In a moment the organ burst forth, and the procession began. Forty clergy were present, and twenty divinity students.

"When the petition had been read in the front of the sacred table, the procession proceeded down the choir, repeating the sublime 24th Psalm. On its return, a pause was made, to allow the middle aisle to be filled with benches for the convenience of the attendant crowd.

"When Morning Prayer began, it was delightful to find that the hearing was perfect; nothing could surpass the clear melodious, gentle echo of the reader's voice. The coolness, also, of the choir was remarked by every one; to which the lofty roof, and the double-glazed windows of ground-glass contributed.

"When I ascended the pulpit, which itself is a beautiful work of art, I was overpowered by the sight. The vast multitude were singing the 100th Psalm, led by the superb organ, of which the fine and rich and mellow tones charmed every ear. . . . The Holy Communion then commenced. The clergy kneeling round the sacred table, all in their surplices, as in cathedrals at home, was a most touching scene. Between 140 and 150 communicants partook of the blessed Sacrament of the Body and Blood of the LORD.

"The entire service lasted about five hours. The impression of the whole scene on the native crowds was extraordinary, and scarcely less on the East Indian population. . . ."

Various additions have been made later—among others, A. W. Blomfield's alabaster reredos with mosaic panels, and the filling of the two blind windows at the east with mosaics by James Powell of Whitefriars.

The west window is by Burne-Jones, 1880, a memorial to Lord Mayo. The throne is to the memory of Bishop Johnson (1878–98). The spire has been taken down, and the top of the tower rebuilt in imitation of the central tower of Canterbury. The statue of Bishop Heber is by Chantrey.

ST. THOMAS'S PRO-CATHEDRAL,
MUS [CAR NICOBAR]

The story of the Church in Car Nicobar has been one of the really encouraging things in post-war Church history. John Richardson, the Apostle of Nicobar, was consecrated Bishop in 1950. The cathedral is the original church at Mus, built of wood, with a thatched roof.

ST THOMAS'S CATHEDRAL, BOMBAY

This is the oldest Anglican church in India. It was begun by President Gerald Aungier in 1672, and the walls had been raised some 10 or 12 feet soon after his death in 1677. In June 1679, Henry Oxinden, deputy governor of Bombay, reported that the church was upwards of one-third built, but that no money was left to finish it: he asked for the payment of the rest of the East India Company's contribution. In 1680 work began again, but in 1683 was at a standstill through lack of funds.

In 1714 the Reverend Richard Cobbe, Chaplain of the Company, arrived in Bombay. On 19 June 1715, he preached a sermon recommending the completion of the church, and talked with the Governor afterwards.

"Well, Doctor," said the Governor, "you have been very zealous for the Church this morning."

"Please your Honour, I think there was occasion enough for it, and I hope without offence."

"Well, then, if we must have a church, we will have a church. Do you see and get a book made and see what every one will contribute towards it, and I will do first."

Cobbe then applied himself to raising money, and subscriptions came in satisfactorily. The first stone of the new work was laid on 18 November 1715, and the church was first used on Christmas Day 1718, when it was "dressed with palm branches and plantain trees, the pillars adorned with wreaths of greens, and the double crosses over the arches looked like so many stars in the firmament". According to Cobbe, it was "a structure deservedly admired for its strength and beauty, neatness and uniformity, but more especially for its echo". It was consecrated by Bishop Middleton in 1816. In 1835 Archdeacon Thomas Carr was appointed first Bishop of Bombay; he was consecrated at Lambeth on 19 November 1837, and was installed on 21 February 1838, in St Thomas's, which then became the cathedral. Government granted Rs 16,000 for building a pinnacled Gothic tower.

In 1861 a new stone pulpit was erected, and in 1864 a new font, designed by a clergyman in England, and carved by James Forsyth. In that year a scheme for remodelling the cathedral was set on foot by Archdeacon Fletcher, and in 1865 plans were published by James Trubshaw of Bombay, the Government architect, a member of the well-known Staffordshire family of master builders and architects, who worked in the Midlands from the early 18th century until the middle of the 19th. He had, he said, tried to combine "a sufficiency of Eastern features and traditions, to make it seem at home in a tropical climate, with ample characteristics of the Faith and people it represents". It was proposed to enclose the old building in a kind of cloister, enlarge the chancel, and raise the roof—"in fact modify the structure very greatly, while yet preserving its main internal features". The alterations would "transform Bombay Cathedral into a building worthy the great and thriving city, to which at present it can hardly be said to be an ornament". The *Builder* (18 February 1865) had an illustration of "Bombay Cathedral as about to be recast", showing a not unimposing pile in very early Italianate Gothic, with a tower and spire recalling the work of Street.

Sufficient money was raised to make a beginning, and the Governor, Sir Bartle Frere, laid the foundation stone. But after three years, the "Cotton Mania" bubble burst, and the work was stopped. All that was completed was the chancel, paid for by public subscription, and the organ chamber, built at the cost of the Government. The chancel, apsidal and vaulted, is rich and elaborate work, in the foreign Gothic style of the 60's. The fountain, outside the west door, was designed by Gilbert Scott.

"The building itself is an example of a new patch on an old garment. The chancel end, built of stone, is of an apsidal form, with windows of Munich glass, modern stalls, and an altar well raised and provided with a red granite cross on a re-table of grey granite, and candlesticks, and frontals of the proper colours for the various seasons. But the nave remains as it was built more than a century ago. This has recently been painted—the walls and ceiling of a French grey, and the pillars white, or with a polish in imitation of marble. The general effect is better than might be expected." (*Mission Life*, 1880.)

In 1906 the organ was restored, and a new pulpit erected. There were further improvements after the Great War.

There are many monuments of the 18th and early 19th centuries, which cannot be described in detail here.

CHRIST CHURCH CATHEDRAL, COLOMBO

A letter from the Bishop was read at a meeting of the Cambridge Camden Society in 1846. He wanted plans for a cathedral.

"My own idea is that a plain cruciform structure would be best; of simple design, good and correct proportion, but not too large, and admitting of addition, by a future generation, if needed: Early English, with a cloister round to serve as verandah, and clerestory windows."

R. C. Carpenter (1812–55) was asked to prepare the design, and the ground plan was forwarded to the Bishop. Carpenter was the architect who came nearest to realizing the ecclesiologists' ideal of a model church: nothing could be better in its way than a church such as St Mary Magdalene's, Munster Square. He was also Nathaniel Woodard's architect for Lancing and Hurstpierpoint Colleges. After his death, his practice was continued by his son R. H. Carpenter, and his pupil William Slater.

In May 1847 the *Ecclesiologist* had an article on church building in Ceylon: Carpenter was then preparing another design for the cathedral. The Bishop wrote on 2 July correcting some points in the article; the *Ecclesiologist* made some comments, and then described Carpenter's new design. The plan was a nave of five bays, transepts, and a choir of two bays, ending in a five-sided apse. An aisle surrounded the whole, opening by arches into a cloister surrounding the whole church. Part of this was available for sacristies: a deep porch was attached at the north-west, and at the west was a narthex. The church was vaulted: the clerestory wall had triple arches opening into a covered external gallery. The style was very late First-Pointed—"perhaps, however, too early for our complete satisfaction. Mr Carpenter has studied to keep the detail of the severest and plainest kind possible; but in spite of this has contrived to give an effect of great stateliness and dignity".

The design, however, was not executed; plans for a far inferior church were made by Captain Pickering in 1852, and the building was begun with Corporal Moore of the 15th Regiment as "chief architect and supervisor". The foundation stone was laid on 15 June. On 15 November the Bishop wrote, "We are now re-building the aisle pillars of solid granite. The bricks we found to be of too soft and crumbling a material for the weight upon them; I determined therefore to pull down carefully the interior walls and arches. It is of course a loss of time, and additional expense of labour; but the expense of the east window is saved by a welcome present. It is given by Mr Horner, of Mells, in Somerset; the glass after a pattern in Salisbury Cathedral, without figures, at my request, as being open to objection in a country where Buddhism and Romanism abound. . . . The tower is now about 60 feet from the ground, and as high as our funds will carry it. It is very strongly built, with good belfry windows in the upper story; and will carry a spire, if our successors are able to add it".

The granite for the foundations, and the slates and tiles, came from England. The Communion plate was given by the clergy of Essex, the organ by Warden Wood, the font by Mrs Wood, the sanctuary chairs by Mudaliyar N. Dias Abeyesinge, and the lectern by Louis Pieris.

The cathedral was consecrated on St Matthew's Day 1854.

A new chancel was added in 1888—H. F. Tomalin architect. The bishop's throne, 1890, was designed by W. J. Tapper. The screen was erected in 1893.

A tremendous design for a new cathedral was made by G. H. Fellowes Prynne in 1915. It was based upon "a combination of Byzantine massiveness and proportions, emphasized with a recognition of Gothic detail . . . and a feeling for models or types of Eastern origin".

New plans have recently been made by Messrs Pinckney and Gott.

HOLY TRINITY CATHEDRAL, RANGOON

In 1861 the Bishop paid a visit, and a site for a church was chosen. The church was consecrated in 1867, and served as the pro-cathedral. It was repainted in 1880, and given new seats and a bishop's throne: it was reopened on 26 September.

On 28 April 1881, the leading engineers inspected it, and made a report. It consisted of nave, chancel, and south-west spire: owing to defective foundations, it had settled, and the south wall was out of the

ST THOMAS'S
CATHEDRAL,
BOMBAY

CATHEDRAL OF THE REDEMPTION, NEW DELHI

ALL SAINTS' CATHEDRAL, ALLAHABAD

CATHEDRAL OF THE REDEMPTION,
NEW DELHI

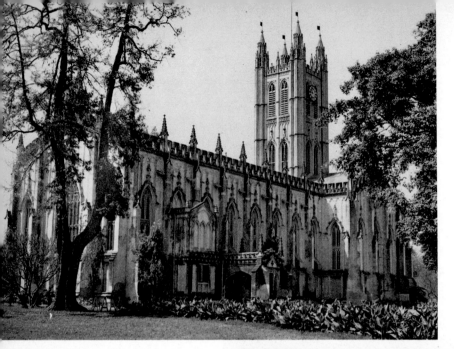

ST PAUL'S CATHEDRAL,
CALCUTTA

ST PAUL'S CATHEDRAL,
RANCHI

HOLY TRINITY
CATHEDRAL,
RANGOON

perpendicular. It could be enlarged to the west; or aisles could be added; or the chancel could be taken down, and transepts and a longer chancel added. The third suggestion would be the best: but as it needed repair, and could never be made really safe, it would be advisable to pull it down, sell the site, and build an entirely new church.

A meeting was held at the end of 1883 to consider the site for the new church. The compound of the mission school was proposed, and agreement was reached on this. After the meeting, plans by Charles Kirk were laid on the table: probably some modifications would have to be made, but he had made the design with the climate in mind, and his aim had been to ensure coolness and ventilation. The architect had waived his claim to the usual commissions, and undertook to supervise the orders necessary in England for the stonework, and its despatch to Burma.

Permission was sought from the Government to sell the old church and the land, and to build with the proceeds the cathedral, a church in East Rangoon, and other churches in the Diocese.

Work was begun in July 1885: the ground was staked out, and advertisements were sent to the papers for tenders for the preliminary work. New designs had been made by R. Chisholm, F.R.I.B.A., of Madras: it was stated that the engineers had taken exception to some of the details, but that the defects would be rectified in the building. The plans were said to be "in a modified early English style midway between Norman and the Decorated style—far lighter than the former and not so florid as the latter". The windows would be so arranged that no direct rays from the sun would enter the building. The roofs of the nave and transepts to be open; the chancel and apse to be vaulted in brick. The design was published in the *Builder*. It was far too ambitious, and though the plan was kept, the cathedral as built bears only a vague resemblance to the design as first made.

The foundation stone was laid on 24 February 1886.

After work had been begun, the width of the nave was increased. When the walls had reached one-third of their height, the sum allotted by the Government was exhausted. Two imperial loans were sanctioned —and these, with the help of diocesan funds, brought the building to completion. The work was superintended by Mr Hoyne-Fox, A.R.I.B.A. The cathedral was opened on 18 November 1894. The loans were repaid from the sale of the site and the fabric of the old church.

The porch was added in 1905; the tower and spire were built in 1913, from a legacy left by Bishop Strachan (d. 1909).

The cathedral was desecrated by the Japanese during the War, and restored afterwards.

THE CATHEDRAL OF THE RESURRECTION, LAHORE

The Lieutenant-Governor secured a site, and designs were made for a station church—All Saints': some money was collected, a committee was formed, and the foundation stone was laid on 11 February 1874, by the Archdeacon of Calcutta. Little progress was made, and the Bishop—T. V. French—decided that the church must give way to a cathedral. When he was on furlough in England in 1883-4, he set himself to collect at least £4,000. J. Oldrid Scott (1842-1913)—the second son of Sir Gilbert—made the plans for a building on a larger scale, using the existing foundations as far as possible. They were, in fact, of little use. The cost was estimated at over £50,000, of which the actual structure would cost £30,000.

The contractors were Messrs Burn and Co.

Work on the superstructure was begun at the end of July 1883: the first consignment of stone from Taraki arrived on 8 August. The construction is mostly of brick: stone, as it had to be brought from a distance, was used sparingly. By October the walls were about 12 feet above ground level, and the western towers were nearly as high as the aisle walls. Four of the bases of the pillars in the choir were in position, and the pillars themselves were ready.

The consecration was on 25 January 1887.

The cathedral is 13th-14th century in style, groined throughout, with an apsidal choir and ambulatory. The font was the gift of the people who had been baptized in the old pro-cathedral. The pulpit was provided by the Guild of Watchers and Workers in England; the stalls and sedilia were given by Mrs Tremlett, Mrs Millett, and some members of St Andrew's, Lahore. The bishop's throne was provided by Mrs Michôd and Mrs Millett, and the reredos by the Duchess of Connaught and the ladies of Rawalpindi. The chancel pavement of black and white marble was given by the Freemasons.

Three windows in the apse, by Clayton and Bell, were dedicated on 3 August 1890, in memory of Bishop French. They included no human figures, as the Bishop had feared that such figures would offend Moslem inquirers.

ST PAUL'S CATHEDRAL, RANCHI
[DIOCESE OF CHOTA NAGPUR]

The church was being built in 1872. "The design was very kindly supplied by our late Judicial Commissioner, and is very simple. The style is Gothic, with lancet windows and arches, supported by stone columns. The steeple stands at the north-west corner, the base forming a vestry. There is a good chancel with an organ chamber on the south side. The church will hold about 1,500 natives when seated (as is the custom with us) on the floor." (*Colonial Church Chronicle*, August 1872.)

Later in the year it was reported to be "rising fast", and the window arches were turned. It was consecrated in March 1873.

ALL SAINTS' CATHEDRAL, ALLAHABAD
[DIOCESE OF LUCKNOW]

The Church Committee of Cannington, a newly planned residential quarter of Allahabad, decided to build a really handsome church, and William Emerson (afterwards Sir William) was chosen as architect. The first stone was laid in 1871. Emerson (1843–1925) began with Habershon and Pite, and was afterwards a pupil of William Burges, whose French Gothic style he followed at first. The influence of Burges can be clearly seen in this church. As money came in plentifully, and as the idea of a Diocese of Lucknow materialized, the plans were enlarged to make it suitable for a cathedral. The choir, transepts, and a temporary nave were finished by January 1877. The contractors were Messrs Frizzoni and Co.

In 1884 the building committee requested the Bishop of Calcutta to take over all responsibility for the completion of the church. He intended to make an appeal, but in June received a letter from an American—A. C. P. Dodge of New York—who promised to send 20,000 dollars in instalments towards the work, as a memorial to his wife.

The choir and transepts were consecrated on 12 June 1887.

Six bays of the permanent nave were consecrated on 12 November 1891: it has since been completed, except for the western towers.

The style is 13th-century Gothic, suggested by the choir of Canterbury, adapted to the Indian climate. The material is white Surajpur stone, with red Mirzapur stone for the mouldings. The five large lower openings of the apse are filled with perforated stone in geometrical patterns "from the best models at Fatehpur-Sikri". The pavement of the choir and sanctuary is of black and grey Jeypur marble with steps of white marble: the transepts, crossing, and ambulatory are paved with black and white Mirzapur stone. The patterns of the pavement were designed by H. S. Talbot, engineer in charge of the work. The alabaster pulpit, by Nicholls of Lambeth, is a memorial to A. S. Harrison, secretary of the building committee; the alabaster font was given by the children of Allahabad. Glass by Shrigley and Hunt.

ALL SAINTS' CATHEDRAL, NAGPUR

The church was projected and sanctioned by the Government of Madras in 1848, at a cost not exceeding Rs 2,000. The Directors were consulted before building was begun. It was erected in 1851: the architect was Lieut. R. H. Sankey, of the Madras Engineers (afterwards Sir R. H. Sankey, K.C.B.). The body measured 36 × 25 × 20 feet, the sacrarium 7 × 12 feet: the style is Gothic.

It was enlarged in 1879, and a tower built partly at the cost of the congregation.

The Diocese was formed in 1902, and the church was enlarged and adapted by G. F. Bodley (1827–1907). The nave was lengthened, the transepts were deepened and doubled, a chancel was built, and an organ chamber and two vestries were added. The work was estimated to cost £2,000.

The collection of subscriptions began in the winter of 1905–6; except for £500 from the Government, all the money came from the members of the church. Bodley said, "If you make the church really devotional, you will find numbers of people coming forward with gifts to beautify it". The gifts included the glass of the east window (by Burlison and Grylls) given by Bishop Eyre Chatterton and his wife; the font, given by the Reverend G. E. M. Tonge; and the sedilia, given by the Viceroy and Lady Hardinge.

The enlarged cathedral was consecrated on 18 February 1914.

ALL SAINTS' PRO-CATHEDRAL, SHILLONG
[DIOCESE OF ASSAM]

Shillong is a small hill-station, which was destroyed by an earthquake in 1897 and rebuilt afterwards. The Diocese of Assam was founded in 1915. The church at Shillong, "which serves as a pro-cathedral, holds 130 people, and is as large as any in the diocese".

Bells were given in 1931 by Lady Hammond, to whose interest and labour various additions and improvements were due, including the altar cross, candlesticks, and vases, which were made in Calcutta from designs by an English architect. Reseating was begun in 1932.

ST ANDREW'S PRO-CATHEDRAL,
SHARANPUR, NASIK

Sharanpur was founded as a Christian settlement in 1854, when the British Government handed over liberated African slaves to the Mission in Nasik. Afterwards, the African colony was removed to East Africa.

The cruciform stone church, with a tower, was adopted as a pro-cathedral when the Diocese was formed in 1929.

CHRIST CHURCH, PRO-CATHEDRAL,
BHAGALPUR

Completed in 1845: Perp., with two-light windows and pinnacles, and a pinnacled west tower, with pairs of lancets in the belfry stage.

A contemporary lithograph of this church makes it look exactly like a church in Tunbridge Wells or Cheltenham—except for a palm tree or two, and a few natives.

The Diocese was founded in 1943.

CATHEDRAL OF THE REDEMPTION,
NEW DELHI

In 1922 the Reverend Thomas Dixon was appointed chaplain: he convinced the congregation that they must build a church that would be worthy of the new city. In 1925 there was a competition, judged by Sir Edwin Lutyens, who chose the plans of H. A. N. Medd. Funds were not at first sufficient for more than a comparatively small building; but after the arrival of Lord Irwin in 1926, the building fund was much increased, largely by subscriptions from England. A new site was chosen, and the foundation stone was laid by Lord Irwin on 23 February 1927. At the time it was still not certain how much money would be available, or how large the church would be, so the stone was laid in the floor of the crossing, to make sure that it would be somewhere in the church. By the end of the next year, the present form of the building was agreed on, and work was begun. The church was consecrated in 1931. The central tower and dome were built in 1935.

The style is Renaissance, and the plan owed something to Palladio's Church of the Redentore at Venice: this suggested the dedication.

The material is white Dholpur sandstone: as the funds would not allow the external facing to be of ashlar, the main walling is coursed rubble masonry: red sandstone is used for the plinth. Ashlar is used for the moulded courses, and the columned porches on the north, south, and west. Internally the whole surface, except for the vaulted ceiling, is of white stone ashlar. The floor is of red and white stone, except for the sanctuary, which is paved with Indian marbles. The high altar is of white marble with coloured marble inlay. The apse is panelled in teak: the reredos has a copy of the painting of the Madonna and Child by Giovanni Bellini. The rood that surmounts it was carved at Bolzano in the Italian Tyrol. At the time of the building, the 1300th anniversary of the baptism of King Edwin was being celebrated at York, and the rood, candlesticks, altar, rails, and pulpit were given by the Province of York. Other gifts were made by all the Dioceses of India and Burma, as a thanksgiving for the work of Lord Irwin.

The Diocese of Delhi was inaugurated in 1947, and designs for the bishop's throne and canons' stalls have been made by the architect.

CATHEDRAL OF CHRIST THE KING, KURUNAGALA, CEYLON

The tower and transeptal chapels—of the Blessed Virgin Mary on the south, and St Thomas on the north—of this cathedral, designed in the Sinhalese style, are almost complete, and were consecrated on the Feast of the Epiphany, 1956. The Bishop's House has since been completed on the north, adjacent to the Chapel of St Thomas, which will be the bishop's chapel. Almost all the money has been raised locally. The nave will be undertaken next.

The altar stands at the crossing. The bishop's throne faces the people westwards: behind it, in the wall, is a statue of Christ the King, 14 feet in height.

ST JOHN'S CATHEDRAL, AMBALA
[DIOCESE OF AMRITSAR]

The first stone was laid on 14 December 1844, but the work was delayed by the Sutlej and Punjab campaigns. The site was then altered, and the foundation stone was laid again in January 1852. The Government gave Rs 40,000, and the materials of the old Kurnal church (chiefly woodwork), and its Communion plate. The new church was consecrated on 4 January 1857, by Bishop Dealtry of Madras, who said that it would form an appropriate cathedral.

The architect was Captain Atkinson, R.E.

The material is brick, the style 14th century. Nave and aisles and chancel, with west tower, and porches in the centre of the north and south sides. Octagonal pillars: clerestory windows of three lights. The black and white marble floor in the chancel, and the screen, were given by the Reverend R. Hine. The pulpit of carved stone came from Delhi.

The first bishop of the new diocese was enthroned in 1953.

ST BARTHOLOMEW'S CATHEDRAL,
BARRACKPORE

On 3 May 1832, a letter from the Government to the Bishop of Calcutta stated that "the Right Hon'ble the Governor General in Council is pleased to grant Sicca Rupees 1,100 as subscription for Government towards the expence of constructing the Church at Barrackpore". The total cost was Rs 14,186. The church was opened in 1831, and consecrated on 24 August 1847.

It was reopened on 29 December 1868, after being enlarged: chancel, verandahs, western portico, and steeple were added, still in the un-learned Classic style that had been used from the beginning by the English in India—the verandahs and portico recalling Soane's Primi-tivist Order, and the steeple more or less 18th century.

The church was repaired in 1951. The diocese was formed in 1956.

The bishop's throne, and the screen behind it, were given by St Paul's Cathedral, Calcutta.

The Church of South India includes the former Anglican dioceses of Madras, Dornakal, Tinnevelly, and Travancore and Cochin.

St George's Cathedral, Madras, was designed by Colonel J. L. Caldwell, the Company's senior engineer in the Presidency: it was consecrated on 8 January 1816. It has an Ionic portico, and a steeple based on that of St Giles-in-the-Fields. The chancel was lengthened in 1864.

The Cathedral of the Epiphany, Dornakal, was consecrated on 6 January, 1939. It is in the Indian style, and the plan was worked out by the bishop, the Reverend T. H. Cashmore, and a retired public works engineer, J. S. Muthaiya.

Holy Trinity Cathedral, Palamcottah (Diocese of Tinnevelly) was built in 1826: chancel and porch 1840, tower 1845.

The Pro-cathedral of the Holy Trinity, Kottayam (Diocese of Travancore and Cochin) was opened in 1842. The first bishop, J. M. S. Speechly, who was consecrated in 1879, brought with him plans made by his architect brother, R. Speechly, for enlarging and adapting it.

ST GEORGE'S CATHEDRAL,
CAPETOWN

*The Portico of the old
Cathedral, since demolished*

SS. MICHAEL AND GEORGE'S
CATHEDRAL, GRAHAMSTOWN

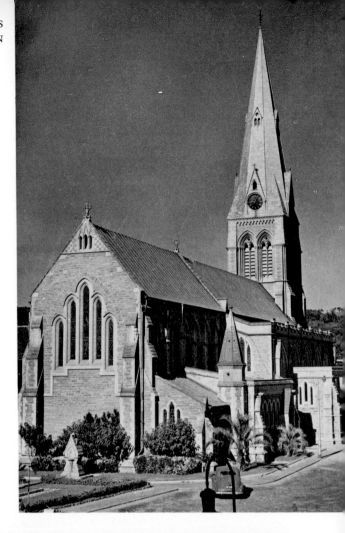

ST MARK'S CATHEDRAL,
GEORGE

2

South Africa

ST GEORGE'S CATHEDRAL, CAPE TOWN

A scheme for building a church was suggested in 1824, but nothing came of it. In October 1827 Bishop James of Calcutta visited Cape Town. A meeting was held, and a subscription list was opened. Promises were received of timber, and labour from carpenters and other workmen. The Governor gave the site, and the Bishop consecrated it; but after he had gone, difficulties arose, and the plan was shelved for two years.

Then Lieut.-Colonel Bell, Colonial Secretary, took up the matter; the foundation stone was laid in 1830, and the church was opened in 1834. The contract was for a building to hold 1,100 to 1,200 people, to cost £12,000, exclusive of enclosure, gates, bells, and organ.

The architect was Findlay.

The portico and tower were copied from St Pancras Church: the interior is said to have been modelled on a plan for a Baptist Chapel in Loudon's *Encyclopaedia of Architecture*. There was a gallery over the altar, the font was in front of it, and pulpit and desk were at the sides of the rails. This kind of arrangement, with one "liturgical centre", is just beginning to come back into favour: but naturally St George's did not meet with the approval of mid-19th-century churchmen. The diocese was founded in 1847: Bishop Gray at once proposed to build a new cathedral, to cost £10,000; but as this was not possible, some alterations were made under Butterfield: the arrangements of the sanctuary were recast "on a dignified and stately plan", and a marble reredos and pulpit were erected.

In 1887 the Diocesan Synod resolved to build a new cathedral, but little advance was made until 1897. The design was made by Herbert

4

Baker (1862–1946): the working out of the design during the actual building was chiefly done by his partner, Francis Masey.

Baker, when he came as a young man to South Africa, had come into contact with Cecil Rhodes, whose idea of developing a distinctively South African type of architecture he tried to put into practice. His early houses are in a style derived from the buildings of the 18th-century Dutch settlers; afterwards he produced the Union Buildings at Pretoria, the Government House at Pretoria, the South African Institute of Medical Research at Johannesburg, and other large-scale public buildings, in what has been called the Imperial Style. The first stone was laid on 22 August 1901, but the foundations and substructure, including the crypt, were not taken in hand until 1904: when they had been completed, operations were again suspended until November 1906. Then the superstructure was begun, consisting of the sanctuary, choir, south chapel and organ loft, the crossing, part of the south transept, the sacristy, and four bays of the nave. By 1908 the eastern part had been carried up to the roof. After Archbishop West Jones's death in 1908, it was decided to build the north chapel to his memory: the foundation stone was laid on 20 November, and consecrated on 28 October 1909. The effigy of the Archbishop is by C. L. Hartwell, the glass by Walter E. Tower. The nave was first used in 1913. The north transept was completed in 1936, at a cost of £12,350, and the north aisle in 1939. The remaining part of the old cathedral was taken down in 1952.

The cathedral is built of hard sandstone from Table Mountain: for the filling-in surfaces of the interior, and the interspaces of the groining, Oamaru stone from New Zealand was used. The roof is of Australian jarrah wood, the high altar of black marble, and the pavement of blue, white, green, red, and black marble. Glass by C. W. Whall, and his assistant Karl Parsons, executed by Messrs Lowndes and Drury.

An altar piece for one of the chapels has been painted by Mrs Charles Wheeler as a memorial to King George VI.

SS. MICHAEL AND GEORGE'S CATHEDRAL, GRAHAMSTOWN

In 1821 Lord Charles Somerset obtained a grant from S.P.G., and in 1823 the Colonial Government passed plans for a church to cost £4,400. The contract was signed on 9 September 1824: the plans were made by W. Jones, a land surveyor, of Cape Town: George Gilbert of Cape

Town was the builder. The work proceeded slowly, as the stone had to be brought in ox-wagons: the nave was first used in 1828. The church was the property of the Government until 1837, when it was handed over to a Church committee, on condition that they put a new roof on it, and kept it in repair. The diocese was founded in 1853.

In 1860 application was made to Gilbert Scott (1811–78) for designs for a tower and spire: they were ready by August 1. Prince Alfred, afterwards Duke of Edinburgh, laid the foundation stone, but the tower and spire were not built until the time of Dean Williams (1874–9).

Bishop Webb said that he hoped to replace the "dilapidated and barn-like chancel and nave" with a more worthy building: £5,000 was needed. The foundation stone of the choir was laid in January 1890 by the Governor. The plans were Sir Gilbert Scott's, worked out by his son J. O. Scott, and carried out by W. White-Cooper. The choir was consecrated in 1893: in 1896 the building was free from debt owing to the efforts of Miss Franks, who raised £8,718 18s. 1d. in England.

In 1905 a legacy of £1,000 was left by Mrs Hayton for building the nave: in 1907 S.P.C.K. promised £2,500, and the Ladies' Association collected £370. The estimated cost was £9,500. On the death of Bishop Webb in 1907 it was decided that his memorial should be the east bay of the nave. In January 1909 the building fund stood at £6,672, and building began in November. On Lady Day 1911 the foundation stone was laid by the Governor-General, and the new nave and north aisle were blessed by Bishop Cornish on the Feast of the Transfiguration 1912.

The walls are of local blue quartz sandstone: the dressings of the tower, and the spire, are of concrete, and those of the rest of the church of Bathurst stone. The pillars of the nave arcade are of black marble: the capitals, arches, and window dressings are of Bathurst, Southwell, and Steenpan stone. The roofs are of teak, except for the tie beams of the nave, which are of English oak. The chancel roof was made and erected by James McLaren. The screen, of teak, was designed by J. O. Scott, and made by African apprentices at the Kafir Institution, under the superintendence of Jacob Stewart. The bishop's throne and the reredos were designed by White-Cooper. Richard Bridgeman of Lichfield carved the pulpit: the lectern is a reduced replica of Scott's at Durham Cathedral. The window at the west end of the north aisle is by Buckeridge and Floyce of London. The other north aisle windows are by James Powell: east and west windows by C. Powell.

The Lady chapel was dedicated in 1952: it was designed by Jones and McWilliams, and executed by Messrs Andrew Carr and Co.

ST SAVIOUR'S CATHEDRAL, PIETERMARITZBURG [DIOCESE OF NATAL]

The first cathedral was ST PETER'S, the foundation stone of which was laid in November 1851: when Bishop Colenso arrived in 1853, the foundations had been laid, but the work was stopped for lack of funds. It was opened for worship in 1857, on the Feast of the Annunciation, and consecrated on St Peter's Day. It is simple Middle-Pointed: the design is supposed to have been made by Mrs Gray, wife of Bishop Gray: Gabriel Eaglestone was the stone mason. The glass was given by William Sewell, the founder of Radley.

It was here, on 5 January 1866, that the Dean read the sentence of excommunication of the Bishop. In January 1868 the Supreme Court deprived the Church of the properties of which Colenso had been trustee: the Dean was turned out of the Deanery and the cathedral, and the other clergy lost their churches. The Bishop continued to minister in St Peter's, and was buried there in 1883. In 1897 the Vestry decided to join the Church of the Province.

On the day following the Supreme Court's judgment in 1868, the Dean called a meeting of the clergy, and some of the laity, who decided to build a church. W. Marshall at once offered lands and buildings to be sold to help the building fund, and the Dean was urged to visit England and make an appeal. Financial support for the new cathedral, and offers of help from churchmen, made it possible for the Dean to lay the foundation stone of ST SAVIOUR'S before he left, on 3 February. The building was ready for worship by Ascension Day, though it was without porch, vestry, and baptistery. Bishop Macrorie landed at Durban in February 1869, and afterwards consecrated the cathedral. It is "plain brick outside, but inside dignified and church-like". The memorial reredos to Dean Green, who died in 1906, was erected in 1909. The original furniture was ordered from the Kafir College, Zonnebloem.

It is now proposed to return to St Peter's, and either to enlarge or rebuild the church.

ST PAUL'S CATHEDRAL, ST HELENA

The foundation stone was laid in 1851. The *Ecclesiologist* (April 1850) criticized the design: "We think that Mr Ferrey might have thrown far more life and variety into the design than he has done. . . . We in England can see many churches—so that the inferiority, it may be, of our own parish church is not a matter of such moment as it would be to the islanders of S. Helena, to whom this building will be for ever their one type of Architecture and Ritualism."

It is a small E.E. church, of nave, chancel, porch, and vestry, with a western bell gable. Benjamin Ferrey (1810–80) designed a good many churches like this. (The design is also attributed to Mrs Gray, wife of the Bishop of Cape Town, who was, according to her husband, "architect to the diocese". But Ferrey's authorship seems to be established.)

SS. ANDREW AND MICHAEL'S CATHEDRAL, BLOEMFONTEIN

Bishop Gray arrived here on 3 May 1850, and at once a deputation came to present a list of subscriptions: the site was fixed. The foundation stone of a church was laid in that year, and work was begun; but in 1854 British troops and officials left, the church was abandoned, and the walls decayed.

The diocese was founded in 1863.

Bishop Twells wrote (19 May 1864): "I am drawing plans for the church and went out to inspect the ruin and complete it in my mind's eye. I think much better of the situation and its possibilities than I did. It is 60 ft. by 25 ft.; this we must finish and consider as the choir of the future cathedral."

By Easter 1865 the iron roof and the windows had been sent out: it was finished in 1866, and consecrated on St Andrew's Day. The architect was Dudley Male: the cost was £2,000. The font was designed by Mr (afterwards Archdeacon) Croghan.

"The interior of the church, aided by the bold and handsome arches which conduct to the side chapel and porch respectively, presents a striking effect, being much more spacious and well-proportioned than the exterior seems to warrant." (*The Church News.*)

In 1872, on the death of Bishop Gray, three memorial windows were placed in the north aisle.

In 1876 an iron extension was made at the west: the cost, £500, was met by J. G. Hubbard, afterwards Lord Addington.

In 1881 £3,000 was given in England for building a permanent nave: the plans were made by Mr Hilder, a devout church architect, "whom pulmonary weakness had driven from England". The plans were placed in the hands of Arthur Byrd, who followed them as far as possible. He afterwards joined the Brotherhood of St Augustine.

The walls were of brick laid in clay: the arches of brick set in cement. The pillars were of brick, but poor materials caused the collapse of a pillar on the north, and £1,000 was needed to rebuild them in stone instead. This was given from England. The contractor for the brick and stonework was J. Goodman of Bloemfontein. The nave and aisles were dedicated on 7 June 1885. The glass in the aisles is by Kempe. The west window, a memorial to Queen Victoria (1904), was made by Messrs William Pearce of Birmingham, who also undertook the glass of the clerestory.

By 1905 many additions had been made: an arcade between the choir and Lady chapel, a war memorial, the chapter house, and the tower.

ST PETER'S PRO-CATHEDRAL, VRYHEID
[DIOCESE OF ZULULAND]

The town of Vryheid was founded in 1884, and a small church was built within a few years. Bishop Vyvyan, who was consecrated in 1903, soon decided to move from Eshowe to Vryheid, the geographical centre of the diocese, and it was agreed to build a new church. It was hoped to erect a cathedral with a nave to seat 400, a side chapel, and choir and sanctuary. But the number of Church people in the diocese was then very small, and no help was obtainable from outside the parish. Plans had therefore to be modified, and finally Baker and Fleming designed the present building, to hold 100, with a small choir and sanctuary. S.P.G. gave £200, and S.P.C.K. £70 towards the cost. The foundation stone was laid in 1911, and Bishop Vyvyan consecrated the cathedral on 28 April 1912.

It is a dignified little church, of red brick, in a plain 13th-century style. The lectern was a Boer War memorial: the processional cross of Rhodesian orange-wood was carved by African schoolboys.

ST JOHN'S CATHEDRAL, UMTATA
[DIOCESE OF ST JOHN'S, KAFFRARIA]

The diocese was founded in 1873.

An iron church was transported from Durban in 1877. A brick pro-cathedral on a stone foundation was consecrated on 18 September 1900: the money had been raised by the exertions of Dean Sutton.

In January 1901 Bishop Key died in England. He had approved designs made for a cathedral by G. H. Fellowes Prynne (1853–1927) the architect of many suburban churches in England, mostly designed in a style derived from Sedding: sometimes successful, sometimes less so. This design is in his usual style.

Bishop Watkin Williams laid the foundation stone. It had been decided to build in the European town, and not on the site of the pro-cathedral. Mr Homes gave the last three years of his life to training African masons: after his death there was a pause. In 1903 Brother Maynard, s.s.j.e., an architect, came from England, and the work progressed rapidly.

The consecration was on 30 September 1906. The nave only was completed: the foundation stone of an eastward extension was laid in 1956.

ST ALBAN'S CATHEDRAL, PRETORIA

Archbishop West Jones wrote in his diary in 1877: "The unconsecrated building serving as a church is miserably small, and cannot accommodate a fourth of the people. To-night there will be a meeting, a kind of social reunion, at which Bishop Webb and I shall have to stir up the people to raise funds for a new building, making ourselves responsible for about £500, which the new bishop will have to raise in England."

A new site was secured, and a church was built.

William White (1825–1900) made a design for a cathedral in 1890. It was to have been cruciform, with a central tower—to have been finished eventually with a spire—and apsidal ends to the transepts and chancel. The material was to be local red bricks; about 35 moulds were sent out for plinths, string courses, windows, doors, and arcades. The pillars, capitals, and bases to be of local stone.

White was one of the architects who were approved of by the

Ecclesiologist. His churches, often of brick, are, generally speaking, simple, devout, and well arranged from the ecclesiological point of view.

The foundation stone was laid, but the scheme did not come to anything.

In 1905 Sir Herbert Baker was chosen as architect, and the choir of his new cathedral was consecrated at Easter 1909. The old building remained as a temporary nave.

The choir and aisles are of local stone, vaulted in concrete. Glass by Whall.

The foundation stone of the nave was laid on 6 November 1955. By the end of 1956 the framework of the nave roof was complete, and work was in progress on the inner concrete roof. The masons were working on the walls. By February 1957 it was reported that the roof had been sprayed with dark grey acoustic plaster: the stone work had reached the sills of the windows, and the window frames were in position. The vault of the south chapel was in place. The architect is Wilfrid Mallowes. Baker's design is not being followed.

Unfortunately a fire at the Church Hall in June 1956 destroyed various things that had been stored there from the cathedral: nearly half the pews, the font, the Lady chapel altar, a bell, several windows and memorials, and the foundation stone which Bishop Bousfield laid in 1890.

ST MARY'S CATHEDRAL, JOHANNESBURG

G. H. Fellowes Prynne, early in this century, made a design for a church with a hall by the side of it. The hall was built, and used for worship: it had an ecclesiastical-looking front, with a Perp. window and two spirelets.

Then it was decided to build the church on a different plan. Sir Herbert Baker made designs, which were carried out by Frank Fleming after Baker had left South Africa. The diocese was founded in 1922.

The foundation stone was laid on Ascension Day 1926, and it was consecrated in 1929. It is built of local stone in a Romanesque style. The windows in the apse were designed by Karl Parsons. Other glass by A. J. Davies.

Fellowes Prynne's hall has been taken down.

ST ALBAN'S CATHEDRAL, PRETORIA

ST MARY'S CATHEDRAL,
JOHANNESBURG

ALL SAINTS'
CATHEDRAL,
ONITSHA, NIGERIA

ST GEORGE'S CATHEDRAL, FREETOWN, SIERRA LEONE

CHRIST CHURCH CATHEDRAL, LAGOS

DIOCESE OF LEBOMBO

1. PRO-CATHEDRAL OF SS. STEPHEN AND LAURENCE, LOURENÇO MARQUES

In 1899 a gift enabled the first bishop of the diocese, William Edmund Smyth, to buy a plot of land in the high part of the town, and he built there the only permanent church in the diocese at the time. Only the chancel was completed: the nave remained an iron room.

It was taken down in 1919, and a stone and brick pro-cathedral, designed by Baker and Fleming, was dedicated in 1920.

2. ST AUGUSTINE'S CATHEDRAL, MACIENE

In 1943, this church, opened in 1938, became the cathedral. It is very simple, and consists of nave, aisles, and apsidal sanctuary.

ST MARK'S CATHEDRAL, GEORGE

In 1845 £200 for a church was placed on the estimates presented to the Council of the Cape. It was "rapidly rising" in 1849, and was consecrated on 7 December 1850. The design was made by Mrs Gray, wife of the Bishop, and was based on Littlemore, near Oxford: the building was done by masons brought from Scotland by the Bishop. A chancel was added in 1860 at a cost of £466.

In 1925 a new chancel and vestry were designed by Baker and Kendall, and built by Messrs Rogers of George. The south transept was built in 1934, and the north transept and Lady chapel were consecrated on 15 June 1954. The chapel is a memorial to the first Bishop of George, the Right Reverend Henry Bindley Sidwell, and also a war memorial. Four windows by Hugh Easton have been inserted.

ST CYPRIAN'S CATHEDRAL, KIMBERLEY

In 1870 the Reverend J. W. Rickards made the first church: it consisted of the rooms of a house in Park Street, with the yard, and the stable at the back: the yard was roofed over, the stable was the vestry, and the room above it was the choir. In 1879 it was decided to import an iron church from England: when first erected, it was blown over: then it was re-erected, and dedicated on Low Sunday 1880.

In 1901 an effort was made to rebuild. In 1907 Bishop Gaul laid the foundations of the nave of a new church, of brick and stone, in the Dutoitspan Road: on 13 May 1908 the nave, transepts, and baptistery were dedicated. The money for the completion was collected gradually. It became a cathedral in 1912.

In 1913 an effort was made to wipe off the debt, and to finish the chancel and tower. The town council decided to remove the buildings which blocked the frontage on Dutoitspan Road. De Beers promised £500. In September 1913 the Governor laid the foundation stone of the chancel. The War delayed matters, but in 1919 it was decided to complete the cathedral as a war memorial.

It consists of nave and aisles, transepts, and a chancel with chapels: the style is 13th century. The architect was William Timlin, a South African.

ST GEORGE'S PRO-CATHEDRAL, WINDHOEK
[DIOCESE OF DAMARALAND]

When South-West Africa was a German colony, there were only a very few Anglicans in Windhoek: the territory was visited from time to time by the Coadjutor Bishop of Cape Town, or by an itinerant priest. But after the conquest of the territory by the South African troops in 1915, and the taking over by the Union of South Africa of the government and of the railways, a fairly large number of Anglicans came into the territory, and the diocese was formed in 1924.

St George's was consecrated by Bishop Fogarty in 1925, about 18 months after the formation of the diocese. The plans were drawn up by an official of the Public Works Department.

It is built of sandstone, and has "something of the air of an English country church". It is very small, with seating for only 80 people. (It should not be necessary to repeat that size does not determine whether a church is, or is not, a cathedral.)

It is well furnished, with a carved reredos in memory of Bishop Fogarty, and an altar which was the gift of St Peter's, Cranley Gardens. The bell, dated 1813, is one of four from St Mary, Northgate, Canterbury, which Bishop Fogarty acquired for churches in the diocese.

3

West Africa

ST GEORGE'S CATHEDRAL, FREETOWN, SIERRA LEONE

The foundation stone was laid in 1817 by Sir Charles MacCarthy. The cost was about £5,000. It was opened on 13 January 1828: the tower was completed later. The nave was rebuilt in 1876: the Governor laid the foundation stone of the chancel on 24 February 1905.

ALL SAINTS' CATHEDRAL, ONITSHA
[DIOCESE OF THE NIGER]

The foundation stone was laid on 9 November 1949, and the Lady chapel was consecrated on 10 May 1952.

The architect is Richard Nickson.

The design incorporates ironstone buttresses, concrete panel-walls, and semi-parabolic arches. There are no glazed windows. It is "a happy blend of African and European skill". Local blacksmiths made the wrought ironwork for the gallery balustrades, Akwa carvers the woodwork of the doors, Akwete weavers the cloth which hangs on the east wall, and Lagos carpenters the seats and sanctuary furniture.

HOLY TRINITY CATHEDRAL, ACCRA

The first S.P.G. missionary, Thomas Thompson, left New Jersey in 1751, and landed on the Gold Coast in 1752. Philip Quaque, the first African priest of the Anglican Communion, returned to Africa from England in 1766, and worked for over 50 years as a missionary, and as chaplain to the Factory at Cape Coast Castle. The climate was almost always fatal to European missionaries in the early days. S.P.G. restarted its work in 1904, and the Diocese of Accra was founded in 1909.

Holy Trinity, Accra, was built in 1893, at the cost of the Government, for the Government officials and traders. When provision for Government chaplains was no longer made, it was given to the Diocese, on condition that it was kept in repair. It became a cathedral in 1949.

The design was made by Sir Aston Webb (1849–1930), the architect of the new front of Buckingham Palace, the Admiralty Arch, the Royal Naval College, Dartmouth, Christ's Hospital, Horsham, etc. He was not normally a church architect—though of course his school and college buildings include chapels, and he restored St Bartholomew the Great, Smithfield, and designed the French Protestant church, Soho, and a few parish churches.

Holy Trinity is built of yellowish-brown sandstone, and consists of an aisleless nave of five bays, with south porch, and north-west tower with broach spire; and chancel of two bays. The chancel buttresses are gabled, and linked with arches. It is simple 13th century in style—uncompromisingly English and Northern. The local legend is that two sets of plans were mixed up, and that the church intended for Accra stands in some chilly spot—but we are not told where.

CHRIST CHURCH CATHEDRAL, LAGOS

Missionary work was begun in Lagos in 1852. The original Christ Church was erected in 1867–9, on the site now occupied by the cathedral. The foundation stone was laid in March 1867, and the building—which was of brick with a slate roof—was dedicated by Bishop Crowther, the first African bishop, on 10 June 1869. The cost was about £2,000. The tower was completed in 1878.

By the time that the control of Christ Church passed from the C.M.S. to the African clergy, in 1919, the building had become inadequate for the large congregations that regularly attended. A building committee was formed, and plans for a new church, of cathedral status, were put in hand. The building, which was erected in three sections, was designed by an African architect, Mr J. Bagan Benjamin, in a Gothic style that it would be unfair to criticize from the point of view of those who demand strict correctness. The construction is of concrete blocks, and the cathedral can hold a congregation of about 1,100. The cost, approximately £50,000, was met by the efforts of the congregation, and by generous gifts from many sources, African and European.

Work was begun on the first section—which involved the demolition of the chancel of the old Christ Church—on All Saints' Day 1924. The foundation stone—a block of white marble prepared at Newcastle-on-Tyne—was laid by the Prince of Wales on 21 April 1925; and the first section, comprising the chancel and the vestries, was dedicated on 16 June 1929.

Work on the second section—the eastern portion of the nave—was begun early in 1934; the foundation stone of this part was brought from Canterbury Cathedral. The Rt. Reverend Melville Jones, Bishop of Lagos, dedicated this section on 18 October 1935.

The final section, consisting of the rest of the nave, and the tower, was dedicated on 1 May 1946.

ST MARY'S PRO-CATHEDRAL, BATHURST
[DIOCESE OF GAMBIA AND THE RIO PONGAS]

The foundation stone was laid by the Governor, Sir R. B. Llewellyn, on 6 January 1900. The building was completed in 1901, and consecrated by Bishop Taylor-Smith of Sierra Leone in December of that year. It is partly built of the stones of the old Public Works mess-room building, which had been used for worship before the building of the church: these materials were given to the congregation by the Government, together with a subsidy of £500. The total cost was about £3,000.

In 1935 the Diocese of Gambia and the Rio Pongas was created, and St Mary's was designated the pro-cathedral.

It is simple Gothic, and consists of nave and apsidal chancel. The bishop's throne was made by members of the congregation.

When the Diocesan Constitution is accepted by the Province, St Mary's will become the cathedral church: it is hoped to extend it with a side chapel, vestries, and other additions.

ST STEPHEN'S CATHEDRAL, ONDO
[Diocese of Ondo Benin]

Opened in 1892. The diocese was founded in 1952.

ST STEPHEN'S CATHEDRAL, BONNY
[Diocese of Niger Delta]

The first church was opened on 1 January 1872. A new church was opened on 27 January 1887. The bishop's throne, the gift of the children of Bonny, was made of teak from an old wreck.

4

Central Africa

ST MARY AND ALL SAINTS' CATHEDRAL, SALISBURY [DIOCESE OF MASHONALAND]

The foundation stone of the pro-cathedral was laid in 1892, and the first part was finished by January 1893. It was enlarged in 1900 and 1911.

The foundation stone of the permanent cathedral, designed by Sir Herbert Baker, was laid on St George's Day 1913, by Lady Milton. The choir, apsidal sanctuary, and two chapels were built: the wood and iron nave of the pro-cathedral remained. A bay of the nave was added later. It was completed in 1938.

It is Romanesque, vaulted, and domed in concrete. Baker designed a circular tower, like those of Ravenna—suggested by the prehistoric round tower at Zimbabwe.

ST PETER'S CATHEDRAL, LIKOMA [DIOCESE OF NYASALAND]

Archdeacon Chauncy Maples was building a church in 1886. On 2 September 1889, he wrote, "I have been busy this week in drawing plans for the stone church which the Bishop allows us to begin building." On 14 April 1890, he mentioned the bricks that Dr Laws was burning for them at Bandawe; but the church had not yet been begun in 1892. In that year, the temporary church, the library, the dispensary, and most of the dwelling houses, were burned down. The first Bishop of Nyasaland—W. B. Hornby—was consecrated on St Thomas's Day 1892.

Chauncy Maples planned to build a new, permanent church, but did not live to see it: he was consecrated bishop in 1895, and was drowned almost immediately afterwards.

In 1899, George Frank George, an architect, joined the Universities' Mission, and took charge of all the building work, all amateurs falling in line under him. He rebuilt the whole station in stone.

Early in 1903 he brought his band of masons and carpenters, all African, who had been trained and instructed by himself and Albert Crabb, and who had already built the churches at Kota Kota and Unangu, to collect material for the cathedral. The granite was quarried on Likoma, but all other materials had to be brought from the mainland—bricks, lime, and timber. Only the cement, iron for the roof, and glass came from England. The foundation stone was laid on 27 June 1903.

All the workmen were either Christians or catechumens, and a service was held each morning before work began.

The cathedral consists of a long nave, with western baptistery and towers, shallow transepts, an apsidal choir with aisles and ambulatory and vestries, and an eastern Lady chapel. It is 320 feet from east to west, and 85 feet wide at the transepts.

The architect was afterwards ordained: after retiring from Central Africa, he was vicar of St Francis', Dollis Hill (1939–42), where he is commemorated.

CATHEDRAL OF THE NATIVITY, NDOLA
[DIOCESE OF NORTHERN RHODESIA]

Dedicated on Christmas Day 1931. Some of the furniture from Bwana Church—which was abandoned as the result of the closing of the mine there—was brought to Ndola. A small Romanesque church.

A site for a cathedral has been given at Lusaka, and the Archbishop of Canterbury launched the appeal for funds in 1955. The Bishop of Northern Rhodesia writes in the U.M.C.A. review for 1955–6: "The Government has given us a fine site in the centre of the new, growing capital on which to build. It means that we must start building in the fairly near future or give up our site to others. . . . The need is great for a cathedral to act for the diocese as a focus of unity in worship and a source of spiritual power."

The architect is R. E. G. Hope of Ndola.

HOLY TRINITY CATHEDRAL, ACCRA, GHANA

ST PETER'S CATHEDRAL, LIKOMA

ST MARY AND ALL SAINTS' CATHEDRAL, SALISBURY, SOUTHERN RHODESIA

ST JOHN BAPTIST'S PRO-CATHEDRAL, BULAWAYO [Diocese of Matabeleland]

A temporary church was begun in 1894; the chancel was opened in 1895, and the nave in 1898.

The permanent church was begun in 1910: Gothic, of red Pasipas stone, and costing over £14,000. The architect was Francis Masey, who died before the completion of the church in 1913.

ST JAMES'S PRO-CATHEDRAL, MASERU
[Diocese of Basutoland]

Built in 1905–6: the architect was F. Masey. A small apsidal Romanesque church.

5

Africa, Missionary Dioceses

CHRIST CHURCH CATHEDRAL, ZANZIBAR

The Reverend A. N. West bought part of the slave market, and gave it to the Universities' Mission; Jairam Senji, a Hindu merchant, gave the site of the whipping-post. The plans for the church to stand on the site were made by C. Forster Hayward (1830–1905), a friend of Bishop Steere. The Bishop acted as master-builder and clerk of the works. The foundation stone was laid on Christmas Day 1873.

In 1876 Chauncy Maples wrote: "The church building goes on rapidly; the walls are now 40 feet high, and we are busy with a kind of clerestory gallery and the roof centring, arching of the windows, construction of the turret, trimming of the columns, placing of the capitals, &c. For all this being carried on I am responsible in the Bishop's absence. He has left definite instructions, and I hope, with the assistance of Wallis and Woodward, to be successful in carrying forward the work as he wishes it to be done."

The first service was held on Christmas Day 1877, before the roof was on. The roof, devised by the Bishop, was constructed of pounded coral mixed with a certain proportion of Portland cement: it is a pointed barrel of 28½ feet span. The work was finished in 1879.

Some marble was sent from England—the large columns of the sanctuary arch (monoliths from Devonshire), and the shafts in the windows of the apse. The floor is paved with black and white marble, with concrete under the movable teak benches. The font and the marble altar with mosaic panels were the work of Messrs Burke and Co. The west window glass, by Murray, under the direction of the architect, was inserted in 1881; the glass in the apse is by Heaton and Butler. Lectern, cross, vases, and candlesticks were supplied by Jones and Willis in 1882. In 1907 carved teak stalls, with copper panels and paintings, were dedicated in memory of Bishop Smythies. The copper panels were designed by Miss Agnes Vyse, and executed by herself and Henry Ross.

The cathedral is basilican in plan: the style is a mixture of Gothic and Arabic, as Zanzibar is a Moslem island. The altar stands on the chord of the apse, where the whipping-post once was. The bishop's throne and the carved stalls are behind it. At the west is a gallery "for such Arab ladies as could not, according to Eastern etiquette, mingle with men on the church floor".

When J. W. Wild in 1846 made an Islamic design for the English Church at Alexandria, the *Ecclesiologist* had been furious: "With what eyes can the proud and supercilious Mohammedan look upon us thus pilfering our churches from that religion of theirs which we profess to call a blasphemous cheat; with what eyes the venerable Eastern Church, proud of her unchanged traditions; with what eyes the Western Church, in whose glorious heritage of Pointed Architecture we partake? ... To build a Christian church in a land where a false religion is predominant, and Christianity trampled down, in the style of that false religion, for the sake of flattering the followers of that religion, is more than a solecism of taste, it is a gratuitous, though we fully believe an unintentional, bruise to our religious feeling." By the 70's, no one seemed to mind. But it is certain that Arabic-looking churches have not disposed the Moslems to look favourably on Christianity.

SS. MARY AND BARTHOLOMEW'S CATHEDRAL, MASASI

The first Christian settlement was made in 1876, and the stone chancel of a church was built, with a temporary nave. A new and larger church was opened on Christmas Day 1881. The place was raided in 1882, and afterwards abandoned.

On St James's Day 1905, the first stone of the new church was laid. The plans were made by W. E. Tomes, who went out to superintend the work. The material was granite from the hill Mtandi, on the slopes of which the station was situated. A few masons were brought from Zanzibar to teach the Masasi. In 1906 the work that had been done was destroyed in a native rising. Work was begun again afterwards, and an ordination was held in the half-finished church in 1907. The consecration was on 3 August 1909. The brickwork of the pillars was brought from Mkomahindo, the first station; and the stones of the altar from Mbemba, the second station. The diocese was founded in 1926.

The extension to the west was begun in 1929, under A. Makins, a former member of the Mission. The plans were made by F. C. Eden (1864–1944); a few additions suggested by Archdeacon George, during his visit to Masasi on his way back to Nyasaland in 1928, were incorporated in the design. The work was helped by the parish of All Saints', Clifton, which made a large donation to the building fund as part of its war memorial.

DIOCESE OF MOMBASA

1. THE MEMORIAL CATHEDRAL, MOMBASA

In 1900, J. H. Sinclair, H.M. Vice-Consul at Zanzibar, who had been trained as an architect, was asked to prepare a design for a church: in 1901 a government official proposed modifications which would enable it to be built for between £5,000 and £6,000. In December a plan was agreed upon—adapted by Sinclair from a design made by Messrs Christian and Purday. The style is Moorish. The dome rises from an octagonal central tower, each side of which is pierced by three slender lights. At the west are two towers surmounted by smaller domes.

The church was completed in 1904, and dedicated on 31 May 1905. The cost was about £4,400. In 1907 the pulpit and font were erected; they were executed in white marble by the Italian Sculpture Marble Co., Carrara, from designs by Sinclair. The perforated panels in the pulpit were copied from panels at Ravenna.

The dome and the transepts are a memorial to Bishop Hannington; the chancel is a memorial to Bishop Parker, and the nave to the Reverend Henry Wright.

2. ALL SAINTS' CATHEDRAL, NAIROBI

The second cathedral of the Diocese of Mombasa. In 1911 the Bishop decided to leave Mombasa, and take up residence here. In 1914 a public meeting was held, under the chairmanship of the Governor, at which it was decided to appeal for funds for the building of a church. The plans were made in 1915 by Temple L. Moore (1856–1920), the architect of many sober, graceful, and rather austere churches built towards the end of the last century, and at the beginning of this.

He planned a church to consist of nave and aisles, with an open narthex at the west; crossing, transepts surmounted by towers, and aisled choir and sanctuary, with a chapel alongside the north aisle, and vestries in a corresponding position on the south. The material was to be grey local stone, with Italian roof tiles, and the work was to be supervised by Messrs H. O. Ellis, of London and Nairobi.

It was decided to begin by building three bays of the nave and aisles: the foundation stone was laid by the Governor on 3 February 1917, and the completed portion was dedicated on 31 July 1918.

On 3 May 1922, the Governor laid the foundation stone of the north tower, which stood for eight years isolated and incomplete. In 1924 the church became a cathedral. In 1930 the nave was finished and joined to the tower: the south transept was added in 1934.

In 1946 an appeal was made for funds to build the eastern parts, which brought in about £5,000; but the Provost left, and nothing more was done for a time. In 1949 a further appeal, for £30,000, was launched; by the end of the year £10,000 had been received, during 1950 another £10,000 was contributed, and at the end of 1951 the total was £31,000.

New plans were made by Messrs Cobb, Archer and Scammell. The choir, as planned by Temple Moore, would have been rather narrow, and he had provided no chapter house, and inadequate vestry accommodation: the revised plans included what was needed, lengthened the choir by one bay, and eliminated the choir arcades, thus providing a chancel of considerable width, with a hammer-beam roof.

The Government House quarry, from which the original stone had come, was worked out; more of the same stone was found at Langata, which was used for the new work.

The foundation stone was laid on 1 October 1949, by Sir Philip Mitchell, and the completed work was consecrated on 21 March 1952. There is glass by A. J. Davies (1877–1953), made at Bromsgrove.

CATHEDRAL OF THE HOLY SPIRIT, DODOMA
[DIOCESE OF CENTRAL TANGANYIKA]

The foundation stone was laid on 23 March 1932, and it was consecrated on 15 July 1933. It is built of granite, quarried locally. The cost was borne by a friend of Tanganyika in England, as a memorial to her brother.

The diocese was founded in 1927, and is supported by the Australian C.M.S.

ST PAUL'S CATHEDRAL, KAMPALA, UGANDA

A church was built in 1890. The first cathedral was built in 1881, opened on 31 July 1892, and blown down in 1894. The second—"a forest of poles"—was built in 1895, and pulled down in 1901.

The building that took its place was a cruciform church of burnt brick for the foundations, and sun-dried for the walls—designed by K. Borup, the missionary engineer, who trained the Baganda in brick-making, carpentry, and handicrafts: he superintended the whole of the work. When the cost had been estimated, it was agreed that all the Christians should contribute according to their means; the regents gave Rs 500, and the lesser chiefs in proportion. Men dug clay from the swamps, and carried it up the hill, and the women gathered wood for the burning of the bricks. The foundation stone was laid on 18 June 1902, by the young King Daudi Cwa: the consecration was on 21 June 1904. It was 210 feet in length, consisting of nave, aisles, transepts, and chancel: there were 18 circular brick columns on octagonal bases, bearing pointed arches. The roof was covered with thatch, with three thatch spires: it was ceiled internally with polished reeds sewn together in regular straight lines. This cathedral was struck by lightning in 1910, and destroyed.

The present cathedral was designed by Arthur Beresford Pite, Professor of Architecture at the Royal College of Art—the architect of Christ Church, North Brixton, and of the Anglican Church at Bucharest.

It cost £28,000; £10,000 of this was raised in England by Bishop Tucker, and the rest was collected in Africa. It was consecrated on 13 September 1919. "The style is Gothic and is based upon the large brick Gothic churches of North Italy. . . . No attempt has been made to depart from English Liturgical requirements on a simple and dignified scale."

The plan is nave and aisles, transepts, central dome on granite pillars, and apsidal, aisled choir. The woodwork is of Uganda teak, of local workmanship. The tower at the west end has not yet been built.

In the burial ground are the bodies of Bishop Hannington and Alexander Mackay.

ALL SAINTS' CATHEDRAL, CAIRO

Bishop MacInnes, Bishop in Jerusalem, proposed the rebuilding of the old All Saints' in 1916. It was demolished in 1926: the new cathedral is on a different site.

The architect was Adrian Gilbert Scott, F.R.I.B.A.: the local supervising architects were Messrs C. R. Bawden and Newnum, and the general contractors Messrs Hettena Bros., of Cairo. The reinforced-concrete piers, arches, and domes of the cathedral were designed by Mr Burnard Green, M.INST.C.E., and carried out under the resident engineer, Mr Simmons. The style is "a free rendering of Ecclesiastical Classic", adapted to the Egyptian climate, with windows on the floor level. The cathedral was consecrated on 25 April 1938.

The memorial window to the Eighth Army is in the Lady chapel.

ALL SAINTS' CATHEDRAL, KHARTOUM
[DIOCESE OF THE SUDAN]

The architect was Robert S. Weir, of London; John Latimer was clerk of the works; and Capt. Done, R.E., director of Military Works for the Sudan, helped in supervising the building.

The cathedral is cruciform: the south transept forms a chapel, the north is the Gordon memorial. At the south-west is a tower, with baptistery in the base. At the west of the nave is a narthex with gallery over. The walls are of sandstone of two colours—yellow, and pale red—from Jabel Auli, close to the White Nile; the vaulting is of small local red bricks; the outer roof of reinforced concrete covered with red tiles. The floor of Sudanese marble; screen and stalls of timber from the Bahr-el-Ghazal.

The building was incomplete when the Bishop of London consecrated it on 26 January 1912: the last tile was placed on the roof on 20 May 1913.

The *Sudan Diocesan Review*, Autumn 1956, contains an appreciation of Sir Wasey Sterry: "When Mr Schultz Weir was appointed Architect of the Khartoum Cathedral, Judge Sterry became his friend and counsellor, giving him most valuable advice about local conditions. He also had a great deal to do with choosing the subjects of those lovely stained glass windows in both the side chapels, and indeed with those in the choir and sanctuary. It was he who composed the words in brass lettering on the west wall of the Gordon Chapel."

A memorial brass to the architect is to be placed in the cathedral. He worked in London under Norman Shaw and Ernest George and Peto, had travelled in Greece, Turkey, and Italy, and made a special study of Byzantine architecture and iconography. He did little church work; but Woolmer Green church, in Hertfordshire, is his.

In 1935 a proposal was made for building a cathedral at Juba in the Southern Sudan, and plans were prepared for a building to cost about £45,000. After the war, the building committee set to work again, but it was agreed that the proposed plans would be too expensive. On 30 August 1953, the site was dedicated, and a cairn of stones with a large wooden cross was erected in the centre. In 1955 Arthur Llewellyn Smith designed a cathedral to cost £35,000, and an appeal was issued; but it was soon realized that even this would be too ambitious. The second plan was therefore given up, and another proposed—much simpler, and estimated to cost about £10,000.

ST LAWRENCE'S CATHEDRAL, TANANARIVE, MADAGASCAR

A temporary cathedral was opened on St Peter's Day 1877.

The foundation stone of the permanent building was laid on 13 September 1883: it was consecrated on 10 August 1889. The cost was about £9,000, which was raised by S.P.G., S.P.C.K., and the friends of Bishop Kestell-Cornish. The architect was William White.

It is of stone, 13th century in style, cruciform, with octagonal towers at the ends of the transepts, and one (not completed) over the baptistery: the chancel is apsidal.

The roof of the chancel was decorated in 1911. The wrought-iron screen is a memorial to the Reverend A. M. Hewlett.

ST JAMES'S CATHEDRAL, PORT LOUIS, MAURITIUS

After the capitulation in 1810 the Council of the Colony proposed to build a church at a cost of £15,000. The foundation stone was laid, but the grant was not paid and the church was not built.

Then the Government gave the Powder Magazine, which had been built about 1780. On 16 June 1812, the Civil Chaplain called for tenders

CHRIST CHURCH
CATHEDRAL,
ZANZIBAR

HRIST CHURCH
CATHEDRAL,
ZANZIBAR

ALL SAINTS' CATHEDRAL,
NAIROBI

THE MEMORIAL
CATHEDRAL,
MOMBASA

THE CATHEDRAL OF
THE HOLY SPIRIT,
DODOMA,
TANGANYIKA

ALL SAINTS' CATHEDRAL, CAIRO

ALL SAINTS' CATHEDRAL, KHARTOUM

ALL SAINTS' CATHEDRAL, CAIRO

ST JAMES'S CATHEDRAL,
PORT LOUIS, MAURITIUS

ST PAUL'S CATHEDRAL,
KAMPALA, UGANDA

for building a church on the site. It was probably found that the task of demolishing the old building would be too costly: anyhow, the Council decided to keep the Powder Magazine, and it was used as a church without alteration.

In 1821 Colonel Barry, chief secretary of the island, called for tenders for structural alterations and necessary fittings: on 21 August an estimate was given by Mr Gastembide, which was approved by the Government architect. The alterations were to include front porch, tower, two vestries, a gallery, the furnishing of the nave and chancel, and the repair of the roof. Gastembide undertook to complete the work by 1 March 1823, failing which he would forfeit a proportion of the contract sum. When the time was completed, the work was only half done, and the question of forfeit was referred to the Procureur General. Gastembide's services were dispensed with.

Then the roof gave way, and the church was closed in 1829: it was opened for worship again on Christmas Day 1831.

In 1846 it was agreed to erect a new building, and £13,000 was voted. But before the plan was carried out, Colonel Blanchard, the officer commanding the troops, submitted a proposal for adding transepts, and making some minor alterations. The Colonial Secretary and the senior chaplain objected; but the work was done.

The church was consecrated by Dr Chapman, first Bishop of Colombo, on 26 June 1850. The first Bishop of Mauritius—Ryan—was appointed in 1854, and the church became the cathedral.

In the time of Bishop Royston (1872-90) a cement floor took the place of the wooden one, and chancel stalls and a stained glass window were introduced. Damage was done by a hurricane on 29 April 1892. In the time of Bishop Gregory (1904-19) the ceiling was removed from the old part, windows were placed in the openings in the nine-feet thick walls, the walls were lined with teak, and a new floor was laid—wooden blocks, and a central passage of black and white marble.

St Paul's, Mahé, is the pro-cathedral of the Seychelles.

HOLY CROSS PRO-CATHEDRAL, LIULI
[Diocese of South-West Tanganyika]

Designed by Archdeacon George, begun in 1923, and consecrated in 1926. It is built of granite, quarried locally, with brick for windows and doorways, and consists of nave with north and south chapels, and apsidal Lady chapel separated from the body of the church by an open arcade, against which stands the high altar, under a baldachino. The altar of St Stephen's Chapel was a gift from the parish of St Stephen's, Lewisham.

6

Canada

A. PROVINCE OF CANADA
NOVA SCOTIA
1. ST PAUL'S CATHEDRAL, HALIFAX

A proclamation in 1749 called on English people to emigrate to Nova Scotia: as the result, 13 transports and a sloop of war left home. The surveyors who laid out the new town were instructed to set apart land for a church. St Paul's was afterwards built, the frame being brought from Boston. The foundation stone was laid by the Governor, the Hon. Edward Cornwallis, on 13 June 1750, and the church was opened for service on 2 September. It was copied from St Peter's, Vere Street: both the Governor and the Reverend William Tutty mention this. Tutty wrote to S.P.G. on 17 March 1750, mentioning the church—"it is exactly the model of Mary'bone Chapel": and Cornwallis, writing to the Lords of Trade two days later, said, "the plan is the same with that of Mary-bone Chapel".

It was built at the expense of the Crown. The Reverend John Breynton wrote to S.P.G. on 8 December 1755, "The Church is now completely finished without, and makes a very handsome appearance, and it is ceiled and plaistered within, and pewed after a rough manner, by the Inhabitants." In December 1760 it was "almost finished, in a neat and elegant manner". The Lieutenant-Governor wrote on 14 January 1762, that the General Assembly had passed a law for finishing the church at an expense of £1,200, and had also joined in a subscription for an organ. The porch was repaired in 1780.

On 12 August 1787, Dr Charles Inglis was consecrated as Bishop of

Nova Scotia—the first bishop for the Anglican Church overseas. St Paul's became his cathedral.

Painting, whitewashing, and plastering was done by William Lawlor in 1788, and the cupola was repaired in the same year. Two new porches were built in 1793.

In 1811 it was decided to erect additional pews, to extend the church by 15 feet 6 inches, and to build a new steeple of the same material and dimensions as the old one. The work was finished by the end of 1812, at a cost of £2,200. The contractor was Charles Dunbrack, who did the work under the superintendence of Edward Pryor. A short time before, crimson velvet hangings for the Communion table, pulpit, and desk had been obtained from England.

Repairs were done in 1824. Between 1868 and 1872 the chancel and aisles were added. (See *The Church of St Paul in Halifax, Nova Scotia: 1749–1949*, by Reginald V. Harris, 1949.)

Bishop Binney, who was consecrated in 1851, found that he was not very happy at St Paul's: he was High, and St Paul's was Low. A few months after his arrival, he had consecrated a chapel of ease to St Paul's in the southern part of the city—a wooden Gothic building, with a tower and spire, which had been opened on 14 May 1848. This was made a parish church in 1856, under the title of St Luke's, and in September 1864 the Bishop made it the cathedral of the diocese.

A site for a permanent cathedral was given in 1871 by Justice Bliss, and another local churchman offered $10,000 if it was begun within a certain time. 1887 was the centenary year of the diocese: Bishop Binney died in that year, but the foundation stone was laid by Bishop Medley of Fredericton on 12 August.

The designs were made by A. E. Street, the son of G. E. Street, one of the most important of English 19th-century architects. Street, jun. studied under his father, and completed some of his works, but was not an architect of any great inspiration. His designs for Halifax were in 13th-century style: the plan was to have been an aisled nave, with north-west tower and spire, and south-west porch with a baptistery to the west of it; transepts, a sanctuary with aisles, and eastern vestries. The scheme came to nothing, but, close to the site, the Bishop built a chapel—St Stephen's—which might be used, after the erection of the cathedral, as a chapter house and synod hall: regular services were held in it.

2. ALL SAINTS' CATHEDRAL, HALIFAX

In December 1905 St Luke's pro-cathedral was destroyed by fire; it was decided not to rebuild it, and the congregation amalgamated with those of St Stephen's and St Alban's.

Work was begun on the present cathedral site in September 1907; the foundation stone of 1887 was transferred, and laid on 9 October 1908. The cathedral was consecrated on 3 September 1910.

The architects were Messrs Cram, Goodhue, and Ferguson of New York, and the builders Messrs S. M. Brookfield Co. of Halifax. The plan consists of nave and chancel of equal height, with narrow aisles and a tall clerestory; transepts, and smaller transepts further to the east: the west end and the central tower were left unbuilt. The style is 15th century, and the general appearance recalls such churches as Paley and Austin's St George's, Stockport. America has many such churches.

Damage was done by the two great explosions in Halifax—in 1917 and 1945. When the cathedral was surveyed after the latter, it was found that the earlier explosion had damaged the fabric more than had been realized. During the next few years, a new temporary west end was erected, and the two western bays of the nave, the great transepts, and the walls of St Stephen's Chapel were reconstructed. The restoration of the east window and the sanctuary was begun in August 1953, and completed in May 1954.

The fittings include: lectern, given by Samuel M. Brookfield, the head of the firm that built the cathedral: dean's stall in memory of Dean Llwyd, who died in 1933: choir stalls made by Bromsgrove Guild Canada Ltd: bishop's throne, the gift of the bicentenary Church Congress held at Halifax at the time of the opening of the cathedral: carved oak altar in memory of Bishop Binney: carved reredos dedicated on 11 August 1929: glass in the east window, by the firm of C. E. Kempe, a memorial to the 1914–18 war. The altar and reredos in St Stephen's Chapel were designed by F. E. Howard of Oxford.

ST PETER'S CATHEDRAL, CHARLOTTETOWN, PRINCE EDWARD ISLAND

A church in 14th-century style, opened in 1868. Bishop Binney, having no cathedral in the island, directed that his throne should be placed in the sanctuary.

HOLY TRINITY CATHEDRAL, QUEBEC

In 1799 Bishop Mountain wrote to the Archbishop expressing his disappointment: in spite of all his efforts, a Court House was to be built on the site of the Recollet Chapel, and no mention of a church had been made by the Government. He also wrote to the Duke of Portland: the only church accommodation was the Jesuit Chapel, which was small, dark, and dirty. The Duke authorized Sir Robert Milnes, Lieutenant-Governor of Lower Canada, to appropriate the site of the Recollet Chapel, and to supply £400 annually towards the erection of a church. Commissioners were appointed.

The foundation stone was laid on 11 August 1800. The architects were Captain Hall and Major Robe, of the Royal Engineers. Robe wrote: "The general dimensions of this church were in great measure taken from those of St Martin's-in-the-Fields, James Gibbs' masterpiece in Trafalgar Square, London, but the state of materials and workmanship in Canada made a plain design necessary."

In the autumn of 1800 the Commissioners asked the Governor for further advances, as the £400 was not enough. The estimate of the cost of building, independent of some furnishings and the pay of the master mason, was about £5,000.

Another memorial from the Commissioners, in April 1802, asked for more. They said that economy was being practised: the spire was to be of wood instead of stone. They also wrote in July, hoping that His Majesty would follow up his bounty with plate, an altar cloth, a bible, and prayer books. An order for silver was given to the royal treasury—but the gifts did not arrive until 2 November 1809.

Another request for money was made in May 1803. The consecration was on 28 August 1804. The expense had been about £18,000.

By 1811 the church needed repair. On 22 September the Bishop wrote to Sir George Provost, asking whether a further grant could be given. The Administration promised to write to the Secretary of State, but there was no result. On 6 June 1814, the Bishop wrote to the succeeding Secretary of State, and a few weeks later sent an estimate of £6,797 for repairing and finishing the church. In 1815 Sir Gordon Drummond, administering the Government of Lower Canada, represented the dilapidated state of the church; and assistance was given in 1816.

It is a pleasing specimen of a late Georgian church, very plain without, and elegant within—of the Ionic order, with a plaster vault, internal eastern apse, and Venetian east window.

An additional gallery was built in 1833.

ST JOHN'S CATHEDRAL, NEWFOUNDLAND

On 1 September 1840, the Bishop—Spencer—wrote to the Secretary of S.P.G. on the subject of a cathedral: "The parish church in the large and populous town of St John's has been built above 40 years; and, having been constructed of very frail materials, is now in so dilapidated a condition, that to repair it properly would eventually occasion a greater expense to the parishioners, than the erection of a new church." The new church should, at least in some degree, partake of a cathedral character. The resources of the community were inadequate, and therefore he appealed to S.P.G., S.P.C.K., the Universities, and the "many true and liberal friends of our Ecclesiastical system in the opulent towns of the Kingdom". The sum required would be about £5,000.

The letter was read to the Oxford Architectural Society, and the secretary was directed to apply for such further information as an architect would need. The reply gave some information about prices. Stone fit for mullions, copings, etc., could not be got in Newfoundland, but must be obtained in England or in Nova Scotia. Good workmen were to be found in the island, especially stone-masons—the Government having imported some for the erection of the Government House. Only so much of the church was to be built as would be necessary for the immediate performance of Divine Service: the tower and spire, and all ornament, could wait.

J. M. Derick sent out a plan which was not adopted. The Bishop entered into a contract with an Irish stone-merchant to supply the plan and the wrought stone. The Bishop's scheme languished, and his successor, Bishop Feild, found the subscriptions exhausted. A quantity of stone window-frames, some mouldings, and a few scattered quoins and dressings, all worked in Ireland, were the sole remains of the scheme: they were piled up in a wharf by the side of the harbour. Then the old wooden church was burned.

In 1846 the Bishop came to England to procure plans: these were made by George Gilbert Scott. In the spring of 1848 an experienced clerk of the works, and a body of masons, who had gained experience at the College of Perth, began the church.

The *Ecclesiologist* reviewed the designs in April 1848: "Under these conditions, a most impracticable climate, no available native materials, an unpliant ritual, and the need of retaining a parochial character,—we think that such a combination, as in the parallel case of a tropical climate, would have justified an attempt at development. Mr Scott has, however, chosen to build by precedent: and the result, though scrupulously correct, appears to us deficient in the indescribable character, the moral feeling, if we may so say—of originality. Under such circumstances, Christian art could afford to be plastic. St John's Cathedral, as designed by Mr Scott, reminds us of a first-rate University prize poem. There is authority for every detail and phrase; it is learned and dignified, but perhaps cold: it displays the artist's reading and study more than his genius." The spire "somehow or other wants verve and force; that indescribable outline which would give it individuality".

Scott imagined that the ecclesiologists had a spite against him—one of the reasons being that his favourite 13th-century style was too early. In fact, they spoke well of him on the whole, and soon came themselves to approve an earlier style than the Middle-Pointed which had been their original ideal. The truth is, that some of Scott's earlier churches are rather dull. During the 50's and 60's he produced some really impressive churches: who, after seeing, let us say, St Andrew's, Leicester, could suggest that the Victorians could do nothing but copy mediaeval work? But his earlier, English-looking 13th-century efforts are not very interesting, and the *Ecclesiologist* was not really being unjust.

Only the nave was built at first. In 1880 the building of the choir and transepts was entrusted to G. G. Scott, jun. (1839–97), who was to follow his father's plans "with such modifications as he thought desirable". J. W. Wills was clerk of the works. A body of masons was brought from England. The freestone was exported from Giffnock Quarries near Glasgow.

In 1883 it was reported that "the aisle walls are ready for the wall plate, and the transept walls are up somewhat higher. Inside, the piers for the tower arches have been brought nearly to their height, and the arcades of choir and north transept finished, and the walls above are brought up to the clerestory string course".

The reredos was erected in 1885: it was designed by Hay and Henderson, and executed by John Rhind of Cambridge Street.

CHRIST CHURCH CATHEDRAL, FREDERICTON, NEW BRUNSWICK

HOLY TRINITY CATHEDRAL,
QUEBEC

ST JOHN'S CATHEDRAL, NEWFOUNDLAND

On 8 July 1892, the cathedral was destroyed by fire. The choir and transepts, rebuilt by G. G. and J. O. Scott, under the superintendence of J. W. Wills, were rededicated on St Peter's Day 1895. The woodwork of the choir, executed by Harry Hems of Exeter, was finished in 1896. The restoration of the nave was not completed until the beginning of this century.

The reredos was designed by Sir Giles Gilbert Scott.

CHRISTCHURCH CATHEDRAL, FREDERICTON

John Medley, the first Bishop, was a High Churchman, and wished to build a cathedral that would be an ecclesiological model. The plans were made by Frank Wills, of Exeter and Salisbury, who came to Canada in 1845. He afterwards went to America, and was partner with Dudley; he worked on behalf of Ecclesiology in the States, designed a good many churches, and was author of *Ancient English Ecclesiastical Architecture, and its Principles applied to the Wants of the Church at the Present Day* (New York, 1850).

The design was suggested by Snettisham Church, Norfolk. The foundation stone was laid on 15 October 1845. The material is local stone, with Caen stone for the windows and interior details; the roof of New Brunswick pine.

In October 1847 the *Ecclesiologist* reported that the design had been altered for the better. The roof of the choir had been raised; the central tower had been abandoned, and transeptal towers, one at least of which was to have a spire, had been substituted. The walls of the nave and aisles were built in 1847, and roofed in 1848. The two towers were abandoned, and Butterfield made a plan for the choir, and a central tower and spire. The Bishop visited England and obtained subscriptions: he promised himself to pay for the roof and windows, and for the carriage of the stone. In 1849 it was reported that the Bishop had modified Butterfield's design for the tower windows, giving them greater simplicity, while preserving the general effect. He had also made the walls of the tower incline inward fifteen inches on each side. In 1852 he went to England again, and obtained various gifts. On 21 May he spoke to a meeting of the Exeter Diocesan Architectural Society on church building in his diocese, mentioning the cathedral. He described the materials, and then spoke of the tower: "He had been very desirous to surmount it with a stone spire, but, after carefully considering the question, he had come to the determination to let well alone, and not to run an unnecessary risk by putting on so great an additional weight. The spire, therefore, was of wood, protected by galvanized iron, and the entire height was 170 feet. The windows, except the east window, were completed; the west window had been most ably executed by Mr Warrington, and the others by the late Mr Beer, and the east window was entrusted to Mr Wailes, who had kindly offered to give one of the eight compartments into which it was divided, and to complete it, so that he (the Bishop) might take it out with him in August".

In this year the plan was again altered, and the aisles which were to have embraced the tower were changed to transepts. The Bishop had the glass of the east window inserted when he arrived back; the balance of the cost was subscribed by members of the American Church. The woodwork was executed by Mr Mitchell.

The cathedral was consecrated on 24 August 1853.

In 1879 two windows by Clayton and Bell were inserted at the west of the aisles.

On the night of 3–4 July 1911, the cathedral was struck by lightning, and the spire, the organ, and the bells were destroyed. During the subsequent restoration, the foundations of the tower were strengthened.

CHRIST CHURCH CATHEDRAL, MONTREAL

One result of the visit of Bishop Inglis in the summer of 1789 was the obtaining of the dilapidated chapel of the Jesuit College for the use of the Anglican congregation. It was repaired and furnished, and opened in December under the dedication of Christ Church. In 1803 it was burned, and the foundations of a new church were laid in 1805: the new building was opened in 1814. It had a Doric portico, and a tower surmounted by an iron balustrade, with clock stage and spire above.

The organ, installed in 1816, was built by Thomas Elliott of London, who had in 1801 built organs for Holy Trinity Cathedral and the Roman Catholic Basilica at Quebec. Archdeacon Mountain, later Bishop of Quebec, wrote in his *Journal* that he had seen at Montreal "a large and handsome church which had cost a hundred thousand dollars with an organ which cost eight thousand five hundred dollars".

The church was completely destroyed by fire on 9 December 1856.

The new cathedral was erected on a different site. Frank Wills made the plans: the contract was given to Messrs Brown and Watson of Montreal on 7 July 1856. Wills died in 1857, and Thomas Seaton Scott of Montreal (1836–95) was appointed to succeed him on 29 April. The foundation stone was laid on 21 May.

In 1859 the *Ecclesiologist* reported: "We hear most satisfactory reports of this cathedral, which is nearly completed. Messrs Clayton and Bell's glass in the east, and the south transept windows is fixed, and is greatly admired. The former contains our Blessed LORD and the Evangelists; the latter the raising of Lazarus, and the Angels announcing the Resurrection to the Maries. That for the north transept will follow in the spring. Several painted windows, including the choir clerestory, are executed by Mr Spence, who has likewise coloured the choir roof. The capitals of the nave arcade are carved in imitation of Canadian foliage, and English foliage is introduced into the choir stalls. The triple sedilia, which we understand stand in the north wall of the sanctuary, are described as very rich. The north transept is appropriated as the baptistery, and is carved by Mr Williams of Manchester. The organ is from Mr Hill's manufactory."

It is indeed a very satisfactory example of "correct" mid-19th-century church building. It was opened on 27 November 1860, and consecrated in 1867.

The tower sank while building was in progress, and the spire had to be taken down in June 1927: it was rebuilt afterwards.

The high altar and carved stone reredos are a 1914–18 war memorial. An inlaid cross is formed of stone from Calvary, the Mount of Olives, Iona, Canterbury, and the site of the earliest Anglican church in Canada. A window in the Chapel of St John of Jerusalem, by Charles W. Kelsey, was erected in 1957.

B. PROVINCE OF ONTARIO

1. ST JAMES'S CATHEDRAL, TORONTO

A meeting was held in 1803 to consider the building of a church at Toronto (then known as York). The S.P.G. Report of 1807–8 stated that it was almost complete: the pews, 32 in number, were soon to be finished. Lieut.-Governor Gore had promised to erect a pulpit at his own expense, so soon as a proper artist could be found. The church was very small, of wood. It was enlarged in 1818.

It was designed by William (really Wilhelm) von Moll Berczy (1748–1813) a Saxon, who went to London in 1790, and became an agent for a land company. Two years later, he took a band of German settlers to New York State; but after some dispute he transferred them to Upper Canada in 1794. He seems to have been in Toronto in 1796: he moved to Montreal in 1805, and later to Quebec. The National Gallery of Canada has two paintings by him, one of which is a conversation piece in English style, painted in Quebec in 1809. He died in New York.

In January 1831 it was decided to build a new church: the committee was instructed to have plans drawn for a building of stone, costing not more than £5,000, not less than 75 feet wide. The plans were made by James G. Chewatt, and the contractor was John Ritchie. The foundation stone was laid on 27 June 1834: it was completed, save for the tower, later in the year.

On 6 June 1839, it was burned down, and plans were made for a new and larger church. In the summer of that year John Strachan was consecrated Bishop: when he returned from England, he found the church rebuilt—of stone, with a wooden tower. It was consecrated on 4 August, and was made the cathedral.

It was burned on 7 April 1849, and the Bishop issued an *Address to the Parishioners of St James's Parish, Toronto*, on the subject of rebuilding. Appended to it were *Recommendations by the Church-building Committee of the Church Society in regard to Churches and their Precincts.*

The foundation stone of the new cathedral was laid on 20 November 1850. The architect was Frederic William Cumberland, who was born in London in 1821, and was educated at King's College. He studied architecture (under Barry) and engineering, and was first a railway engineer, and then in the engineering department of the Admiralty. He went to Canada in 1847, and became partner with William G. Storm (1826–92). He designed Osgoode Hall and University College, Toronto. His interest in railways remained, and in 1860 he became managing director of the Northern Railway. He died in 1881.

Thomas Ridout was associated with him in the building of the cathedral, and the contractors were Metcalfe, Wilson, and Forbes. It was opened on 19 June 1853: the cost was $94,000, not including the tower.

The style is 13th century, of the type that one associates with the older

London suburbs, such as Paddington: it consists of nave, aisles, and porches, and an apsidal chancel with vestries. There are triplets of lancets in the aisles and celerestory, and traceried windows in the apse: the aisle buttresses are surmounted with pinnacles. In 1865 the tower was raised 35 feet, and the building was finally completed in 1874, by Henry Langley (1837–1907).

The side galleries were removed in 1889, and the choir was moved to the chancel. In 1914 the wooden floor was removed, and replaced by concrete, with red tiles in the nave, and tiles and marble in the chancel.

The glass is chiefly by Clayton and Bell.

2. ST ALBAN'S CATHEDRAL, TORONTO

Bishop Strachan bequeathed 400 acres of land to assist in building a cathedral. In 1872 the Synod contemplated building it as his memorial, but nothing came of it. Bishop Sweatman revived the scheme, and secured about 4½ acres outside the city, in Seaton Village. This was soon incorporated within the city limits.

The Bishop had not proposed to build until the cathedral establishment had been set up, and sufficient money raised. But building was proceeding so fast, and prospects seemed so good, that he changed his mind. In 1885 the trustees of the property offered $2,000 on condition that the choir was erected within 18 months. The Chapter accepted the offer, and building was begun.

Services were held in the basement from 1887: in 1889 the choir was roofed in. It was built of red Credit Valley stone and Ohio freestone: apsidal, with aisles of three bays. The cathedral, as planned, was to have had a fantastic pinnacled tower, very tall and slim, at the south-west, and a much lower tower, with spire, at the north-west. The architect was Richard Windeyer.

The cathedral project was never very popular, and no more than the chancel was ever built. There were ambitious schemes for completion by Cram, Goodhue, and Ferguson of Boston and New York, with Symons and Rae as supervising architects; but these remained on paper.

There was a fire in 1929, and the church was reopened after repair on 15 September. But the Synod had decided on 30 May of that year that it was not to be a cathedral. It took the title of the Church of St Alban the Martyr, the former Cathedral; and St James's became the cathedral once again.

ST PAUL'S CATHEDRAL, LONDON
[DIOCESE OF HURON]

The original church, built in 1835, was a frame building—"one of the finest, and certainly one of the neatest, churches in the provinces". It was burned down on Ash Wednesday 1844.

The foundation stone of the present church was laid by Dr Strachan, Bishop of Toronto, on 24 June of the same year, and it was opened on Ash Wednesday 1846. The architect was William Thomas, who was born at Stroud in 1800, and practised at Leamington, where he designed Lansdowne Crescent and Circus, and houses in Brandon Place. He published *Designs for Monuments and Chimney-pieces*, 1843. His brother John (1813–62), who became well known as a sculptor, helped him for a time. Thomas emigrated to Canada, and settled at Toronto, where he designed St Michael's (R.C.) Cathedral and the Gaol. He died in 1860.

The style of St Paul's is "mixed Gothic, in which early English predominates. Many of the details, both in design and workmanship, are very beautiful, and reflect credit on the constructors". It is of brick, with a wide nave, originally galleried, and a pinnacled tower, with a panelled upper stage, 130 feet high.

The Diocese of Huron was formed in 1857, and St Paul's became the cathedral. The chancel was extended in 1869, and vestry and organ chamber were added.

The foundation stone of a new cathedral was laid on 5 June 1872: by 1874 the chapter house had been built, and services were held in it. Bishop Hellmuth moved his seat there in 1877, but in 1882 it was restored to St Paul's. In 1893–4 the galleries were taken down, transepts and a new chancel were erected, and buildings were added for parochial and diocesan purposes. Messrs Spiers and Rohns of Detroit were the architects, and Messrs Moore and Henry of London the superintending architects.

Font of Carrara marble is a memorial to Dean Innes, who died in 1903. Pulpit 1924: new altar, reredos, and sanctuary panelling 1955.

ST GEORGE'S CATHEDRAL, KINGSTON, ONTARIO

It was resolved on 9 January 1792 to employ Archibald Thomson to build a church, 12 feet high, at a cost of £108. It was glazed and plastered by October, and pulpit, desk, Communion table, pews, cupola, and bell had been added by the autumn of 1794. In 1795 a gallery was built. In 1802 the church was enlarged, and given another gallery.

In 1823 the first steps were taken for replacing the old wooden church. The new building, from designs by Rogers, was begun in 1825: it was opened in 1826 and consecrated in 1828. The cost was £10,000, which was raised from the rent of Church lands, contributions from the parish, donations by the rector and the assistant ministers, and a royal gift of £1,500. The Tuscan portico and octagonal tower with cupola were added in 1846.

A Victorian writer expressed the opinion that it was "built before the revival of correct taste in Church architecture, but nevertheless a really fine specimen of the Queen Anne style".

In 1892 it was reopened after being enlarged with transepts, a central dome, and an apsidal chancel by Power and Son (John Power, sen., born in 1814, and John, jun., born in 1848). It was damaged by fire on 1 January 1898, restored by the same firm, and reopened in 1901. The interior was renovated in 1953.

ST MATTHEW'S PRO-CATHEDRAL, TIMMINS
[Diocese of Moosonee]

The first pro-cathedral was at Moose. John Horden (afterwards Bishop) arrived here on 26 August 1851. There was "a neat little church, with a suitable tower". The Methodists had had a mission here, but had abandoned it: Horder took possession of it. The diocese was formed in 1872.

Our Mission News (August 1886) mentioned "a fine cathedral at Moose, the spacious chancel of which was opened on Whitsunday last".

The next pro-cathedral was Holy Trinity, Cochrane, which was opened on 6 June 1909. This was destroyed by fire in 1911. It was rebuilt in 1913, but was condemned as unsafe in 1943. The former church at Timmins was pulled down, and a new one was consecrated on 30 November 1947: it had been made the pro-cathedral. It consists of nave with low north-east tower and spire, and an apsidal chancel. The window of St Paul is by Yvonne Williams.

ST LUKE'S CATHEDRAL, SAULT STE MARIE
[DIOCESE OF ALGOMA]

The work of the Anglican Church began in 1832 as a mission to the Indians, but a permanent church was not built until 1870. This was a small building of local sandstone, in a very simple E.E. style.

In 1873 Algoma was founded as a missionary diocese, and the first Bishop, the Right Reverend F. D. Fauquier, made Sault Ste Marie his headquarters, with St Luke's as his church—though it was some years before it became known as the pro-cathedral.

In 1896 the church was extended to the east and west, and a tower and transepts were added.

In November 1952 the interior was destroyed by fire. The church has been rebuilt, enlarged, and beautified, and has been constituted as a cathedral.

Part of the original church of 1870, and the tower and south transept of 1896, remain on the south.

CHRIST'S CHURCH CATHEDRAL, HAMILTON, NIAGARA

The Reverend J. G. Geddes arrived at Hamilton in 1835, and found that services were being held at the Court House. On 13 June a Vestry meeting was held at the office of John Law, Esq., "for the purpose of furthering the erection of a Protestant Episcopal Church". Three sites were offered: the one on James Street was accepted, and a building committee was appointed. The architect chosen was Mr Wetherall, and the contractor was Jonathan Simpson. Difficulties arose during the years 1836–8, but the church was eventually opened on 31 July 1839. It was consecrated in 1842. The tower and spire were unfinished, but the ladies made an effort and raised $1,000—which stimulated the rest of the parish, and they were completed without delay.

The church was extremely handsome, entirely 18th century in appearance. There was an elaborate and effective steeple, with a vestibule at the base: on the north and south sides were doorways with pilasters and pediments, and at the west a Tuscan portico. The sides of the church had long arched windows, divided at gallery level, and pilasters.

After seven or eight years it was found to be too small, and plans

CHRIST CHURCH
CATHEDRAL,
MONTREAL

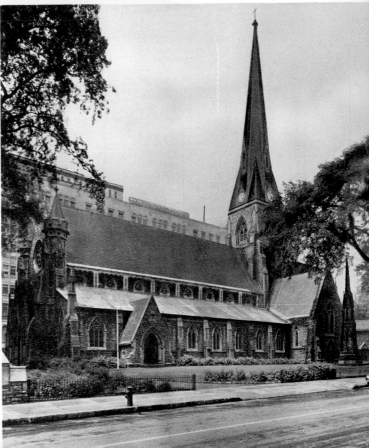

ST JAMES'S CATHEDRAL, TORONTO

ST PAUL'S CATHEDRAL, LONDON, ONTARIO

ST GEORGE'S CATHEDRAL, KINGSTON, ONTARIO

CHRIST'S CHURCH CATHEDRAL, HAMILTON, NIAGARA

were made for rebuilding: but it was eventually decided to build another church on the south side of the town.

In 1852 it was enlarged with a new chancel and a portion of a new nave, "to form the commencement of a handsome and commodious church which might last for generations, and in point of style and dimensions be somewhat in keeping with the population, wealth, and prosperity of the city".

In 1873 a subscription list was opened, and $22,000 was raised; but as $20,000 more was needed, it was resolved to borrow that amount, and to proceed with the work. The Dean and churchwardens later found themselves in difficulties over this loan.

The Diocese of Niagara was created in 1875, and Christ's Church became the cathedral. The Reverend J. G. Geddes—still here after 40 years—was appointed Dean. The new building was opened on 20 February 1876. It was said of the Dean that "he regards this splendid building with the warmth of love which a father bears towards a beautiful daughter" (*Dominion Churchman*, 1879).

It is a pity that Wetherall's handsome classical church was suffered to remain for so short a time; but the present cathedral is a good example of Victorian Gothic that is not ashamed to be elaborate. English churchmen with aesthetic leanings are rather embarrassed by this kind of work, and try to tone it down; but Canadians appreciate it.

The architects were Leith and Langley of Toronto.

The chancel was rebuilt and enlarged in 1924. The east window—based on a suggested restoration of the shattered window of Guisborough Priory—has glass to the memory of the first Bishop, Thomas Brock Fuller (1875–85). Of the other windows, one—"an example of early Canadian work"—was exhibited in London at the Exhibition of 1862, and was particularly admired by the Prince of Wales. The west window of Faith, Hope, and Charity (1876) is by Heaton, Butler, and Bayne.

The Caen stone reredos, with 18 canopied statues and four reliefs of the life of Our Lord, is by J. Wippell and Co. The cost was £2,500.

CHRIST CHURCH CATHEDRAL, OTTAWA

The first church was built in 1833: in 1841 the Vestry decided to enlarge it.

The present church was erected in 1872: the architect was King

Arnoldi—a member of a German family which settled in Canada in the 18th century.

The diocese was founded in 1896.

The chancel was designed by A. J. Hazelgrove, 1932.

It is in Middle-Pointed style, with a clerestoried nave and aisles, and a north-west tower with broach spire.

c. Province of Rupert's Land
ST JOHN'S CATHEDRAL, WINNIPEG, RUPERT'S LAND

The first church was built in 1822, the second in 1833–4. In 1856 Bishop Anderson visited England to raise funds for building a cathedral: the Hudson's Bay Company and S.P.C.K. gave £500 each.

The old St John's was pulled down, and the new building was erected according to plans that the Bishop had brought from England—the church in 1861, and the tower in 1862. The plans had to be reduced, and the tower, which had inadequate foundations, had to be taken down in 1875.

In 1907 a beginning was made of raising funds for a new cathedral. Plans were obtained from a firm of architects in England, but they would have been too expensive. Early in 1913 the old building was found to be unsafe: the last service was held on 7 November.

The money was raised, and early in 1925 Parfitt and Prain were appointed architects: the Sutherland Construction Company gave the lowest tender. The foundation stone was laid on 29 June, and the new building was finished by the end of 1926. In December 1928 the Dean and Chapter accepted G. Parfitt's plan for sanctuary panelling, bishop's throne, and stalls. The east window (by Cakebread and Robey) was dedicated in April 1932.

The font is of Italian marble, a memorial to the first Bishop of Rupert's Land. The pulpit was carved by R. Dien; it is made of oak from the old Bishop's Court, built in 1844, and was presented in 1907.

ST JOHN'S CATHEDRAL, SASKATOON

The first church was built in 1902, and dedicated on 18 January 1903. It was enlarged by a nave in 1904, a tower was added in 1908, and there was a further enlargement in 1909.

At a Vestry meeting in November 1910 it was recommended that a new site should be purchased. In 1912 the old church and rectory were moved to the present site, and on 6 May a tender for the erection of a new and much larger church was accepted.

The foundation stone was laid by the Duke of Connaught, then Governor-General, on 2 September 1912. The architects were Messrs Thompson, Daniel, and Colthurst. (Thomas Brammall Daniel, born in 1873, was articled to J. D. Harker of Manchester. He was the architect of one or two other buildings in Saskatoon, and some in the East End of London.)

In 1913, before the building was completed, the great boom in real estate declined, and work had to be stopped. Money was borrowed to cover in the building, but the first service was not held until 7 October 1917. It became a cathedral in 1924.

The base of the walls is of Saskatchewan granite; the exterior walls are of Redcliffe brick made in Alberta, and the interior brick is from Manitoba. Window tracery, and all ornamental work, is of buff terra cotta by Doulton and Co. Steel work is used in the tower and spire, and in the roof trusses. The plan is cruciform, with tower and spire between the chancel and south transept.

The interior walls were covered with buff stucco in 1954: screen, pulpit, lectern, altar, reredos, and font are of terra cotta.

Embedded in the pillars are a cross given in 1932 by the Friends of Canterbury Cathedral, a finial dislodged from the choir of Exeter Cathedral in the raid, and a stone from Glastonbury Abbey.

ST JAMES'S CATHEDRAL, PEACE RIVER
[DIOCESE OF ATHABASCA]

A log church was built in 1910.

In 1936 an anonymous donor offered to build a small permanent cathedral: it was consecrated on 10 July. The architects were Twizell and Twizell of Vancouver.

The former Diocese of Mackenzie River had as pro-cathedral first St David's, Fort Simpson, and then St Paul's, Chipewyan. Fort Simpson was built by the Reverend W. W. Kirby, "largely by his own hard manual labour".

ST PAUL'S PRO-CATHEDRAL, REGINA
[DIOCESE OF QU'APPELLE]

The Diocese of Qu'Appelle—originally known as Assiniboia—was founded in 1883, and the first Bishop was consecrated in 1884. It includes the southern half of Saskatchewan, with a piece of S.E. Alberta.

The original pro-cathedral was ST PETER'S, QU'APPELLE, a very simple brick Gothic church with a low north-west tower and spire—built in 1885, and consecrated on 30 June.

In 1911, 25 acres of land in Regina were bought by the Church, and in 1912 a committee of Synod made a plan for the diocesan buildings, which were to include St Chad's College, a cathedral, bishop's house, schools, a synod house, clergy house for the Railway Mission, etc. St Chad's College was opened in 1914.

St Paul's, Regina, was made the pro-cathedral on 18 May 1944. The first church was built in 1883: it was a small wooden building. The foundation stone of the present St Paul's was laid on 18 September 1894, and the first service was held in the nave on 24 January 1895. In 1905 the Vestry decided to build the transepts and chancel, which were completed in 1906.

It is of brick, in a very simple Gothic style. There were extensive renovations a few years ago.

CATHEDRAL OF THE REDEEMER, CALGARY

The S.P.G. Report for 1884 mentions the building of a church costing about £500. This was a wooden building. The permanent church was later built by the side of it—plain E.E., with nave and chancel of equal height, and a three-sided apse. It was completed in 1905.

ST ALBAN'S PRO-CATHEDRAL, KENORA
[DIOCESE OF KEEWATIN]

Keewatin—"the Land of the North Wind"—is a missionary diocese. "The town of Kenora, situated at the north end of the Lake of the Woods, is our principal town, and here also is our pro-cathedral of St Alban and our See centre.... We have no city in the diocese, and no town with more than one priest" (*Canadian Churchman*).

ALL SAINTS' CATHEDRAL, EDMONTON

The Parish of All Saints' grew from the work of the Reverend William Newton, who arrived in Edmonton on 28 September 1875. The Roman Catholics and Methodists had been there for a generation, and the planting of the Anglican Church at first seemed almost impossible. But in 1914 the new Diocese of Edmonton was carved out of the Diocese of Calgary, and All Saints' became the pro-cathedral.

In 1919 the church was burned to the ground. In 1921 the crypt of a new cathedral was opened, in which the congregation worshipped until 1956. The pro-cathedral had meanwhile become the cathedral of the diocese.

The corner stone of the present building was laid by the Bishop of the Diocese, the first sod having been turned by the Archbishop of Canterbury in 1954. It was consecrated on 10 May 1956. The new cathedral has been built to the south of the crypt: it is of modern design, in keeping with most of the other architecture of Edmonton—the Oil Capital of Canada. It is of brick inside and out: the south wall, which is against a large building, is of solid brick: the north side is almost entirely of glass.

The ceiling of the chancel is finished in panelled oak: the ceiling of the nave is panelled in acoustic tile, with beams tinted light blue. The woodwork throughout is of oak.

The cost was approximately $300,000: the architects were Blakey, Blakey, and Ascher.

ST MATTHEW'S CATHEDRAL, BRANDON

The first Anglican service was held at Brandon in 1881. In 1882 a site for a church was purchased, and an English architect, Fitzroy Dixion, who had just arrived, drew up the plans. E. McCroskie, another architect from England, supervised the building. S.P.C.K. contributed to the cost. The city directory for 1883 described it: "The English Church of St Metthew, an elegant structure of Gothic design, is situated near the south-east corner of 11th Street and Princess Avenue. The position is a very central and commanding one, and the high gables and bell turret of the pretty little church can be seen rearing itself conspicuously above its more rectangular surroundings from every part of the city. The cost of this site and buildings amounts to about $7,000,

E. McCroskie and Co. being the architects. The interior of the building is made attractive by the roof, choir stalls and ceilings being of stained pine, the east window of ornamental glass representing a scene in the 'Crucifixion', and the reredos composed of five lancet recesses of carved wood filled in with tapestry. The reredos is the gift of the first organizer of the congregation, L. M. Fortier, Esq. The church was dedicated on 1 October 1882 by the Lord Bishop of Rupert's Land. . . ."

It was of brick, plain E.E. in style, and was twice enlarged. Part of it is now St Hedwig's Roman Catholic Church.

The site for the new St Matthew's was bought in 1909 and 1910, and the foundation stone was laid on 2 October 1912. The architect was Mr Elliott of Brandon. The new church was dedicated on 1 February 1914. The first Bishop of the new diocese was consecrated in 1924, and St Matthew's became the pro-cathedral. It was consecrated on 10 May 1945, after the debt on the building had been paid off, and was made a cathedral in 1952.

It is of brick, and consists of nave and aisles, transepts, a central tower, and chancel with vestries and organ chamber. The west window is the kind of angular Perp. that one associates mainly with early 20th-century Nonconformist chapels in England: the rest are lancets.

Repairs were done between 1948 and 1952; an oak reredos was dedicated by the Archbishop of Canterbury in 1954. There are many memorial windows.

Here are knapped flints from Brandon, Suffolk, and fragments from the Abbey of SS. Peter and Paul, Canterbury (now known as St Augustine's).

ST ALBAN'S CATHEDRAL, PRINCE ALBERT
[DIOCESE OF SASKATCHEWAN]

A church was built in 1886, the money for which was collected in England by Bishop McLean, the first Bishop of Saskatchewan. It was made a pro-cathedral on 22 August 1894.

In 1895 it was decided to build a new and larger church of brick, at a cost of £6,000, as a memorial to Bishop McLean. Some difficulty was experienced in raising the money, and the old church had to be repaired in 1898. In 1901 it was possible to make a beginning, and the new church was first used on Christmas Day 1905. It was dedicated on 4 February 1906.

In 1911 the chancel and vestry were added, and memorial windows to Bishop McLean and his family were placed at the east end. The west window is a Great War memorial.

On 28 June 1944, as no debt remained, the cathedral was consecrated by the Right Reverend Henry D. Martin, D.D., the seventh Bishop of the diocese.

ALL SAINTS' CATHEDRAL, AKLAVIK
[DIOCESE OF THE ARCTIC]

Bishop Lucas of Mackenzie River established a mission here in 1919, and a small church was built in 1920. When Bishop Fleming visited Aklavik in 1937, he received the first gift towards the building of a new and larger church—100 dollars from Loucheaux Indian women. Next came 25 dollars from the fur traders.

The new cathedral, built of timber from British Columbia, and holding about 250, was consecrated on St Peter's Day 1939. The panelling is Indian work, and three Indian women gave a frontal of white moose skin adorned with patterns in porcupine-quill embroidery. The altar piece—"Epiphany in the Snows"—was painted by Violet Teague of Melbourne. The altar candlesticks were a gift from England: the cross is from St George's, Edgbaston. The pulpit contains two panels from St Paul's Cathedral, and some wood from Charing Church, Kent; the lectern has wood from St Nicholas, Biggar, Lanarkshire, and a panel from Turvey Church, Bedfordshire. The glass in the chancel is by Robert McCausland of Toronto, and the baptistery window by Hugh Easton. The painted shields at the ends of the wardens' seats are the work of Clement Skilbeck. The architects were Molesworth and Secord of Toronto.

D. PROVINCE OF BRITISH COLUMBIA
CHRIST CHURCH CATHEDRAL, VICTORIA, BRITISH COLUMBIA

The first church was built by the Hudson's Bay Company in 1853–6. It was of wood and plaster. The first Bishop was consecrated in 1859. He went to England in 1869 to appeal for help for the diocese: during his absence the church was burned down. "It is a matter for much regret that the opportunity was not seized to erect a permanent cathedral, or at least a portion available for present use in durable materials. Plans were prepared by Mr Ferrey, but the funds were not forthcoming, the people of Victoria were unwilling to wait, and in the end another wooden building, of better design and with more church-like arrangements, was erected upon the same lovely site on which the late church stood" (*Colonial Church Chronicle*, March 1873). It was consecrated on 5 December 1872.

Improvements were made in 1890: the east window by Burlison and Grylls, a memorial to the wife of Bishop Hills, was erected, the interior was coloured, and the woodwork was stained.

Towards the end of the 19th century, subscriptions were invited, and $16,000 was raised. Plans for a permanent cathedral were made, with Sir A. W. Blomfield (1829–99) as assessor.

Plans were submitted in December 1891: the local designs were sent to London unopened. Edmund Ferrey chose ten from the whole series, and submitted them to Blomfield: they were exhibited at Church House, Westminster, in May 1892. "New and Old" was a magnificent design by H. Wilson: it is illustrated in the *R.I.B.A. Journal*, 23 February 1907. "Ars" was by A. R. Scott of Paisley. "Duomo" and "Hope" were admired; but the winning design was "Fides", by J. C. M. Keith and Evers of Victoria. They planned a nave, aisles and an outer ambulatory, transepts, choir, sanctuary, chapels, vestries, and library.

In 1913 W. D. Caröe paid a visit, and decided in favour of a new site. In 1914 J. C. M. Keith was preparing plans based on his original designs, but revised to suit the altered circumstances and the new position. Caröe was to be associated with him as consulting architect.

In 1924 the Reverend E. P. Laycock was appointed Archdeacon, with the duty of advising about the construction and furnishing of the new cathedral. The ground was broken on 25 May 1926, and the foundation stone of the first part—nave, transepts, and western towers—was laid by the Bishop of London on 1 September. The contractors were Messrs Parfitt Bros of Victoria. The nave and baptistery were consecrated on 28 September 1929.

The style is 13th century. The exterior is faced with Newcastle Island stone, with "Canmos" stone for the windows, doors, flying buttresses, etc. The roofs are covered with copper. The baptistery floor is of British Columbia marble, and the vaulting of red brick. The Caen stone font came from the old cathedral: the wrought-iron railings and gates

ST JOHN'S CATHEDRAL,
ATOON, SASKATCHEWAN

CHRIST CHURCH CATHEDRAL,
VICTORIA, BRITISH COLUMBIA

ALL SAINTS' CATHEDRAL, AKLAVIK (THE ARCTIC)

ST ALBAN'S
CATHEDRAL,
PRINCE ALBERT,
SASKATCHEWAN

between the nave and the temporary sanctuary are Sir Gilbert Scott's, and stood in Westminster Abbey at the entrance to the sanctuary.

Four south aisle windows are by J. E. Nuttgens, and twelve in the north aisle by James Ballantine of Edinburgh; the western lancets and the rose window are by Percy Bacon of London. The altar from the old cathedral is in the chapel at the east of the north aisle, with the old east window above it.

It was decided to complete the north-west tower to commemorate the connection of Bishop Winnington Ingram with the cathedral. An anonymous gift of £5,000 made possible the building of the lower part of the tower, and a peal of bells, by Mears and Stainbank, was hung in a temporary wooden erection in 1936. In 1951 an appeal was made for funds to build the top stage. The towers were dedicated in 1954. The south-west tower is a memorial to Bishop Schofield, who was largely responsible for the building of the cathedral.

The pulpit, made in England under the supervision of Canon Laycock, was dedicated in 1956.

ST ANDREW'S CATHEDRAL, PRINCE RUPERT
[DIOCESE OF CALEDONIA]

By the end of the 19th century there were fifteen churches in the diocese, "all of wood, and some of them quite handsome structures". The largest was St Paul's, Metlakatla, which was the original cathedral: its history dates back to the foundation of the diocese in 1879. It was "largely designed by Indians".

On 17 January 1906, Bishop Du Vernet moved to Prince Rupert, and held the first services in the town. On Easter Day 1907 he opened St Andrew's church hall, which was used as a church, reading-room, recreation hall, and episcopal residence.

In June 1909 he filed an application for eight lots on 4th Avenue West, which were afterwards sold to him. On 22 December 1912, a new building was opened, designed by Messrs Gordon and Helliwell of Toronto, to serve as parish hall and church. Plans had been made in the previous year for a permanent cathedral of stone costing about £5,000.

The lower part of the present cathedral was built on a permanent foundation in 1913. The upper part was being added in 1925, and was completed in 1929: it is constructed mainly of Douglas fir.

7

DIOCESE OF NEW WESTMINSTER
1. HOLY TRINITY CATHEDRAL, NEW WESTMINSTER

The first church, of wood, was built by John Sheepshanks, after-wards Bishop of Norwich, who came here in 1859. The Church committee met first on 11 December 1860.

A peal of bells was given by Baroness Burdett-Coutts in 1862: there was nowhere to put them, and a movement to build a tower came to nothing. In September 1865 the church was burned to the ground. An appeal was made to England, and a new church of stone was built at a cost of about $11,000. The first stone was laid by Governor Seymour, and it was consecrated on 18 December 1867. "A creditable stone structure with nave, chancel, north aisle, and south transept, disfigured somewhat by a square wooden tower built to receive a peal of bells, presented by the Baroness Burdett-Coutts."

The first Bishop was consecrated in 1879.

In 1881 Dean Stanley gave a cross made of wood from Westminster Abbey, and the four shafts that had supported the altar in Henry VII's Chapel. These were reproductions, based on drawings: the originals were afterwards found, and substituted for them.

The cathedral was damaged by fire in 1898.

In 1911 the Bishop said that a cathedral would probably be built in Vancouver: the work would probably begin with the erection of the chancel or a chapel, or a building which could be used as a chapter house. In 1912 he announced that a sub-committee of the executive of the diocese had authorized Messrs McClure and Fox to prepare plans, estimates, and specifications. A building committee was appointed. Nothing came of this. The diocesan synod in that year discussed the removal of the See house and cathedral to Vancouver.

2. CHRIST CHURCH CATHEDRAL, VANCOUVER

The building of the church was first proposed in 1888: it was to be of stone, to seat from 400 to 500 people. On 11 February 1889, a building committee was formed: it was agreed that a beginning should be made on the basement of the church, which could be used for worship for the time being, and be available afterwards for a Sunday school and parish rooms. Tenders were let to E. Cook for the masonry, and to Charles Hillyer for all other trades. The basement was opened on 6 October.

In 1894 the Vestry agreed to proceed with the building of the superstructure. The foundation stone was laid on 28 July, and the completed church was consecrated on 17 February 1895. It was enlarged early in this century.

In 1929 it became the cathedral of the diocese. E. D. Farmer, who died in 1924, left a memorial sum of money for rebuilding the chancel as a memorial to his wife.

The cathedral is plain 13th century in style, divided into a wide nave and aisles by timber posts, which support a rather heavy and complicated roof.

Diocese of the Yukon

The pro-cathedral was St Paul's, Dawson. As the population of Dawson has dwindled, and that of Whitehorse has grown, it is now Christ Church, Whitehorse, a wooden building.

ST SAVIOUR'S PRO-CATHEDRAL, NELSON
[Diocese of Kootenay]

A temporary church was built in 1892. First steps towards the erection of a permanent building were taken in 1896. The foundation stone was laid on 16 August 1898, and it was first used on 5 December. The consecration was on 27 May 1900. It was a simple church with wooden arcades; the chancel was not built. It was destroyed by fire on 25 January 1928: only the walls remained. It was afterwards rebuilt.

ST PAUL'S CATHEDRAL, KAMLOOPS
[Diocese of Cariboo]

The first services were held here in 1880. A permanent church was begun in 1888, and first used on 24 February 1889.

In 1936 the Bishop of Cariboo said that Kamloops was the natural place for the See city of the diocese, and that St Paul's would become the cathedral. A friend in Montreal had given a bishop's chair, and he hoped for further furniture for the chancel. He would appoint a committee to make plans for any alterations or additions to the church.

7

West Indies

CATHEDRAL OF ST JAGO DE LA VEGA, SPANISH TOWN, JAMAICA

The Spaniards built three churches here—the Red Cross, the White Cross, and an Abbey Church—which were destroyed by the Cromwellian soldiers when the town was captured in May 1655. A church was built after the Restoration on the site of the Red Cross, and the church and churchyard were granted to the incumbent and parishioners by royal letters patent on 20 December 1666.

This church was destroyed by hurricane in 1712, and rebuilt afterwards: the inscription now on the west front of the tower reads:

D.O.M.

This Church dedicated to ye Service of Almighty God was thrown down by ye dreadful Hurricane of August ye 28th Anno Domini MDCCXII, and was by ye Divine Assistance, through ye piety and at ye expense of ye Parishioners, more beautifully and substantially rebuilt upon its old foundation in ye thirteenth year of ye Reigne of our Most Gracious Sovereigne, Queen Anne, and in ye Government of His Excellency the Lord Archibald Hamilton, in the year of our Lord MDCCXIV.

The tower was built in 1817, of brick, like the body of the church. It is of three stages, surmounted by an octagonal wooden lantern of two stages, with a spire.

The organ was erected in 1755.

The diocese was founded in 1824, and the church became the cathedral.

The Middle-Pointed chancel and sanctuary were added in 1848–53, at a cost of £4,570, towards which £1,600 was provided by the Government. The architect was John Calvert; the tradesmen were, Richard Cowan contractor for the masonry, James Campbell carpenter and joiner, James Jones carpenter, and Joseph Waldron builder. The addition is 50 feet in length, with clerestory and aisles, clustered columns with moulded arches, and angel corbels supporting the roof.

The glass in the east window (1848) is by Jones and Willis. The new chancel, and the body of the church, were provided with seats which, for their date, have a curiously Gothick look.

The cathedral was repaired in 1901, damaged by the earthquake in 1907, repaired in 1908, damaged by the hurricane of 17 August 1951, and repaired again afterwards.

There is a large collection of monuments, including three by Bacon: (1) Thomas Earl of Effingham, Baron Howard, and Catherine his wife (1791); (2) Anne, wife of Sir Adam Williamson, Governor (1794); (3) Dr Francis Rigby Brodbelt (1795). A fourth, that of Dr Richard Batty (1796), has been destroyed: it showed "a pensive figure, bending over an altar, on which is sculptured a pelican feeding her young, and upon it an antique lamp with flame". Only the head of the pelican survives.

The monument of Sir Basil Keith is by J. Wilson, and that of Elizabeth Mary, Countess of Elgin and Kincardine (1843), by Sir John Steell.

The organ, in the 18th-century west gallery, dates from 1849: it has a pleasant Gothic case.

ST MICHAEL'S CATHEDRAL, BRIDGETOWN, BARBADOS

The first church of St Michael (which stood where St Mary's now is) was built in 1655. In 1660 it was decided to build a new church. The churchwardens were to fell timber, and a clerk of the works—William Burdon—was appointed: he was to receive 1,500 lb. of sugar per year, over and above his salary as parish clerk, "for his care and paynes for keepinge of a just account of all workmen and labourers yt shall be employed about the work of building ye new church".

On 20 June 1661, a contract was signed with Captain Robert Cullimore, who was to build a new church "according to the dimensions indented and shown on a plot", for 250,000 lb. of sugar, to be paid in three instalments. In 1662 the wardens were empowered to buy timber from the parish land for the roof. By August 1664 the church was nearing completion, and the churchwardens were ordered to select timber for the pews. By October it was sufficiently complete for meetings to be held in the vestry. Cullimore was paid 20,400 lb. of sugar for extra work. The old church was abandoned; the new was consecrated in September 1665.

The hurricane of 10 October 1780 destroyed the church. In 1783 a petition was sent to the Committee for the distribution of the Parliamentary Bounty granted for the relief of the sufferers from the hurricane: £8,000 was needed for rebuilding the church.

On 1 June 1784, a resolution was passed for the payment of the money due to the clerk of the committee for rebuilding the church—£139 13 4. On 5 November the Vestry agreed with Sam Nusum to contract for the pitch pine lumber requisite and wanting for the roof at £15 per 1,000 feet. The contractor, or superintendent of the works, was Mr Griffiths. An inspector was later appointed to examine his work, with which the Board were not satisfied. In 1785 an Act was passed for raising £10,000 by means of two lotteries: £5,000 to be for the rebuilding of St Michael's, and £5,000 for Christchurch, St George's, St Thomas's, and St Lucy's.

The church was completed in 1789.

When the first bishop was appointed, it became the cathedral. When a capitular body was formed, stalls were provided for the canons. Bishop Mitchinson had plans prepared for a new cathedral, but nothing came of the scheme.

An apsidal chancel has been added, with an iron screen. The nave has been reseated. The organ (1923) is at the south-east of the nave.

ST GEORGE'S CATHEDRAL, KINGSTOWN, ST VINCENT
[DIOCESE OF THE WINDWARD ISLANDS]

The earlier church was destroyed by a hurricane in 1780.

The present church was built in 1820 at a cost of £47,000, of which the Government gave £5,000. It is simple Georgian in style, with two rows of arched windows.

The chancel and transepts were built in 1880–7 under David S. Osment. The cupola was blown down by a hurricane in 1898, and battlements were added to the tower afterwards.

The pulpit is of polished mahogany. The chandelier is said to have been given by George III. The windows in the chancel, by Kempe, were given by the widow of Lieut.-Governor Dundas, who died in 1880.

ST JOHN'S CATHEDRAL, ANTIGUA

The first church, of wood, was built in 1683–4: it stood about 60 feet to the south of the present site. In 1718 an Act was passed for erecting a new church: this was of stone, and was completed, except for the steeple, in 1725. The addition of the steeple was proposed in 1771, but not finished until 1788.

A drawing of the south side of this church shows a good-sized building with arched windows: the angles have rustic quoins. In the middle is an outward break, with the doorway. The west tower is rather low, surmounted by a cupola.

The diocese was founded in 1842. On 8 February 1843, the church was destroyed by an earthquake. "The tower was rent from the top to the bottom. . . . Almost the whole of the north-west wall of the gallery fell out in a mass. The north-east wall was protruded beyond the perpendicular. The Altar piece, the public monument erected to the memory of Lord Lavington, and the private monuments . . . fell down piecemeal inside. A large portion of the top east wall was precipitated into the Churchyard, carrying along with it two of the east iron windows. . . . A large pile of heavy cut stones and masses of brick fell down at the south and at the north doors. . . . Thus within the space of three minutes, the Church was reduced to a pile of crumbling ruins, the walls that were left standing being rent in every part, the main roof only remaining sound, being supported by the hardwood pillars.

"Having been constituted a Cathedral Church and Episcopal See . . . it was the intention of the members of the Vestry at their next meeting, proposed to be held on the 27th instant, to have entered into a contract for improving the Chancel and elevating the stone work of the Tower, completing the same with four minarets in a manner suitable for a Cathedral. . . ." (*Memorandum of the Awful Earthquake.*)

The Council and House of Assembly allowed £500 for temporary repairs, and the ruined building was used for the enthronement of the Bishop on 17 May; but it was beyond repair, and it was decided to build a new cathedral. A sum of £40,000 was assigned to the purpose from the loan of £100,000 made to Antigua by the Imperial Government. There were various private donations, and a further sum of £1,150 was loaned by the West India Bank.

The foundation stone of the new cathedral was laid by Sir Charles Fitzroy, Governor-in-Chief of Antigua, on 9 October 1845. It was first used on 10 October 1846, but the towers and the exterior were not entirely completed until August 1847. It was consecrated on 25 July 1848.

The architect was Thomas Fuller ("son of Mr Fuller of Bath"). The committee imported twelve carpenters and eight masons from England. The workmen numbered 170, under the superintendence of W. Roue of Bristol, the clerk of the works. The glass was supplied by Messrs Dix and Williams of Bristol, where the mahogany pulpit, desk, stalls, and bishop's throne were carved. Three windows were painted by Wilmshurst, and the roof was covered with patent galvanized tiles made by Messrs Morewood and Rogers of Upper Thames Street. The walls are built of magnesian limestone from the north of the island, with an interior frame of hard wood lined with pitch pine—a precaution against earthquake. Roof of pitch pine: the ceiling of the nave coved and panelled, and those of the aisles flat and panelled. The floors laid with lias stone obtained from Mr Treasure of Bath.

The style is Roman: the plan, nave and aisles with two western towers with cupolas; transepts, and apsidal chancel. The columns are octagonal with moulded capitals and bases: the description in the *Builder* mentions elliptical arches with moulded archivolts, corbels, and keys, but these were omitted.

It is a very late example of this kind of church. Even the *Builder*, which had no particular prejudices about style, thought it necessary to apologize for it, saying that the style was the choice of the committee: the *Ecclesiologist* did not deign to notice it at all, though it was quite a noteworthy piece of church building, except by making one contemptuous remark: "A mere overgrown Pagan church, of the school of St Marylebone and St Philip's, Regent Street, with two dumpy pepper-box towers".

The silver candlesticks of the high altar were given by Colonel Peter Lee, who died in 1704: the chandelier was the gift of the Reverend Philip Darby in 1740. The mahogany altar of 1893, made by Henry Crosbie, a local joiner, has been moved to the war memorial chapel: the present high altar, also of mahogany, is by Jones and Willis.

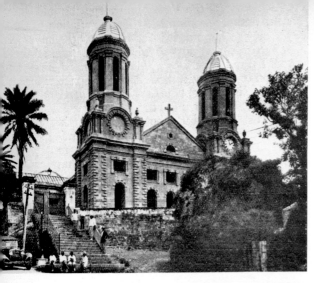

ST JOHN'S CATHEDRAL, ANTIGUA

ST GEORGE'S CATHEDRAL, GEORGETOWN, BRITISH GUIANA

GEORGE'S CATHEDRAL, KINGSTOWN, ST VINCENT, WINDWARD ISLANDS

CHRIST CHURCH CATHEDRAL, NASSAU, BAHAMAS

ST JOHN THE BAPTIST'S CATHEDRAL, BELIZE, BRITISH HONDURAS

The iron gates to the churchyard were erected in 1789: on the stone piers are metal Renaissance statues of St John the Baptist and St John the Divine, said to have been taken from a Martinique ship during the Seven Years' War, 1758–63.

ST GEORGE'S CATHEDRAL, GEORGETOWN, BRITISH GUIANA

The first church was built in 1809. The second was begun in 1838, and consecrated in December 1842. It is described in a letter from the Reverend J. F. Bourne in the *Ecclesiologist* of December 1847, which gives a vivid picture of this early Victorian parish-church-cathedral. "It is a somewhat heavy building, plaistered and painted stone colour, without clerestory, without buttresses, except at each angle of the building; with two long rows of Early-Pointed windows, containing wooden frames, and the ordinary square glass lights, opening like two leaved doors; the upper row of windows lights the lofty gallery. It has also a very short chancel with two eastern windows of stained glass by Ward and Nixon, the upper, a circular, and the lower a wide window with a very flat-Pointed arch and wooden monials. . . . The tower is large, at the west end, with octagonal turrets at the corners terminating in four pinnacles; and when in progress, was found to be so heavy, that the upper portion, above the belfry-floor, was completed in wood, including boarded battlements. . . . Internally, the building is divided into nave and aisles by two rows of "green heart" pillars, covered with stucco to represent clustering columns whose onerous duty it is to support the large galleries and the purlins of the roof. The ceiling of the central portion, or nave, is arched, and Pointed arches are formed thereupon in stucco between each pair of columns. . . . There are no sedilia, no stalls: there is not even a throne for the bishop; but when it is the *cathedral*, the fleur-de-lis is taken from the top of the north chair and a small wooden mitre is fixed in its place. . . ." A window by O'Connor for this church was exhibited at the Great Exhibition in 1851.

It was taken down in 1877, and a temporary church was erected.

Sir Arthur Blomfield made a design for a cathedral in 1881. It was to have been cruciform, with two towers at the west, and an octagonal central tower. The walls were to have been of Portland cement concrete, with quoins, string courses, and cornices of brick, and the details of the lower arcading, and other ornamental portions, of terra cotta.

Columns of cast iron, clustered and banded; roofs of pitch pine from North America, covered with galvanized iron.

The cathedral which was actually built from Blomfield's plans in 1889–92 is very different.

A concrete wall rises six feet nine inches from the ground: the framework of the superstructure is wood, the interstices are filled with plaster panels. The labour was supplied by skilled Creole carpenters. It cost more than $100,000, and is said to be the largest wooden church in the world.

The font—an angel with a shell, like that of Inverness Cathedral and the windows in the baptistery, were the gift of the Bishop. The wrought iron chancel screen was given by Mrs Woodgate Jones, and the side screen by the ladies of the Colony. The electrolier in the chancel was given by Queen Victoria, the altar rail by Professor Austin of Salt Lake City, the altar cross by the clergy of Antigua, and the lectern by the clergy of Barbados.

CHRIST CHURCH CATHEDRAL, NASSAU

On 20 March 1721, a meeting of the Council agreed to build a church, and a wooden frame was ordered from New England: this arrived in April 1723. A Vestry was elected, who chose two churchwardens, and an estimate was made for completing the church: the Council voted that certain customs duties should be used, and the church was finished in 1724.

The Reverend William Smith, who arrived in 1733, had it "put into a tollerable good order", but by 1738 it was "in a very tottering condition", and a fund was opened to build a new church of stone. A sum of 600 pieces of eight was raised by subscription. But it was not until 1749 that a bill was presented to the Legislature for building and beautifying the new church, and in 1750 it was still without a roof or floor. After a rebuke by the Governor in a speech at the opening of the session of the Legislature, further money was raised, and in 1753 the House of Assembly passed another bill "for raising and levying certain taxes for the finishing and beautifying the church in the City of Nassau". The church was finished in 1754. In 1758 King George II gave a bible and prayer books, cushions and a carpet for the altar, and pulpit cushion and cloth, all of crimson damask with silk fringe; two linen cloths and two surplices.

In 1773 the Reverend John Hunt represented to the Governor and Council that the money collected was not enough to build a steeple, and prayed for a sum of money from the public revenue. The steeple was built in 1774, and on 4 June of that year Hunt, writing to S.P.G., described the church as a handsome stone building.

In 1784 loyalists from the American colonies made several gifts, including a bell. The church was consecrated by Bishop Lipscombe of Jamaica and the Bahamas in May 1825.

In 1827 the steeple, which had become dangerous, was taken down: the present tower—very plain Gothic, with angle buttresses and pinnacles—and the west porches were built in 1830.

In 1834 an Act was passed by the Legislature for the rebuilding of the church: commissioners were appointed, and the foundation stone was laid by Sir Francis Cockburn, the Governor, on 26 September 1837. The new building—Gothic in style—was opened for divine service on 19 April 1840, and consecrated by Bishop Spencer on 5 June 1845.

The Diocese of Nassau was created in 1861, and Christ Church became the cathedral.

In 1864 an extension at the east end was begun. A new organ was ordered in 1865, to stand in a chamber on the south; the enlargement was completed in 1866. Windows by Messrs Cox and Sons of London were erected in 1868. These were broken by a hurricane in 1929, and in 1942 they were further damaged by a fire near the cathedral. On 20 March 1949, new windows were dedicated—the work of M. Fassi-Cadet of Nice.

Various other improvements have been made at the east end in recent years, and the organ has been moved to the west gallery.

HOLY TRINITY CATHEDRAL, PORT OF SPAIN, TRINIDAD

In 1797 Sir Ralph Abercromby took possession of Trinidad for the British, and installed his A.D.C., Sir Thomas Picton, as Governor. A wooden church was built in 1802; this was burned down in 1808, after which services were held in the Town Hall.

On 29 August 1809, the Governor petitioned the King for help, asking for £110,000 for various public buildings, including a church. Parliament granted £50,000, of which it was determined to use £20,000 for a church and a gaol. The gaol alone cost £30,000. A drawing for the church was obtained in England, based on the model of the chapel at Pentonville Prison,[1] with some few alterations. The building of the church began in 1810, a little to the north of the present building, in the centre of Brunswick Square (now called Woodford Square): this was a contravention of the law, and against the wishes of the inhabitants, as the square was a public recreation park. A meeting of protest was held, and a petition was presented to the Governor, but the building went on, and reached the top of the walls. Before the roof could be put on, another petition was presented to the new Governor, Sir Ralph Woodford, in 1813. He agreed in condemning the position of the church, and eventually a public subscription was raised to meet the cost of pulling down the half-finished building, and restoring the square to its former condition. The foundations were discovered under the grass when static water tanks were erected during the early days of the 1939–45 war.

Steps were soon taken to build a new church, and plans were drawn by Philip Reinagle, a son of the artist, who was also the architect of the Roman Catholic cathedral. On 30 May 1816, the foundation stone was laid by Sir Ralph. The church was complete, at least externally, by 1818: the inscription over the south door is:

AN. DNI. 1818—REGNI—R—GEORGII—TERTII—58

It is said that British workmen were employed on the building—probably from the Garrison; and stone came from Hollington Quarries near Cheadle in Staffordshire.

The church was not ready for consecration until 1823. One reason seems to have been lack of money, as Sir Ralph had to go to England to raise more. Another was that there was no bishop available. There was a correspondence between the Governor and the Reverend J. H. Clapham, who said that he could not consecrate the church. However, he eventually consented to do so, and the consecration took place on Trinity Sunday, 25 May 1823. The form of consecration was apparently drawn up by the Governor himself. He took a great interest in the church, and a list of "furniture and appurtenances for the Church", in his own handwriting, dated 22 May 1823, still survives. In the following November he gave "six covers of silk crimson damask for the Communion table, two dozen damask napkins", more than 51 volumes of

---

[1] Not, of course, the present Prison, which was built in 1840–2 from plans by Sir Charles Barry. The original Prison was founded in 1807.

Bibles and Prayer Books and a complete outfit for the beadles—hats, staves, and gowns.

The church is Gothic, with a hammer-beam roof.

Mr Coleridge, who accompanied his relative, Bishop Coleridge of Barbados on his first visitation, in 1825, wrote: "The church itself is one of the most elegant and splendid things in the Empire. It is wainscoted with the various rich woods of the island, the western door, the organ and staircase, being all in a corresponding style of richness and propriety. The tower, perhaps, wants elevation."

The altar, pulpit, and desk were originally in the middle of the south side, the pulpit being entered from a staircase in the porch through one of the openings that are still to be seen in the wall. Opposite it, over the north door, was the Governor's state pew, with "a truly grand staircase constructed agreeably to the nicest rules of arts". At the west end were galleries, with the organ: in the centre of the church were four large pews for His Majesty's Council, the garrison, and visitors. The altar piece was a large picture, painted and presented by the daughter of Colonel Birch, afterwards Madame Lamartine.

On 20 September 1825, there was an earthquake, "by which the whole church suffered, but the tower most". One of the pinnacles fell through the roof, two others were "twisted in an extraordinary manner", and the damage was so great that the tower had to be partly rebuilt.

At some time during the 19th century the internal arrangement of the church was changed, and pulpit, stalls, organ, and altar were erected at the east end.

In 1870 the clergy and laity resolved that Trinidad should be separated from the Diocese of Barbados, and the first Bishop of the new diocese, Richard Rawle, was consecrated on 29 June 1872: he was enthroned in Holy Trinity on 6 August.

It was his intention to build a chancel, and a local firm, Wharton and Stollmeyer, submitted plans, which were rejected. The Bishop wrote on 27 May 1882: "What to do about the cathedral chancel I know not, probably it will stand over to be erected after my death." A design by C. A. Bassett-Smith of London was accepted, and work began in January 1895. The foundation stone was laid in April, and on 9 May 1897, it was dedicated. The work cost about £6,000, and was a memorial to Bishop Rawle. It comprises a chancel, a cloister, bishop's vestry, bishop's chapel, ambulatory, and two other vestries.

The stone pulpit was given in 1902 in memory of A. G. Da Silva.

The reredos was erected in 1926. Correspondence with the firm of Bassett-Smith began in the previous year. It was shipped to Trinidad in April 1928, and dedicated on 20 October, as a memorial to Bishop Hayes, Bishop from 1889 to 1903. On either side of the altar it is inset with mosaics by James Powell.

An earthquake on 4 December 1954, caused considerable damage to the building and the organ: afterwards the roof was repaired and the church completely renovated.

The memorial to Sir Ralph Woodford, the founder of the church, was erected by "the inhabitants of Trinidad, deeply sensible of the substantial benefits which his long administration of the government conferred upon the colony". It is the work of Chantrey, executed in 1839, and represents Sir Ralph reclining on a couch and reading the Bible.

ST JOHN THE BAPTIST'S CATHEDRAL, BELIZE, BRITISH HONDURAS

In 1810 Lieut.-Colonel Smyth made an offer to the magistrates that, if they approved, he would make himself responsible for finding a clergyman to take charge of the settlement, and would give up the parade ground, on the south of Belize, for the building of a church. But the magistrates had their own plans, and refused. They appointed a committee "to inquire into the best method of obtaining a Clergyman from England, and of building a church, to be built of imported brick, and to be 50 by 80 feet in extent". A public meeting was held in 1811, and the committee's recommendations were accepted. In 1812 the foundation stone of the church was laid, and building was begun. The bricks came from England as ballast in the holds of trading ships: many of them were from London. The church was in use by 1813, though it was not yet complete: a tender for the roof was accepted— £370—and a subscription was opened to raise funds for completion. By 1816 the work was finished, but there was still a debt, and a further subscription list was opened. The response was satisfactory, and the church was enlarged in 1819. A large sum voted out of the public funds had not been needed. In that year it was decided to obtain an organ, and Communion plate was presented in 1820.

This is how the church was described in the *Honduras Gazette* in 1826: "The building is of brick; it has an embattled tower and a spire.

The roof projects and is slated. The interior is chaste and beautiful. It stands in the form of a cross, having the grand entrance at the northern extremity of the transept. An octagonal pulpit faces the grand entrance, which is ascended by a flight of geometrical stairs winding round its front and so contrived that one-half of its ascent is an octagonal platform which forms a reading desk; immediately underneath is the clerk's seat, which is also octagonal. The pews are divided by a mahogany railing and are cool and commodious. The Communion Table is semi-circular, standing on an elevation of a corresponding shape, which is railed in at the eastern end of the building. In the gallery at the western extremity is a fine toned organ.

"The floor of the aisles and transepts is tesselated, and that of the Altar finished in a similar manner, but the lines are intersecting segments of circles. On the North and South sides are two tiers of windows (the uppermost semi-circular), ornamented with brows, which terminate in heads; each of the top tiers is surmounted by a Cherub. Behind the pulpit in the Southern transept is a deep gallery, for the accommodation of the girls of the Free School, beneath which is the vestry. To the centre of the ceiling is attached a passion flower of colossal proportions, hanging from which is an elegant chandelier of considerable value.

"On either side of the Communion Table is a handsome tablet suspended by bronze and gold chains and held by cherubs in glory.

"Over the centre Eastern Window is an Eye, with a glory radiating from it. Under the chandelier stands a beautiful mahogany Font, flat at the top, supporting a silver Baptismal Basin.

"The furniture of the Desk, Pulpit, and Communion Table are covered with crimson velvet, richly ornamented by gold fringes and tassels, with cushions to correspond. . . ."

The church was the scene of the coronation of three Kings of the Mosquito Nation: George Frederick in 1816, Robert Charles in 1825, and George Augustus Frederick in 1845. The rite followed closely that prescribed for the coronation of a British Sovereign.

The diocese was formed in 1891. The spire was removed about 70 years ago.

Belize was damaged by a hurricane on 10 September 1931. The cathedral was unroofed, the south wall was cracked. The altar and other furnishings were "all mixed up at the east end", and the east window was destroyed. Only the silver bowl of the font was recovered afterwards. The structure was soon repaired. On 30 June 1935, a new east window and reredos were unveiled. The glass was the gift of the Diocese of Jamaica. The reredos—of local mahogany, with carving of the adoration of the Magi—was the work of Harold Youngman, A. H. Hellyer, Miss F. Huddleston, and others: it was the gift of Lady Burdon, in memory of Sir John Burdon, the late Governor. The colossal passion flower and the eye unfortunately fell victims to the hurricane.

ST ANDREW'S CATHEDRAL, SYDNEY, N.S.W.

CHRIST CHURCH
CATHEDRAL,
NEWCASTLE,
N.S.W.

8

Australia

A. PROVINCE OF NEW SOUTH WALES
ST ANDREW'S CATHEDRAL, SYDNEY

The foundation stone of the first church was laid by Governor Macquarie on 31 August 1819. A Gothic design had been made by Francis Howard Greenway. Greenway, a pupil of John Nash, had set up in Bristol, with his brothers, as "stonemasons, architects, and builders, etc." in about 1805. In 1809 they became bankrupt. Some time afterwards, Francis was accused of forgery, pleaded guilty, and was sentenced to death at Bristol Assizes on 23 March 1812. The sentence was commuted to one of transportation, and he was taken to Australia. Governor Macquarie pardoned him, and employed him in designing and erecting public buildings for the colony.

Greenway's enemies disapproved of this design: one "from phrenetical and illiberal views, pronounced it too grand, and like the style of ancient superstition which the battering rams of reason should destroy". The work was stopped by J. T. Bigge, who was sent as a royal commissioner to report on the state of the colony.

In 1837 Governor Bourke had the original foundation stone taken up and relaid on the present site. A new design for a church had been made by James Hume—a Presbyterian, "quite ignorant of church architecture". But the idea was Bishop Broughton's. He wrote in 1844: "I formed the design in 1837.... At that time I was more proud of my production than I have been since, or am now, subsequent study of church architecture having revealed to me many mistakes and anachronisms." The new church was 15th century in style, cruciform, with "a short prim quaker-like nave", and a copy of Magdalen tower at the west. Broughton sent home for accurate drawings of the tower. The nave and aisles were to be modelled on St Mary's, Oxford.

8

Work went on for the next two years, but the drought of 1839 brought great distress, contributions fell off, and the work came to an end in 1842.

In 1845 a committee was formed which raised £4,000 in a year; new estimates were made, another architect—Edmund Thomas Blacket—was appointed, and work began again in April 1846.

Blacket was born in London in 1817. In 1842 he and his wife landed at Sydney on the way to New Zealand, and had to wait for another ship to complete the journey. He "used the time to deliver letters of introduction to influential people, who were so impressed by the attractive personality of this handsome young man of twenty-five years that they persuaded him to remain in the colony" (Morton Herman, *The Architecture of Victorian Sydney*, 1956, p. 9). He had been brought up as a Nonconformist, but later joined the Church of England. He "made a careful study of ecclesiastical art, and examined and surveyed the best ancient examples throughout England," but he had no professional training in architecture. In Australia "his first office was the unthankful one of correcting, or shaping into some practicable and better form, the blunderings of predecessors on unfinished churches, as well as of fighting against the whims and prejudices which ignorance and false principles of economy in individuals and church committees opposed to him. But when the soundness of his judgment, and the correctness of his taste were better known, he commanded an influence, to which those whom he had to deal with (and in many cases they were of very intractable materials), were always obliged in the end to yield." He died in 1883.

In redesigning this church, he scrapped the Magdalen tower, extended the nave, and designed two western towers. "While the matter was still under debate Bishop Selwyn came on a visit from New Zealand, and his emphatic advocacy of the two towers was accepted as the final decision." The narrowness of the transepts was unsatisfactory, but as it was impossible to demolish what had been already built, he designed a low central tower, broader than it was long, like the tower of Bath Abbey, at the crossing. Buttresses were added to the old work. The *Ecclesiologist* on the whole approved, though it was thought that a central spirelet would be preferable to the lantern tower.

A meeting was held on 26 April 1847, for the purpose of raising funds. The report of the building committee described the alterations in the plan. The contract for the portion of the building then in progress would be completed in October; the architect was preparing the plans and specifications for a third contract, and tenders would be advertised for as soon as the state of the funds permitted.

In 1848 the nave and north transept were completed to the springing of the arches of the windows, and a contract was entered into for carrying the walls of the nave, extending from the south transept to the middle of the western window, to their full height, including the tracery of the windows.

The report of the committee issued in 1850 said that this had been done, and that a fifth contract had been accepted—for the completion of the north aisle walls, and for the elevation of those of the northwestern tower and north transept to a similar height, including the tracery of the north aisle windows. "The next portion of the work to which your committee propose to direct their immediate attention, is the erection of the columns necessary for the support of the clerestory walls, and the lantern tower—the completion of the tracery of the east window, and that of the choir-aisle windows."

Blacket had had to resign, in consequence of having been selected by Her Majesty's Government as Colonial architect. T. W. Shepard had been appointed as clerk of the works to carry out his design.

The discovery of gold in 1851 disorganized the community, and the rise in wages, and in the cost of materials, made it necessary to postpone much of the work that had been undertaken.

The report of the committee for 1852–3 stated that during the past two years the piers had been built, the choir windows and buttresses completed, and the contract for the choir and transept arches entered into and half completed. The sum expended, to date, had been £6,686.

The *Sydney Morning Herald* of 18 March 1862, reported a meeting held to promote the completion of the cathedral. The Governor made a short speech, and the secretary read a report. The committee had last met the subscribers three years ago, when money was urgently needed to roof the building. Since then, £3,487 had been received, and used for the roof. Upwards of £3,000 had been paid or secured for providing windows. These were described: the Reverend E. Coleridge of Eton had been asked to undertake the artistic management of the work. The committee had now to appeal for funds for the fitting up of the interior: the design had been decided on. The cost of this work would be about £4,000: the floor—the marble for which was on its way from

England—would cost about £1,000. It was hoped that some portions of the work might be given by individuals. The glass was by Hardman.

The cathedral was consecrated on 30 November 1868.

The pulpit—carved by John Ferris of Little Norton Street—was given by Robert Towns. The font, with basin and capitals from Otago, and pillars of granite from Gabo Island, cost £250. The marble and tile work in the chancel was executed by Fields of London, under G. G. Scott, for £867. The paving of the nave and aisles, by Minton, was completed in 1869. The alabaster reredos was designed by J. L. Pearson. The monument to Bishop Broughton was carved by J. Dinham.

The central tower was completed in 1873, and the contract for the two western towers was made in the same year; they were finished in 1874.

Part of the site, which was taken over by Governor Bourke, was given back to the Church in 1936. Plans were made for extending the cathedral: the first premium was awarded, in 1938, to R. A. P. Pinckney and A. F. E. Gott.

In 1949 the altar was moved to the west end, and an entrance made at the east.

CHRIST CHURCH CATHEDRAL, NEWCASTLE

The foundation stone of the original Christ Church was laid by the Commandant, Captain James Wallis, on 1 January 1817. The design was made in 1816 by James Clohasy, a convict: Wallis altered the plan by lengthening and widening it. Governor Macquarie described it as a handsome neat built church with a spire: the spire was taken down in 1820, for fear of gales, and a plain bell cote erected instead. The altar piece was painted by a convict named Lycett.

A writer in the *Sydney Gazette* (15 August 1818) was delighted with the church: "The suitable paintings and ornaments on the inside, united with simplicity, order, and cleanliness, excite in the pious mind, the most heavenly and devout sensations, and enrapture the human soul." It was, in fact, a very plain building: the windows were wide and ogee-headed, and there was a very shallow eastern apse.

The first Bishop, Tyrrell, was consecrated in 1847, and was installed in Christ Church on 31 January 1848.

A committee for building a permanent cathedral was formed in 1881, and in 1883 the Bishop (Pearson) said that a start had been made on digging the foundations: the cathedral was to be built of brick at a cost of £20,000 from the designs of John Horbury Hunt of Sydney.

Hunt was one of the founders of the Institute of Architects of New South Wales, and was president of it for many years. He "was an architects' architect, which accounts for his success with fellow professionals, but in the broader world he was unpopular and often had a bad press. One journal could comment on his 'dramatic force and energy' whilst simultaneously analysing the drama to find behind it only 'extreme prolixity . . . and incessant redundancy. . . .' In the early nineties Hunt could triumph over even such attacks, but he was not able to adapt himself to a changing world. As his old friends dropped off he could not make others, and he died a lonely bibliophile and a poor man in 1904." (Morton Herman, *The Architecture of Victorian Sydney*, 1956, p. 151.)

The foundations were finished in 1885 at a cost of £5,000, after which the work stopped for six years. The old church was becoming dangerous, and a temporary pro-cathedral was opened on 11 December 1884.

In 1891–93 the lower part of the nave walls was built at a cost of £10,000. At this time the old church was pulled down. A tender of £14,800 was received for completing the walls and erecting the roof; but as only £6,500 was in hand, it was decided to suspend the work temporarily after £8,000 had been spent, if sufficient funds were not then available. Arrangements were made in 1894 for a loan, but the contractor refused to proceed with the second part of the contract, and the work once again came to a standstill.

Bishop Stretch, who was appointed Dean in 1900, called in J. H. Buckeridge of Sydney, who made a plan for roofing the nave at the level which the walls had reached, and building the east end, on a larger plan, for about £10,000. The nave was roofed, and the transepts were built, together with a temporary wooden chancel, and the new work was dedicated on 21 November 1902. The contractors were Howie and Son.

During the next few years, windows, a baptistery, organ, and bishop's throne were provided.

In 1907 there was a "creep", which damaged much property in the town, and particularly the cathedral: the walls cracked, and it was thought that the west end of the nave would have to be pulled down. However, the damage was repaired, and there has been no serious movement since then.

Then further plans were made by F. G. Castleden of Newcastle, and carried out by H. P. Connolly: the transepts were roofed, and the choir, choir aisles, and vestries were erected: this work was dedicated on 9 March 1910. The cost was about £4,500. New fittings included sedilia of Australian marble, stalls, marble paving, and a carved high altar of rosewood. Through the gift of Mr and Mrs Hudson Berkeley, the Dean's warden, a reredos was erected, and three arches were pierced through the wall behind it, after the model of Abbey Dore: the ambulatory was continued round the east end, and a small chapel built in memory of Bishop Tyrrell. These additions were dedicated on 5 May 1911.

In 1912 the walls of the east end were raised to their full height, and the east window was put in place. The completed chancel was dedicated on 13 November 1912.

In 1922 a war memorial chapel was planned: Mr and Mrs Hudson Berkeley gave £9,000, and the Parnell family and Commander Gardiner made large donations. The chapel was built at the north-east corner, of Sydney freestone, at a cost of about £15,000: it was dedicated on 27 September 1924. The architect was F. G. Castleden.

It was then decided to raise the walls of the nave to their full height. A bequest of £5,000 from Mr Hudson Berkeley, who died in 1924, made it possible for the work to begin. It was carried out in 1927-8, and the crossing arches were also built. The new work was dedicated on 29 September 1928.

All that now remains to be done is the raising of the transepts to their full height, and the erection of the central tower.

The original part is ordinary—but the result of all this work is a cathedral with an extremely impressive exterior. It is the largest in Australia.

The font is of red and white marble, with an oak cover: the glass in the baptistery, and most of the rest of the glass in the cathedral, is by the firm of C. E. Kempe.

The altar piece, the gift of Miss L. E. Nicholson, was dedicated on 7 March 1938: it is similar to the one which Edward VII placed in Whippingham Church, Isle of Wight, to the memory of Queen Victoria —the Last Supper, carved in white alabaster by Messrs R. L. Boulton and Sons. The standard candlesticks are 16th-century Italian.

There is a window on the north by Burne-Jones, executed by Watts.

The reredos of the Warriors' Chapel has fourteen terra cotta panels by George Tinworth. The cross, candlesticks, and lamp are the work of W. Mark of Melbourne. Here is the recumbent bronze figure of Alfred Forster, who was killed in the Great War—the son of Lord Forster, the Governor-General, who laid the foundation stone of the chapel. He and Cecil Thomas the sculptor were wounded by the same shell: Forster died, but Thomas recovered, and made a bronze figure of his friend which was given to All Hallows' Barking. Lord and Lady Forster then gave the order for this figure: no name is inscribed, as the intention is that it should represent all whom the chapel commemorates. The bust of Lord Forster is also the work of Cecil Thomas.

ST SAVIOUR'S CATHEDRAL, GOULBURN
[Diocese of Canberra and Goulburn]

The site was granted by the Crown for Church purposes in 1842, and there was an earlier building. A proposal to build a cathedral was made in 1861, before a bishop was appointed, and a design was made by Goold of Sydney.

Mesac Thomas, the first Bishop, claimed that he had collected £18,500 for the building of the cathedral: the total cost was £25,000, without the tower and spire, and exclusive of special gifts for furnishings or windows. The Bishop consulted architects in England, including J. L. Pearson, who submitted a design. Finally E. T. Blacket was chosen.

The foundation stone of this Middle-Pointed cathedral was laid on 15 January 1874. Blacket died in 1883, and the building was completed by his sons, A. and C. Blacket. It was dedicated and licensed on 29 April 1884: when the debt was paid, it was consecrated—on 24 September 1916.

The contractors were Messrs R. and J. Turner, Duncan, Nelson, Le Breton, Stone and Brigdale, H. Langley, A. A. Marshall and Co., and F. C. W. Richard. The capitals and bosses were carved by Tinkler of Sydney, and the medallions and reredos by W. P. Macintosh of Forest Lodge. The material is local (Bundanoon) standstone, with pillars of Pyrmont freestone.

The font, of Caen stone, was designed by J. A. Chatwin of Birmingham (1829–1907), and carved by John Roddis: the cover, of Queensland maple, was made by F. W. Tod of Sydney. The pulpit of Caen stone was carved by John Roddis from a design suggested by Bishop Thomas:

it was the gift of the Bishop's friends in Warwickshire. The bishop's throne is from Blacket's design. The reredos, given by Mrs Thomas, is a reproduction in Oamaru freestone of da Vinci's Last Supper. The original altar is now in the Bishop Thomas memorial chapel: the present one is by Jones and Willis, 1916. Tiles by Minton. Glass by Hardman, Ashwin and Co. of Sydney, Lyon Cottier and Co., and A. Handel. Two windows were sent out by Heaton, Butler and Bayne in 1885.

The Soldiers' Memorial Chapel was erected in 1922 at a cost of £5,523, from designs by Messrs Burcham Clamp and MacKellar: the materials are all Australian, and the work was executed by the firm of James Turner, Goulburn, the chief craftsman being P. H. Nourse.

When the Federal Capital of Canberra was established, five acres near Parliament House were set apart for building an Anglican cathedral. The plans, obtained by a competition costing £2,363, were for a range of buildings of concrete, in the Lombardic style: the architect was Harold Crone. "It is doubtful if this particular design will ever be carried out."

ST PETER'S CATHEDRAL, ARMIDALE

Bishop Broughton first visited Armidale in 1845, and determined to build a church of St Peter, and to station a priest there. A wooden church was consecrated by Bishop Tyrrell of Newcastle on 26 May 1850: nine years later, money was being raised to enlarge it.

The Diocese of Grafton and Armidale was founded in 1863: the first Bishop—Sawyer—was consecrated early in 1867, but was drowned almost as soon as he reached Australia. His successor, Bishop Turner, was installed in St Peter's in 1869.

The permanent cathedral was opened on 3 June 1875. Nave, transepts, and chancel of the same width as the nave, with a vestry on the south. Almost entirely of brick—the style Early Geometrical. The chancel is separated from the nave by a "very bold arch with several rings of brickwork, the bricks being so set as to produce a kind of chequer in relief". The east end is lit by five single lights, the west by four. The windows leaded in patterns: seats of cedar.

The architect was J. Horbury Hunt of Sydney.

The Dioceses of Grafton and Armidale were separated in 1914.

CHRIST CHURCH
CATHEDRAL,
GRAFTON,
N.S.W.

ALL SAINTS' CATHEDRAL, BATHURST, N.S.W.

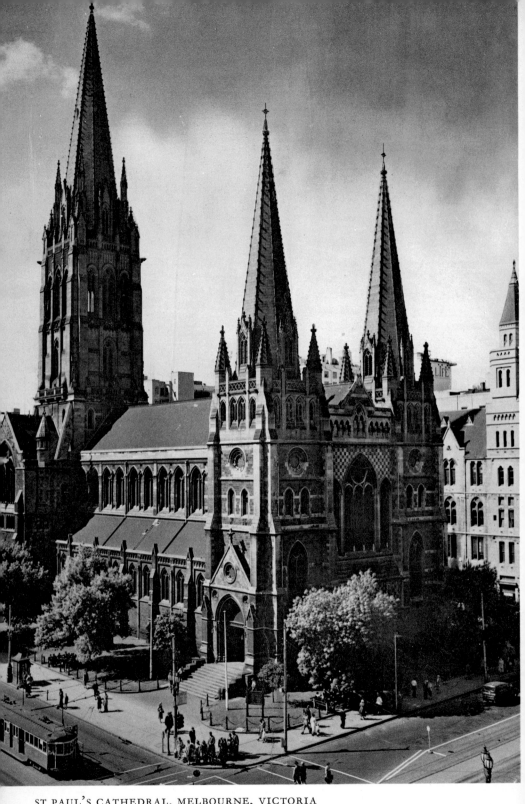

ST PAUL'S CATHEDRAL, MELBOURNE, VICTORIA

ST PAUL'S CATHEDRAL, MELBOURNE, VICTORIA

ST JOHN'S CATHEDRAL,
BRISBANE, QUEENSLAND

ALL SAINTS' CATHEDRAL, BATHURST

The foundation stone of the church was laid by Bishop Broughton on 24 January 1845; it was used from July 1848 onwards, and consecrated on 14 December 1849. It is of brick, in what Professor Pevsner has taught us to call the *Rundbogenstil*—an unattractive word, but it does cover all the varieties of Romanesque—Italian, Rhenish, and Norman—that were used, with more learning or with less, by several architects during the 30's and 40's. Bathurst is rather a good specimen. It was described in 1851 as "a good Norman church of brick and stone dressings, with tower engaged in the north aisle, and well-developed chancel". The tower, finished in 1852, is decidedly imposing: it contains the oldest peal of bells in Australia (1855). The north aisle was enlarged in 1869.

The first Bishop of the Diocese was enthroned in 1870. The chancel was extended in 1874, and a clerestory has been added.

At the time of the consecration of Bishop Long in 1911 the fabric was in a very poor condition: the walls had settled and cracked, and the roof was dangerous. £2,000 was spent in patching it up; but after the Great War it was decided to reconstruct the whole building. A foundation stone was laid in 1920, but the cathedral hall was built first, and a beginning was not made until 1925. The first section was completed in 1927. The plans for the new building were made by Louis R. Williams of Melbourne: the style is described as "not a mere attempt to reproduce some type of mediaeval Gothic, but a free and artistic essay carrying the Spirit of the Age as well as the Spirit of the Ages". The material is brick, locally made: what has been built so far is the choir, sanctuary, choir aisles, and eastern ambulatory, vestries on the north, and the Warriors' Chapel on the south. The superintending architect was A. N. H. Sambrook of Bathurst: the contractors were D. McNaughton and Sons of Sydney. Glass by W. Montgomery; screens, bishop's throne, sedilia, etc., by Foy and Gibson; wood-carving by N. Reding—all of Melbourne. The cost of the fabric—£7,000—was provided by Walter McIntosh, in memory of his brother: all the fittings and furniture were gifts.

The new cathedral when complete will have a nave with narrow aisles, western narthex, N.W. mortuary chapel, and two other chapels, and a tower over the east of it.

ST PAUL'S PRO-CATHEDRAL, HAY
[DIOCESE OF RIVERINA]

The Diocese was founded in 1884. St Paul's is an unpretentious brick church built in 1885, with chancel and nave of the same width, porch, vestries, and a small tower. The east wall has a painting of the Ascended Christ, by the Right Reverend E. A. Anderson, Bishop from 1895 to 1925.

CHRIST CHURCH CATHEDRAL, GRAFTON

The first church was built here in 1854 at a cost of £310.

William Collinson Sawyer, the first Bishop of Grafton and Armidale, arrived in Australia late in 1867. He visited Grafton for a few days, went to Newcastle, returned on 11 March 1868, and was drowned on 15 March, after taking evensong in the old wooden church.

His successor John Francis Turner, himself "an architect of no mean order", had plans prepared for a cathedral at Grafton. But the parishioners considered that the cost would be too great, and he devoted himself to building the cathedral at Armidale. When this was done, he had a modified plan made for Grafton, with smaller estimates, and the foundation stone was laid on 24 June 1874. But nothing more was done until 1880. In 1881 contracts were let for the walls and roofs, and the sanctuary, choir, transept, and part of the nave and aisles were dedicated on 25 July 1884.

The architect was J. Horbury Hunt. The contractors were Messrs Reynolds Bros for the brickwork, and G. Lawson for the woodwork. The foundations are of stone, the walls, pillars, and arches of brick, made locally by Samuel George. The style is Victorian First-Pointed.

In 1934 the completion of the nave was begun: it was made possible by a gift from the Reverend Lendon Bell. The tower and spire are not yet built, the chapter house awaits completion, and the vestries need to be extended. The glass of the east window, by Lyon Cottier and Co., is a memorial to Bishop Turner (1869–93).

The Dioceses of Grafton and Armidale were separated in 1914.

B. PROVINCE OF VICTORIA
ST PAUL'S CATHEDRAL, MELBOURNE

The original cathedral was St James's, originally in Little Collins Street, but afterwards rebuilt in King Street, and rededicated on 19

April 1914. It was begun in 1839, built by convict labour, completed in 1841, and opened in 1842. It is built of squared blocks of stone: the windows are semi-circular-headed, with moulded architraves and key-stones. The tower has an octagonal top stage capped with a dome. The *Ecclesiologist* was, of course, contemptuous: "a tall gaunt martello tower, with a morion cap upon its summit. This extraordinary steeple, joined to the dark armour-coloured stone of which the church is built, gives it a most martial air." The architect was Robert Russell.

In 1868 it was stated that "the architect sent out by Mr Scott to super-intend the erection of the cathedral at Christ Church, New Zealand, will, probably, send in plans" (i.e. R. Speechly).

A committee for building a new cathedral was appointed in 1869. Plans were made by Messrs Terry and Speechly, whose estimate was £75,000, exclusive of the tower and the internal fittings. Nothing came of this, and after eight years William Butterfield (1814–1900) was appointed instead.

Butterfield was a solitary, austere, ascetic man, and his churches express exactly the spirit of the Tractarian leaders. Generally speaking, the larger churches are more successful than the small—in some of which the deliberate crudities have to be seen from rather too near, and are slightly embarrassing even to those with robust Victorian tastes. But the larger churches, with their low aisles, tall clerestories, rather low chancel arches, and tall chancels, are magnificent. The seats are generally almost fanatically low—kneelings rather than sittings: and the whole thing is a perfect setting for the ritualistic worship which is out of fashion now, but attracted enormous congregations in the 19th century. How we should have enjoyed being at St Ninian's Cathedral, Perth, on the day of its consecration in 1850, seeing the choir and clergy cluster round the brass lectern, and hearing them thunder out the *Urbs Beata Jerusalem* as arranged in the *Hymnal Noted*. Or worshipping at St Matthias', Stoke Newington, with Monk at the organ.

The foundation stone was laid on 13 April 1880, by the Governor, the Marquis of Normanby. In the course of the work Butterfield resigned, and a local architect, Joseph Reed, took his place: he super-vised gratuitously the completion of the building, and was responsible for most of the internal fittings. The consecration was on 22 January 1891.

The material of the exterior is sandstone and limestone from Barra-bool Hills and Waurn Ponds, near Geelong, diversified with broad bands of bluestone. The pillars are of Pyrmont stone from Sydney. All the internal work is of Tasmanian blackwood. Most of the glass is by Clayton and Bell.

The western bay is divided from the nave by a tall arch, as at St Alban's, Holborn. There were to have been two western saddleback towers, and an octagonal central tower and spire. In 1924 the Cathedral Erection Board called for designs for completing the cathedral: the competition was won by James Barr of Sydney. He finished off the two western towers with a low upper stage, pinnacles, and a spire, and built a tall central tower and spire (319 feet), supported by steel on a concrete base. The master builder was Clements Langford. The effect is very un-Butterfieldian.

The interior shows the original design, apart from the woodwork, and a few other features. There are various elaborate furnishings: Australian churchmen are not shy of admiring intricate carving, mosaic and marble, and have not been affected by the polite Good Taste that is now fashionable among English deans and chapters and diocesan advisory committees. Churches like this in England are a sore trial to those who believe only in limewash, clear glass, and artistic hangings.

The font (Butterfield's design) is of Australian granite, with a carved blackwood cover given in 1927. There is also a marble immersion font.

The pulpit and archbishop's throne were carved on the spot, by five men in seven months. The screen was designed by Walter Butler, and carved by Philip Gawler, in 1912.

The east end bears a general resemblance to that of Keble Chapel at Oxford. The reredos is of Venetian glass mosaic, with the Crucifixion above, and the Last Supper in the middle; immediately above the altar is a white marble cross with angels in mosaic, and St Peter and St Paul at the sides. The Chapel of the Ascension has also a reredos of glass mosaic, in memory of Sir William and Lady Janet Clarke.

CHRIST CHURCH CATHEDRAL, BALLARAT

The foundation stone was laid in 1854, by Archdeacon Stretch of Geelong; but building operations were postponed until 1857, by which time the stone had disappeared. The church was opened on 13 September 1857. The cost was about £2,000: the style is plain E.E. Chancel and transepts were added in 1868.

In 1886 it was decided to erect a new cathedral. A beginning was made, and the foundation stone was laid on 30 November 1888, by Sir Henry Brougham Loch, Governor of Victoria. The diocesan offices in the basement of the cathedral were dedicated on 8 June 1904, and the chapter house was completed in 1908, and dedicated on 10 November. But nothing more was built.

To meet growing needs, a wooden building was erected at the back of the School, which was later moved and attached to the north transept of Christ Church: it is now the choir vestry. From the materials of the old vicarage, demolished to make room for the new cathedral, a room was built next to the Sunday school.

A further effort at carrying out S. F. Johnson's plans for the new cathedral were made in 1905, but nothing came of it.

In 1923 the church was remodelled, and a porch and baptistery were built. In 1929 a new organ was installed. Since then a sanctuary has been added, and there have been additions to the furniture, including reredos, panelling, and pulpit canopy.

ALL SAINTS' CATHEDRAL, BENDIGO

The foundation stone was laid on 22 January 1855, and the church was opened in October 1856. Of local freestone, in 13th-century style: a tower and spire were intended, but not carried out. The cost was £4,500.

After 19 months it was unroofed by a cyclone, and so much shaken that it had to be rebuilt at a cost of nearly £3,000. Later, the chancel was rebuilt at a cost of £1,200.

The pulpit, designed by Sir Gilbert Scott, is from Westminster Abbey.

In 1931 John Gawler and Louis Williams were asked to make plans for a new cathedral, which were accepted. The choir has been completed.

HOLY TRINITY CATHEDRAL, WANGARATTA

The original church was built in 1856, and enlarged with transepts in 1873: the first bishop of the diocese was enthroned here in 1902.

The design for the cathedral was made by Messrs Butler and Bradshaw of Melbourne: most of the drawing, and all the supervision of the work, were done by W. R. Butler, who also designed some of the furniture. The foundation stone was laid on 14 December 1908, and the first stage of the work—three bays of the nave and aisles—was dedicated on 24 August 1909.

The chancel, sanctuary, Lady chapel, and vestries were built in 1923-4. Two benefactions made this possible: over £11,000 from Francis Heach, and £5,000 from Jonathan Thomas Bell. The contractor for both sections was W. McKnockiter.

As part of the celebration of the centenary, £35,000 was asked for in three years for the completion of the cathedral: £45,000 has been promised. The plan includes two slender towers with spires.

The external walls of the cathedral are of granite from the Warby Ranges behind South Wangaratta, laid in regular courses: the window tracery—14th century in style—is of Pyrmont stone. The interior walls are of brick, with black pointing: there is a seven-foot dado of black and red brick. There have been many gifts of furnishings and ornaments: the pulpit is a memorial to Bishop Armstrong (1902–27).

ST PAUL'S CATHEDRAL, SALE
[DIOCESE OF GIPPSLAND]

The first church was built in 1856. The foundation stone of the present building was laid by Bishop Moorhouse on 3 December 1882: it was opened on 5 November 1884. It was made the pro-cathedral when the diocese was formed in 1902.

CHRIST CHURCH PRO-CATHEDRAL, ST ARNAUD

The town began with a gold-rush in 1855; but the miners were disappointed and soon went away, leaving only a small community depending on quartz mining. It is now the centre of a farming district. In 1862 the Government granted the site for a church, and the inhabitants attempted to raise the money: people of all denominations subscribed, because, as the local paper said, the new church would be some sort of guarantee of the stability of St Arnaud. The foundation stone was laid by the Dean of Melbourne on 16 September 1862. The architect was Frederick Marlborough Moore, the manager of the Freiberg Company. The cost was £881, excluding the cost of the bricks. The shell of

the building—red brick, with a slate roof—was completed within a
year, but it was not furnished and dedicated until the early 70's. In
1877 two west porches and a vestry were added, and in 1924 the chancel
and sanctuary, and a low tower and spire.

The diocese was formed in 1926, and the Bishop was enthroned in
Christ Church on 30 September.

c. PROVINCE OF QUEENSLAND

ST JOHN'S CATHEDRAL, BRISBANE

The first Bishop of Brisbane was appointed in 1859, and in 1860 a
design for a cathedral was made by William Burges (1827–81). It was
never carried out, but it would have been a beauty. Burges was a
thorough-going mediaevalist, who "imbued his sensitive and poetical
mind in mediaeval lore". He loved French Gothic of the early 13th
century—which appealed to the younger architects of the late 50's and
60's as being strong and manly, in contrast to the tame and effeminate
English 14th-century style which the earlier ecclesiologists had recommended. It could be made, and often was made, coarse and unattractive;
but Burges had a whimsical, humorous mind, which enlivened his
designs in a most refreshing way.

The design for Brisbane was "semi-speluncar", with walls four feet
thick. It consisted of nave and aisles, with a saddle-back tower at the
south-west; apsidal choir, and apsidal north and south chapels. The
aisles were vaulted, the nave had a coved wooden roof. Statues of kings
and queens would decorate the west end, as it was in Queensland; and
the pulpit would stand on dogs. This was typical of Burges: the point,
of course, was that Durandus in his *Rationale Divinorum Officiorum*
says that the dog, who keeps us awake by barking, is a type of the
Christian preacher.

However, nothing came of this. In 1867 the committee chose a design
by D. W. Ryan for a cathedral of nave and aisles, tower and spire,
transepts and apsidal chancel, with vestry and organ chamber, bishop's
room and sacristan's room.

In 1878 the foundation stone of St Paul's, Maryborough, was laid, and
it was opened in 1879. The church—with cemented brick walls, iron
columns, and a slate roof—was to serve as a cathedral. It was designed
by F. D. G. Stanley, colonial architect.

In 1885 the Reverend W. T. T. Webber was appointed Bishop. He had been responsible for building the magnificent church of St John, Red Lion Square, one of the best of the churches of J. L. Pearson (1817–97)—now, alas, a total wreck, and not to be rebuilt. In 1887 the Bishop decided to build a cathedral as a Jubilee memorial, and naturally applied to Pearson for the plans; but lack of funds held up the scheme for ten years. In 1897, after a visit to England during which he received promises of help, he determined to devote himself to the task of raising £35,000, to build the choir and transepts.

The site of the old St John's Church (opened in 1854) was too small; and, as no additional land could be obtained to the east, the Chapter decided to sell the site, and buy a larger one elsewhere. The St John's land, the rectory, the schoolroom, and the institute were sold to the Government for £33,000, and the Chapter undertook to demolish the church. The new site, 2½ acres overlooking the Brisbane River, cost £18,000.

The foundation stone was laid by the Duke of York—afterwards King George V—on 22 May 1901. The Bishop went to England to raise funds, but died before the building was begun. J. L. Pearson had died in 1897, and his son F. L. Pearson superintended the erection, in conjunction with W. D. Caröe. The contractor was Peter Rodger of Ballarat.

The first section of the cathedral was consecrated on SS. Simon and Jude's Day 1910. This consisted of the apsidal choir and ambulatory, Lady chapel on the north, and double aisle—now the chapels of the Holy Spirit and the Blessed Sacrament—on the south; the transepts, and one bay of the nave: the lantern tower was only carried up to the level of the roof. The nave has double aisles: the clerestory windows are in the outer wall of the inner aisles, so that the arcade will intercept the rays of the sun.

The first portion of the stalls was erected in 1913—three canons' stalls on each side, of teak, made in Exeter by Messrs Luscombe and Son; the sculptured work by Nathaniel Hitch of Kennington.

The cathedral is of stone—the outer walls of pink porphyry from the O'Connell Town quarries, five miles away, with dressings from Pyrmont Quarry, near Sydney; the interior of brown Helidon sandstone. There are vaulted roofs throughout, as in most of Pearson's larger churches.

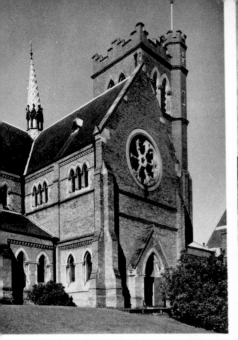

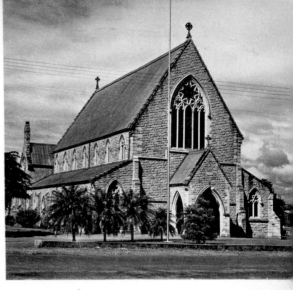

ST PAUL'S CATHEDRAL,
ROCKHAMPTON, QUEENSLAND

GEORGE'S CATHEDRAL,
TH, WESTERN AUSTRALIA

CATHEDRAL OF
SS. PETER AND PAUL,
DOGURA, PAPUA,
NEW GUINEA

'S PRO-CATHEDRAL, BUNBURY, WESTERN AUSTRALIA THE PROPOSED NEW BUILDING

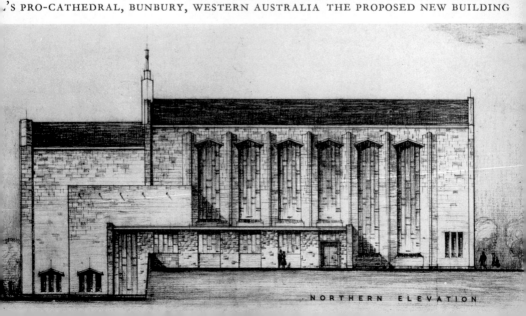

NORTHERN ELEVATION

ST PETER'S CATHEDRAL,
ADELAIDE, SOUTH AUSTRAI

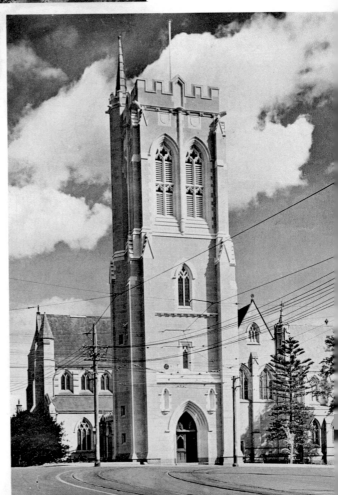

ST DAVID'S CATHEDRAL,
HOBART, TASMANIA

The high altar, Byzantine in style, has three marble slabs from Iona: a stone canopy was designed, but has not yet been erected. In the pavement of the sanctuary are two pieces of the Shellal mosaics—part of the floor of a ruined Christian church of about the 7th century, which was unearthed when trenches were being dug during the second battle of Gaza, in April 1917: the greater part of the mosaic is in the Canberra war museum.

The pulpit, which was carved in Cheltenham, is of Cornish soapstone, and the font of Frosterley marble.

The debt on the building was not paid off until just before Dr W. C. Wand (Archbishop from 1936 to 1944) left for Bath and Wells. Afterwards, a committee was formed to raise funds for the completion of the cathedral; by 1956 something over £250,000 had been raised—about half the amount needed to complete the nave. It is greatly to the credit of the people of Brisbane that they are attempting to build according to the original design. The Governor-General, Sir William Slim, turned the first sod on 21 August 1955, and work was begun on the reinforced concrete floor.

The finished cathedral will have two western towers with spires, not unlike those of Truro Cathedral; a central lantern tower with a pyramid top; and a cloister on the north, with vestries, chapter house, and library.

ST JAMES'S CATHEDRAL, TOWNSVILLE
[DIOCESE OF NORTH QUEENSLAND]

The first church, of wood, was built in 1871. The diocese was formed in 1878.

The first Bishop—George Henry Stanton—decided to build a cathedral, and plans were made by E. T. Blacket. A gift of £1,000 was made by W. Hayes. The foundation stone was laid on 27 June 1887.

There were some delays in the building, but it was finally completed in 1892, and consecrated on 27 October. It is 13th century in style.

Much damage was done by the cyclone in 1903: the restoration was completed in 1904.

Only the choir, ambulatory, and transepts were built. The nave and towers are to be built from plans by Louis Williams. The screen is a memorial of the 1914–18 war, and the bishop's throne a memorial to Bishop J. O. Feetham.

ST PAUL'S CATHEDRAL, ROCKHAMPTON

A wooden church was built in 1862 and consecrated in 1863. It was destroyed by a cyclone, and another church was built on the site now occupied by the parish hall.

In 1875 the foundation stone of a large stone church was laid, but differences of opinion arose, and building stopped. It was begun again in 1879: the Bishop of North Queensland laid a memorial stone on 16 September. The consecration was on 18 October 1883. The diocese was formed in 1892.

The glass in the lancets of the apse was designed by Caroline Townshend and executed by Messrs Lowndes and Drury of Parsons Green. Three of the windows were erected in 1914 in memory of the first Bishop of Rockhampton, Nathaniel Dawes, and the other two in 1921 in memory of Marion Dawson.

CATHEDRAL OF SS. PETER AND PAUL, DOGURA, PAPUA [NEW GUINEA]

The cathedral was begun in 1934, and consecrated on 29 October 1939. It was built entirely by Papuan Christians, as a thank-offering for the blessings that have come to them through the Christian Faith; 170 men, from all the mission areas, gave their services for not less than three months. In addition, about £700 was given by the Christians of the diocese. The total cost was about £4,000.

The work was supervised by Robert Jones, a member of the Mission staff. Plans made by Professor Sydney Wilkinson were found to be too ambitious, and were modified by Mr Jones.

The cathedral, Romanesque in style, is built of reinforced concrete. The transeptal towers are memorials to the two founders of the Mission, Albert Maclaren and Copland King: their lower stages form the Lady chapel and the chapel of the Resurrection. The high altar, of polished granite, was given as a thank-offering for the work of Bishop Newton. The altar in the chapel of the Resurrection—similar in design to the altar in the chapel of the Blessed Sacrament in Brisbane Cathedral—is a memorial to Bishop Sharp, the second bishop of the diocese. Many of the ornaments, and the windows, were gifts: the window of St Lawrence was presented by the children of Australia. The wall paintings at the east end were the work of Canon James Benson, who died in 1955.

The site of the cathedral was a battleground—where the peoples of the beach fought with the peoples of the mountains, and ate the dead afterwards. The pioneer missionaries landed only 48 years before the consecration.

St John's, Port Moresby, is a co-cathedral.

ALL SOULS' CATHEDRAL, THURSDAY ISLAND
[Diocese of Carpentaria]

Albert Maclaren, the pioneer priest, persuaded the Bishop of North Queensland to build a church, as a memorial to the dead and a thank-offering for the living, in memory of the sinking of the *Quetta* on 28 February 1890. The foundation stone was laid on 24 May 1893, and the church was dedicated on 12 November. The chancel and four bays of the nave were built in concrete; the aisles were added later, with temporary walls of wood. The architect was J. H. Buckeridge of Sydney. The *Quetta*'s riding lamp and bell were retrieved, and are here.

It became a cathedral in 1900.

D. Province of West Australia
ST GEORGE'S CATHEDRAL, PERTH

The colony was founded in 1829, and a temporary church was built. In 1835 it was proposed to build a Court House, which could also be used as a church. The design was made by Henry W. Reveley, engineer to the Administration, son of the architect Willey Reveley, who had had some training in architecture, and had been to Italy and Greece. It was opened on 24 March 1837.

In January 1838 a meeting was held to consider the building of a church. By January 1839, £1,140 had been promised, and in February the *Perth Gazette* advertised the contract. Plans and estimates were to be approved by Mr Trigg, the superintendent of public works ("the father of Congregationalism in Western Australia", and the builder of Trinity Church). On 14 February the plans of Joseph Brown, an amateur architect, were accepted: Richard Morrell of Fremantle was to be the builder. The Governor laid the foundation stone on 1 January 1841. In March of the next year the contractor gave up work, and the building was not opened until 22 January 1845: it was consecrated on

15 November 1848. It was plain Grecian, with a west portico and octagonal tower: the side walls had square-headed windows and pilasters.

It became a cathedral in 1857: transepts were added, and dedicated on 10 January 1864.

On 22 June 1877, a meeting decided to erect a new building. It was agreed to consult A. W. Blomfield, and a committee was appointed. On 22 July they considered the plans of various churches sent from England, and liked best those of St Luke's, Chesterton, Cambridge (by W. Smith). But in September they were discussing a Perp. design by Wardell. Finally E. T. Blacket of Sydney was chosen as architect.

Work on the foundations began in October 1879, and was complete by May 1880. Tenders were then invited for carrying the walls up to 18 feet. The north transept window was to be made to contain glass made by Clayton and Bell for the old cathedral. The Governor laid the foundation stone on 2 November 1880.

A second appeal for funds, in February 1881, met with small response. There was also difficulty in getting the stone. This came from the Government quarries at Rottnest, but the convict labour had mostly been transferred elsewhere. Also, much of the stone, when it arrived at Fremantle, had to be rejected. In August 1882 the Government allowed stone to be quarried at the other Government quarry at Fremantle; but there was a lack of skilled labour, and the capitals had to be carved at Sydney, and shipped over.

In March 1883 Blacket died, and his son took his place. He kept to the original plans, except that there was to be only one west doorway, instead of three, and jarrah wood was to be used instead of New Zealand Kauri pine. There was some discussion about the material for the pillars: the architect suggested Melbourne blue stone: others suggested white bricks from Melbourne, Sydney Pierpoint freestone, or iron. In the end, blue stone was used.

By May 1884 the second contract was complete, and tenders were invited for finishing the work. The lowest was that of Keane, the contractor for the third section of the Government railway. By August 1888 the interior was fairly complete, and it was opened on 8 August. Much of the furniture of the old cathedral was used temporarily. The consecration was on 15 November.

The pulpit was erected in 1892, the altar in 1896, and an iron screen which had been made in England. The reredos was erected three years afterwards.

Blacket had planned a tall tower and spire, which had never been built. In 1901 a low tower was erected as a memorial to Queen Victoria: it was dedicated on 22 January 1903. The architect was Talbot Hobbs (afterwards Sir Talbot).

The Soldiers' chapel was built as a 1914–18 war memorial, on the site on which Blacket had proposed to build the chapter house.

ST PAUL'S PRO-CATHEDRAL, BUNBURY

A building on the northern portion of the present pro-cathedral site was opened on 5 January 1845. It served as church and school, and was the gift of T. W. Thomson. The site and the building were afterwards bought from him by the Church for £130.

The Reverend Joseph Withers, who became rector in 1864, soon realized that it was too small, and decided to build a new and larger church. It was completed in 1866, and consecrated on 11 November. It is of brick, 90 feet by 30 feet, with plastered walls and a roof of shingles. Nave and chancel are under one roof, and there is a three-sided apse lit by lancets under gables. The diocese was formed in 1904.

Bishop Goldsmith (1904–17) wanted to build a more worthy cathedral, and a possible site was offered to the Vestry in 1916; but opinions were divided about it, and it was eventually refused.

The church has now become out of repair, and plans for a permanent cathedral have been made by Forbes and Fitzhardinge.

ST JOHN THE BAPTIST'S CATHEDRAL, KALGOORLIE

The foundation stone was laid on 25 November 1908: the church was consecrated on 19 February 1909.

The diocese was formed in 1914.

PRO-CATHEDRAL OF THE ANNUNCIATION, BROOME
[DIOCESE OF NORTH-WEST AUSTRALIA]

A small church, holding only about 100 people.

The diocese, covering over 600,000 square miles, with a very small population, was formed in 1909. In 1921 Archbishop Lowther Clarke of

Melbourne appealed for the building of a cathedral; he said: "A stately church of dignity and reverence will do much for the Christian faith in this new land of unspiritual ideals. Something is wanted to appeal to the imagination." But in 1923 the Bishop wrote: "The cathedral is still unrealized."

E. EXTRA-PROVINCIAL DIOCESES

ST DAVID'S CATHEDRAL, HOBART, TASMANIA

The old St David's was begun in 1816, at the suggestion of Governor Macquarie. On 13 April Colonel Thomas Davey, the Lieutenant-Governor, reported that work had begun. He arranged that the church should stand east and west; but as this would interfere with the appearance of other buildings, Macquarie would not agree. This delayed plans for a while, but the foundation stone was laid by Davey in February 1817. In May he reported that the walls were going up. The first service was held on Christmas Day 1819, though the work was still incomplete. By March 1820 the engineer in charge—Major Bell—reported that the steeple had been carried up to its full height of 110 feet, that the roofing had been finished, and the greater part of the plastering and carpenter's work done, and that the flagstones for the sanctuary and the middle of the church were being cut.

The church was simple Colonial Classic, with a hipped roof, seven round-headed windows at the sides, and a tower with octagonal upper stage and cupola.

In 1866 the Bishop appealed for funds to build a new cathedral: plans were obtained from G. F. Bodley, and the foundation stone of the nave was laid on 8 January 1868. By the beginning of 1869 enough money was in hand to justify the acceptance of a tender for building the nave, aisles, and transepts. The nave was first used on the last Sunday of 1872, though "the floor was like a macadamized road and all the furniture for interior was still to be supplied". It was consecrated on 5 February 1874, with a temporary east end and vestry.

The foundation stone of the chancel was laid on 3 February 1891: the foundations were the only part of the work that the Chapter then felt able to undertake; but in the next year it was decided to build the chancel for £6,696. On 4 January 1892, the foundation stone of the tower was laid. The chancel was consecrated on 18 January 1894.

The contractors were Messrs Cooper Bros and Messrs Stabb Bros, and the work was carried out under the supervision of George Fagg, M.S.A., of Hobart. The timbers and boarding of the roof are of native blue gum, and the paving of the central portions of the choir and chapel is of Sicilian black and white marble.

The pulpit, 1903, was carved by H. R. Franklin of Deddington. In 1905 the Dean brought back from England the dossal, canopy, and side curtains for the altar that Bodley had designed. While in London, he discussed the condition of the chancel with the architect. On a report from Alexander North, the diocesan architect, and in concert with Bodley, the roof was removed, and parts of the walls were rebuilt and strengthened: the work was completed in 1909. The Dean also arranged with Bodley to send out working drawings for the tower and cloister, and for the chancel screen and new organ. The screen was dedicated on 15 November 1916.

In 1928 a sum of money was made available to the Cathedral Board, and it was decided to complete the design. The cloisters and the first section of the tower were completed in 1931, and the tower was finished in 1936.

The cathedral is in Bodley's English 14th-century style, which he had adopted not long before he made the design, after an earlier French Gothic phase. The design for the tower was made later. The original plans included an embattled tower with plain octagonal pinnacles and a spire. The present tower shows Bodley at his most Bodleian. It is fortunate that the builders of 1936 had the piety to keep to his plans, and not to substitute something contemporary.

ST PETER'S CATHEDRAL, ADELAIDE

In 1847, the year of the appointment of the first Bishop, William Butterfield prepared drawings for a cathedral, bishop's palace, and college. The cathedral was to occupy the north side of a square: on the west side was a range of collegiate buildings—schoolroom, refectory, and dormitories. The south side was occupied by the rest of the college, and by lodgings for the bishop's chaplains. The palace was at the southeast, extending along part of the east side, and connected with the cathedral by chapter house and sacristies. The cathedral—of brick, like the rest of the buildings—was to have had an aisled nave of four bays with a clerestory, transepts which did not project beyond the aisle walls, a low central tower, with a cap, supported on tall brick arches, and choir. "Nothing", said the *Ecclesiologist*, "could be more severe than this design, and yet it has a character of its own which it is perhaps impossible to describe: it has just that individuality which we admire in our ancient churches. One thing which contributes to give this effect is its great height in proportion to its dimensions. The building, although plain to excess and of a material so mean as brick, will be religious and imposing from its unusual height and marked outline." But the authorities did not approve of the design, and they wanted stone, not brick. Butterfield, who can never have been easy to deal with, gave up.

A few years afterwards, William Slater made a sketch for a larger and more elaborate cathedral—Middle-Pointed in style and cruciform, with a central tower and spire. But this also was not adopted.

Finally designs were made by E. J. Woods and McMinn, local architects, who adapted Butterfield's plans. The foundation stone was laid on St Peter's Day 1869. The choir, transepts, and one bay of the nave were opened in 1876, and consecrated on 1 January 1878.

The nave was completed later, and the western towers were finished in 1902. In 1903 the Lady chapel was built, the choir was lengthened, and vestries were provided in the crypt—the gift of Mrs Alfred Simms. The porch, and windows, were given by R. Barr Smith.

The cathedral is built of Tea Gully stone and Murray Bridge freestone; the roofs are of slate. It is obvious that some parts of the design are of Butterfieldian origin, and some are not.

The reredos is the work of the Guild of St Swithin. The series of windows of Archbishops of Canterbury is by E. W. Carter (1886–1953). The hanging rood, erected a few years ago, was designed by Andor Meszaros.

ST MARY'S CATHEDRAL, AUCKLAND

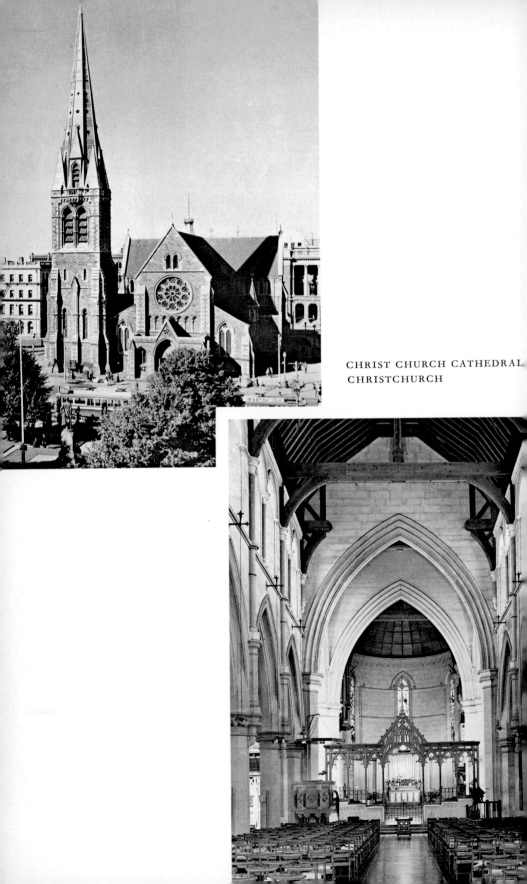

CHRIST CHURCH CATHEDRAL
CHRISTCHURCH

CHRIST CHURCH CATHEDRAL, NELSON

ST PAUL'S CATHEDRAL,
DUNEDIN

ST PAUL'S CATHEDRAL, WELLINGTON,
The architect's drawing of the permanent church

HOLY TRINITY CATHEDRAL, SUVA, FIJI, POLYNESIA

ST PETER'S CATHEDRAL, HAMILTON

9

New Zealand

ST MARY'S CATHEDRAL, AUCKLAND

Bishop Selwyn in 1841 asked the Cambridge Camden Society to furnish him with designs and models for the cathedral and parish churches. An article on the subject was the first in the first number of the *Ecclesiologist* (November 1841). The site of the cathedral would be marked out and consecrated, but the building would not be begun yet. For the parish churches the Society would furnish working models of Norman capitals, sections of mouldings, ornamented piers, door and window arches. One model would be sufficient, because the churches would be 200 miles apart. "Norman is the style adopted; because, as the work will be chiefly done by native artists, it seems natural to teach them first that style which first prevailed in our own country; while its rudeness and massiveness, and the grotesque character of its sculpture, will probably render it easier to be understood and appreciated by them."

On 30 August 1842, the Bishop wrote to the President of the Society, reporting progress. He had chosen a site for the cathedral. "The position will suit a building in the style of Durham, Christchurch, or Romsey. The ground on the top of the hill will not admit of a greater length than 300 feet. The material in this part is a dark brown volcanic stone, which is often found crystallized so as to require little or no facing with the tool. This, with hewn stone for the windows and door cases, would make an admirable building."

The first St Mary's was consecrated on 14 October 1860: it was of wood, with a central tower and spire. There was an enlargement in 1879.

During the incumbency of the Reverend G. H. S. Walpole—afterwards Bishop of Edinburgh—plans were made for building the first part of a permanent church; but these had to be given up.

The parish then erected the present wooden church, which was begun in 1886, and consecrated on 30 November 1888. The architect was B. W. Mountfort of Christchurch: the cost was £5,800.

Benjamin Woolfield Mountfort (1824–98), who had been trained as an architect under Gilbert Scott, came to Canterbury in one of the first four ships, and spent the rest of his life there. Scott's cathedral at Christchurch was built under his superintendence, and he designed other New Zealand churches, including the cathedral at Napier. His fame spread beyond New Zealand. The church of St Saviour, Sandakan, Borneo, was burned down in 1890, and Mountfort was engaged to design a wooden church. Then the public works officer advised brick, and Mountfort designed a brick church. Then good building stone was discovered nearby, and he designed a stone church. The church was finally built under the superintendence of the Reverend W. H. Elton.

Mountfort also designed the Canterbury Provincial Chambers and the hall of Canterbury College. For many years Mr Luck was his partner. He was a photographer, a member of the diocesan synod, and a churchwarden. He died on 15 March 1898.

In 1935 Miss Mina Tait Horton left £65,000 towards the building of a permanent cathedral. A competition in 1938 was won by Charles Towle, A.R.I.B.A. By 1955 the sum available was over £180,000, and the Synod decided to proceed with the building of the sanctuary, presbytery, choir, crossing, and transepts. The present St Mary's will form a temporary nave; the choir and sanctuary will become the Lady chapel.

CHRIST CHURCH CATHEDRAL, NELSON

The first stone of the first church on the site was laid on 26 June 1848, and the church was opened on Christmas Day 1851, and consecrated on 7 March 1858. It was of wood, roofed with shingles—cruciform, with a western tower and spire. The architect was Frederick Thatcher, who was born about 1820, came to New Zealand at the beginning of the 40's, and was afterwards ordained. He visited England in 1859, and returned to New Zealand in 1861. He fell ill in 1865, retired to England, and remained there for the rest of his life. He was secretary to the

Bishop of Lichfield from 1868 to 1882, and prebendary of Lichfield from 1883 until his death in 1890.

The See was created in 1858.

In 1887 the church was remodelled and enlarged from plans by B. W. Mountfort. By 1916 it showed signs of decay, and the spire had to be taken down.

After the Great War, plans were made for a handsome new cathedral in Takaka marble.

A substantial sum of money was collected, and the work was begun. But it proved to be more expensive than had been expected, and building was stopped in 1932 after rather less than one-third had been completed at a cost of £69,000.

It now consists of the nave, to which the clerestory remains to be added: the wooden chancel of the old cathedral is still standing.

The style is 13th century.

CHRIST CHURCH CATHEDRAL, CHRISTCHURCH

The design was made by George Gilbert Scott, and the foundation stone was laid on 16 December 1864. The foundations were completed in 1865, at a cost of over £7,000—after which a period of commercial depression set in, and the work came to a standstill.

The architect sent out to superintend the work was R. Speechly. When he gave up, B. W. Mountfort took his place.

In 1873 the nave was begun, and the tower and spire were built—the gift of Robert Heaton Rhodes. The finished portion was consecrated on All Saints' Day 1881. The supervising architect was B. W. Mountfort, from whose design the porch was erected: he also designed the projecting balconies at the top of the tower.

The spire was damaged by an earthquake in 1888: the Rhodes family met the cost of the repair, which was finished in 1891. The west porch —1894-5—was the gift of Mrs Creyke.

In 1899 the Dean and Chapter decided to complete the cathedral as a memorial of the 50th anniversary of the foundation of Canterbury settlement by the arrival of the first settlers on 16 December 1850. The spire was again damaged by earthquake on 16 November 1901.

"The walls of the chancel of Christchurch Cathedral, N.Z., are beginning to show the beauty of the complete building as designed by the late Sir Gilbert Scott. The spire is to be once more restored, and, once again, through the liberality of the Rhodes family; but in view of possible damage by further earthquakes, a wooden framework covered with copper sheeting will take the place of the stonework at the summit. The cost will be £888." (*Church Times*, 11 September 1903.)

The cathedral was finished in 1904.

The style is Scott's favourite 13th century. The details are mainly English, though there are a few French features. "Retain all the good you have picked up in your wanderings," he wrote, "and use it up in your reformed architecture."

The pulpit is a memorial to Bishop Selwyn.

ST JOHN'S CATHEDRAL, NAPIER
[DIOCESE OF WALAPU]

The cathedral was built through the efforts of Dean Hovell (1878–1905): it was consecrated on 20 December 1888. At the time of the consecration £9,533 had been spent on the site, building, and fittings, and there were liabilities amounting to £1,675.

The chancel and organ chamber of the temporary St John's Church were given to St Augustine's, some of the windows went to St Paul's, Wairoa, and the rest of the building was sold, and erected as a dwelling-house in Harvey Road, Napier.

The new cathedral was designed by B. W. Mountfort, and was in 13th-century style, of red brick, with "stone corbels, crosses, panels, and other ornamental features." It was 180 feet long, with nave and chancel of equal height; the nave had passage aisles. The interior, with its brick walls, traceried chancel screen, altar raised on steps, and eastern quintuplet filled with stained glass, was exactly like that of a large outer London church of the 80's. The New Zealanders appreciated it far more than we appreciate such churches in England.

It was destroyed by an earthquake in 1931—so completely that only one or two small fragments of wall were left standing. A temporary building was erected in the same year, and is still in use.

The foundation stone of a new cathedral was laid by the Governor-General, Sir Willoughby Norrie, in October 1955, and the east end is now being built. The construction will be of reinforced concrete, and the cost will be at least £150,000.

ST PAUL'S PRO-CATHEDRAL, WELLINGTON

At a meeting of S.P.C.K. on 7 February 1865, the Bishop stated that the contract for the cathedral of his diocese had been taken for £3,470. "The new church is a handsome, substantial building (wooden, in consequence of earthquakes), with tower and spire, and a detached chapter house, or vestry; and the interior will admit of much decoration by a judicious arrangement of the beautiful New Zealand woods." It was consecrated on 6 June 1866.

The architect was Frederick Thatcher, as the inscription on the foundation stone bears witness: "Fred. Thatcher (late Curate) Architect of the building." He fell ill after the tenders had been called, went back to England, and never saw the building take shape.

The foundation stone of the new cathedral was laid by Her Majesty the Queen in January 1954. The design was made by Cecil W. Wood in 1942: since his death, Robert C. Munro, of Christchurch, has been in charge.

When the new cathedral is built, the old is to be demolished.

ST LUKE'S CATHEDRAL, SIOTA
[Diocese of Melanesia]

In 1920 Bishop Steward transferred the Mission headquarters from Norfolk Island to Siota in the Solomon Islands: the building of the cathedral in 1928 was the completion of his plan. At the end of 1928 the Bishop wrote: "It is a really fine native building; the timbers, which are the gifts of many islands, were worked by their inhabitants by hand; they are huge, and are reminiscent of the kind of work put into the old Norman churches in England, but larger, I think, than any I have seen. We hope to have a great deal of mother-of-pearl inlaid."

In January 1942 the altar vessels, the Bishop Patteson mat (on which the dead body of the martyred Bishop was placed), the Bishop Selwyn pastoral staff, and the altar vessels, were taken away for safety; and in May other fittings were removed. The cathedral suffered from bombing in July and August; and when it was used as a hospital, after the American occupation, there was a certain amount of vandalism. Afterwards some repairs were done, and an artist in a U.S. Construction Battalion carried out the redecoration of the altar. A new episcopal throne was placed in the cathedral in 1949 as a memorial to Bishop Baddeley.

The Church of ALL SAINTS', HONIARA, was dedicated on 20 September 1952. This is now used as the pro-cathedral, as St Luke's, Siota, has become too dilapidated: the bishop's throne and the Patteson and Selwyn relics have been moved to the new building. When a permanent cathedral is built, it will be at Honiara.

ST PAUL'S CATHEDRAL, DUNEDIN

The foundation stone of the first church was laid on 26 June 1848: it was opened on Christmas Day 1851 and consecrated on 7 March 1858. The architect was Frederick Thatcher.

The diocese was founded in 1869.

Edmund Harold Sedding, of Plymouth, visited Dunedin in 1908, conferred with the diocesan authorities, and inspected the site. He had made preliminary drawings before the visit, and amended them after it. The design was published in 1909. He proposed an admirable Perp. cathedral, of moderate size, "of the character of Gloucester Cathedral". Nave and choir both of three bays. Triforium and clerestory arranged "according to the Gloucester and Winchester type": the upper part of the aisles to be used as a passage, and the triforium to be used for accommodation. Local limestone was to be used for the exterior walling, and Oamaru stone for tracery and moulded work.

Part of the cathedral was built, to an altered design, in 1914–19. The supervising architect was Basil V. Hooper, A.R.I.B.A., A.N.Z.I.A., who was at the time practising in Dunedin, where his practice was mostly in domestic work. He left Dunedin about the time that the work on the cathedral was completed, and was later in practice at Auckland.

The building was made possible by the Harrop bequest of £30,000, to be available if the diocese raised an equal sum. The nave and aisles, of six bays, with crypt below, were completed: the chancel is temporary.

The material is Oamaru stone: the imposing front—which is in fact east, not west—is approached by a flight of 38 steps of Nelson marble. The nave and double aisles have stone vaults: the passage aisles adjacent to the nave are roofed with pointed barrel vaults at right angles to the main building axis, and at the same height as the nave arches and the clerestory windows.

The design of the font is based on the Norman font at Lenton, Nottingham: the stone pulpit, with carved alabaster panels, stands on six shafts of West Coast Green marble. The fine organ (1920) is by Willis. The glass of the eight-light window above the main doorway is the work of Powell of Whitefriars.

HOLY TRINITY CATHEDRAL, SUVA, FIJI
[DIOCESE OF POLYNESIA]

A wooden church was built in 1886. The diocese was created in 1908, and it became the pro-cathedral.

The present building, constructed of concrete blocks, stands on the site of the old Government offices, a few yards away from the site of the first church. It was consecrated on 22 April 1953, and the old building was taken down immediately afterwards.

Only the first part of the cathedral has been completed—the choir, sanctuary, Lady chapel, chapter house, the memorial chapel of St George, and the vestries. The foundations of the nave have been laid, and it is hoped to begin building within a few years.

The cathedral was designed by C. Neville Nettleton, Government architect; the building has so far cost about £30,000.

ST PETER'S CATHEDRAL, HAMILTON
[DIOCESE OF WAIKATO]

The original church was built at the foot of the hill—once a Maori fort. The present building, on top of the hill, was built in 1914–15. It is of ferro-concrete, with nave, aisles, choir, and sanctuary: the west wall was temporary, to allow for later extension.

In 1926 the Waikato area, part of the King Country, and the Province of Taranaki, were cut off from the Diocese of Auckland, and formed into a new diocese with Hamilton as its centre: St Peter's became the cathedral.

Early in 1927 the east window, made in England, was erected as a war memorial. In the same year, by the will of Miss Annie MacPherson, the cathedral benefited by over £5,000: subsequently a choir vestry was built, surmounted by a tower: a bell was hung, and a peal was completed later. A chapel was built at the west end, and the west wall was strengthened.

10

Missionary Bishoprics

SS. MARY AND NICOLAS'S CATHEDRAL, SEOUL, KOREA

Shortly after the death of Bishop Arthur Beresford Turner (1910) a fund was opened to erect a memorial, which it was hoped would take the form of the building of part of a new church or pro-cathedral. By 1920, between £4,000 and £5,000 had been raised, and a leaflet was printed describing the proposed cathedral. The total cost would be £50,000: it was proposed to begin on part of it, at a cost of £15,000–£20,000.

The foundation stone was laid on 24 September 1922, and the consecration was on 2 May 1928.

The design was made by A. S. Dixon, F.R.I.B.A., of Birmingham—the architect of St Basil's, Deritend, St Andrew's, Barnt Green, the Chapel of the Grey Ladies, Coventry, and the Bishop's Chapel at Bishopscroft, Harborne. Bishop Trollope, who was appointed in 1911, had known him when he was Vicar of St Alban's, Birmingham.

The cathedral is Romanesque in style, cruciform, with a central tower, and small towers in the angles of the choir and transepts; apsidal aisled choir. There is an undercroft under the choir and transepts.

COLLEGIATE CHURCH OF ST GEORGE, JERUSALEM

The joint Anglican and Prussian Bishopric was established in 1841: it was one of the three blows which broke J. H. Newman, and finally shattered his faith in the Anglican Church.

A cathedral was designed by Matthew Habershon, an architect who was deeply interested in missions to the Jews, and who wrote books about Prophecy. According to the *A.P.S. Dictionary*, this is the cathedral illustrated in *The Anglican Cathedral Church of Saint James, Mount Zion, Jerusalem*, by J. W. Johns, architect, 1844. Johns, however, nowhere mentions the name of Habershon, nor does he suggest that the design was not his own. He says that he was appointed in March 1841, and left for Jerusalem in April: he made arrangements with Maltese masons to follow him, and arrived in July. Work was begun on the foundations, and Bishop Alexander laid the first stone in January 1842. The first stone above ground was laid by Mrs Alexander on 1 November. Work continued until January 1843, when it was stopped by the Turkish authorities: the walls had reached the height of five feet.

The illustrations show a most peculiar little church: Early English in style, with apsidal transepts and chancel, and a very low central tower with very tall pinnacles.

An article in the *R.I.B.A. Journal* (1930) by George Jeffery, the architect of St George's, says that the first cathedral was consecrated in 1848. The architect (presumably of the resumed work) is said to have been Hillyer, who died within the first year of operations, and was succeeded by a foreman or clerk of the works called Crutchlow. It had been enlarged by the extension of the chancel and the addition of a porch.

The church—Christ Church—bears no resemblance to the published design: it is Perp. in style, and rather square in outline. It is the centre of the work of the C.M.J., and ministers to the British community. The Arabic services originally held there were transferred to St Paul's Church when it was consecrated in 1874.

Bishop Blyth, who was appointed in 1887 as the first purely Anglican Bishop, wished to have a church in which Anglican worship could be worthily maintained. Jeffery visited him in the winter of 1891–2 and discussed plans: on his return to England he made the design, which was accepted in 1892. The general appearance was meant to recall the collegiate foundations of William of Wykeham. Work began in 1894, and the church was built up to the level of the vaults over the south aisle. The window tracery, etc., was made of white marble, at Servezza in Italy. In 1894–6 work was stopped. It was resumed in 1897, and the nave was consecrated in October 1898 by Bishop John Wordsworth of Salisbury.

Many gifts were received from different parts of the Anglican Communion. The font was given by Queen Victoria.

10

The chancel and transepts were built in 1905–10, and consecrated on 1 November 1910, by Bishop Winnington Ingram of London. The bell tower was completed as a memorial to King Edward VII. The screens and stalls were made by Wippell.

St John's Chapel, on the north of the chancel, was decorated, after the British occupation in 1917, by members of the Order of St John of Jerusalem. In 1938 the marble choir screen, given in 1898, was restored, raised, and given a carved oak canopy. The reredos and tester of the high altar were erected in the same year.

In 1948 the church was damaged in the fighting between Arabs and Jews: the pulpit, the gift of the Church of Ireland, was destroyed, and the organ was damaged.

St George's is called a Collegiate Church, not a cathedral, as the Church of the Holy Sepulchre is the cathedral of Jerusalem.

ST THOMAS'S CATHEDRAL, KUCHING, BORNEO

The first church was built by the Reverend F. T. McDougall, afterwards Bishop. In May 1849 he went to Singapore, and consulted Major Faber and Mr Thomson, the military and civil engineers there, about some points. Mr Stahl, formerly carpenter of the *Mary Louisa*, took charge of the erection of the church and mission buildings. It was begun on 25 August 1849, and consecrated in January 1851. McDougall described it: "The pillars of the arches are of palm wood . . .; the planking is a kind of cedar, the mouldings are all Balean and Miraboo. . . . For the font I have procured a large clam shell, large enough to immerse a three or four years old child. . . . The east window is of coloured glass, and given by my friend Mr Jackson, the Assistant Resident at Singapore. The central light will represent the Sarawak cross, a red and purple cross on a golden ground. It is the national flag, and will please the native eye, besides being an appropriate Christian emblem." (C. J. Bunyon, *Memoirs of Francis Thomas McDougall*, 1889, p. 71.)

The church was wrecked in the Chinese insurrection of 1857, and restored afterwards.

William Slater's designs for a cathedral were noted in the *Ecclesiologist* in February 1863: "The plan of the nave is two bays long and 25 feet wide, with narrow aisles. The crossing is of one bay. The transepts have no aisles. The choir is terminated with a circular apse, and has aisles on either side used for sacristies and the organ. The choir will be screened off from the aisles and nave. It is raised four steps above the nave, and the sanctuary rises by three more. The pulpit is placed against the north-east choir pier, and the font at the west door. There is an open galilee porch of two bays at the west end. The material used for the walls is brick, with coloured courses, and incised ornamentation on the voussoirs of the arches. The roofs are of timber, covered outside with shingles. The design is necessarily of great simplicity. Nothing but the plainest chamfers appears in the shape of mouldings. The piers and arches are alike of brick. Externally the roof is uniform, and there is a small tower with an octagonal spirelet in the angle between the south transept and the choir. A clerestory of simple broad lancet lights runs entirely round the church. The transept roofs are hipped, with questionable effect. The whole design, however, is characteristic and dignified, and very suitable for its purpose."

Nothing came of this.

In 1915 Bishop Mounsey said that the deficiencies in the present building were "all too apparent", and that an architect had said that a suitable church could be erected for $100,000. In 1919 Bishop Danson, his successor, wrote that the basilican style would be the most appropriate.

The old wooden building was desecrated by the Japanese during the war, and had become unsafe. The present Bishop, who was consecrated in 1949, decided that a new cathedral must be built.

Plans were made by C. W. Garton, of Messrs Nelson, Garton and Co., of Liverpool. He explained them in the *Borneo Chronicle* of December 1952. He had endeavoured to incorporate a Western plan and lay-out with an outward appearance of Far Eastern influence. The structure was to be of reinforced concrete with an outer and inner skin: the outer was to have a mixture of black granite chippings, hand-polished, and lined out to represent stone: the inner skin might be treated in the same way, or it might be rough-rendered and decorated in a light cream colour. The design included an elongated central dome.

The Duchess of Kent laid the foundation stone in 1953.

But it was decided that these plans would place too heavy a burden on the Church in the Diocese. Mr Church, f.r.i.b.a., of Messrs Swan and MacLaren, Singapore, was invited to submit new plans, which were approved on 11 October 1954. About $200,000 was available, and it was decided to make an effort to raise an equivalent amount: an appeal was launched on 16 January 1955. The response was most satisfactory. St Andrew's, Brunei, gave the roof, SS. Philip and James's, Kuala Belait, provided the cost of the terrazzo tiling of the floor, and the parish of Seria paid for the electric lighting. Each of the seats on the north side of the nave bears the name of the parish which contributed to its cost. There were many other gifts.

The cathedral was consecrated on 9 June 1956. It is of reinforced concrete: the arches are 48 feet high; the tower is 84 feet, with a 24-foot cross. The marble for the apse and the tops of the altars came from Italy. The woodwork is of local timber, fashioned by Chinese craftsmen in Kuching.

ST ANDREW'S CATHEDRAL, SINGAPORE

The foundation stone of the first church was laid in 1834: it was built in 1835-6, and consecrated on 10 September 1838. The cost was $10,910, of which the Government gave $4,000: the rest was contributed by S.P.C.K., the Church Building Fund, the Bishop of Calcutta, and the general public. The architect was G. D. Coleman, who was in Calcutta from 1816 to 1820, and in Batavia from 1820 to 1826: then he settled in Singapore, where he designed and built a considerable portion of the city. He was the first Government superintendent of public works. The Armenian Church of St Gregory the Illuminator is his design.

St Andrew's, a plain building with a Doric portico on each side, was given a tower and spire, "to please the Bishop of Calcutta", by John Turnbull Thomson, Government surveyor from 1841 to 1854. It was struck by lightning in 1845 and 1849, and the church was closed in 1852 and demolished in 1854.

The foundation stone of the present church was laid on 4 March 1856, and it was consecrated on 25 January 1862. The architect was Captain (afterwards Colonel) Ronald McPherson, of the Madras Army —who is buried at Singapore, and is commemorated by the west window, and a cross in the cathedral compound. The building was in the hands of Captain McNair. John Bennett, a civil engineer, was also largely concerned with it, and was responsible for most of the detail: W. D. Bayliss acted as superintendent of the works, and of the convict labourers.

The style is rather crude E.E.: it is said to have been copied from Netley Abbey, but the resemblance is not very obvious. A heavy, ornate tower, without a spire, was planned, but the foundations were inadequate, and the west end began to crack in 1858–9, before the tower had risen above the level of the nave roof. The design was accordingly altered, and it was finished off with pinnacles and a spire.

The church consists of nave and aisles, with western porch under the tower, transeptal porches, and apsidal chancel. The walls and pillars are covered with Madras chunam—a composition made from shell lime without sand; but with it, wrote McNair, "we had whites of eggs and coarse sugar or 'jaggery' beaten together to form a sort of paste and mixed with water in which husks of cocoanuts had been steeped. The walls and pillars after a period of drying were rubbed with rock crystal or rounded stone until they took a beautiful polish and being occasionally dusted with fine soapstone powder, and so leaving a remarkably smooth and glossy surface."

The apse has three very long and wide lancet windows, rather effective in their complete plainness, filled with glass to the memory of Sir Stamford Raffles, John Crawford, and Major-General William Butterworth—the founder of the Settlement, and two of its Governors. The painted reredos—by C. J. Blomfield, a son of Sir Arthur—is in memory of Mrs Hose, wife of Bishop Hose of Singapore, Labuan, and Sarawak, who died in 1904.

The pulpit was given by a former Governor, Sir Cecil Smith: it was made in Ceylon, and dedicated in 1889. The lectern was given in memory of his first wife by Thomas Shelford, who died in 1900: the altar rails are a memorial to him. The choir stalls were given by J. J. Macbean in 1900.

In 1922 the north porch was converted into a chapter house.

Singapore was originally in the Diocese of Calcutta: it was transferred in 1869 to Labuan and Sarawak. In 1881 the Venerable G. F. Hose was consecrated Bishop with the new title of Bishop of Singapore, Labuan, and Sarawak. The first Bishop of Singapore was consecrated in 1909.

II

America

HOLY TRINITY CATHEDRAL, HAMILTON, BERMUDA

The original church was begun in 1844; the chancel, transepts, and one bay of the nave, were consecrated by Bishop Feild of Newfoundland in 1855. The design was made by James Cranston of Oxford, but it was carried out by William Hay of Edinburgh, who made some alterations; the form of the tower piers was changed, so as to give greater strength, and to save expense in the construction of the tower; and the chancel was slightly lengthened. It was completed in 1868, and the nave was consecrated on Ascension Day 1872. It was 13th century in style, with walls of local limestone and a roof of cedar: "except Fredericton Cathedral", said a 19th-century critic, it "surpasses, perhaps, in correctness and propriety, any church in the North American colonies".

It was destroyed by fire on 27 January 1884. The rebuilding was entrusted to Messrs Hay and Henderson of Edinburgh, who made plans for a cruciform church in 13th-century style, on a larger scale than the former building. The foundation stone was laid on 1 May 1886. The building was done by native workmen trained by Alexander Pratt, the clerk of the works; the dressings were executed by masons from Edinburgh. The nave was finished and dedicated in 1894, and the tower in 1905. A spire was proposed, but was not built. Henderson, the surviving partner, died in 1906, and H. O. Tarbolton, F.R.I.B.A., of Edinburgh, was appointed to complete the building: he visited Bermuda to arrange for the remodelling of the plans for the east end, which needed to be made more cathedral-like. The chancel was consecrated by Bishop Llewellyn Jones on 11 May 1911.

The walls are of native limestone, and the pillars of red Peterhead granite: Caen stone is used for the arches of nave and choir, and the mouldings of the windows and doorways: the details of the upper part of the tower are of Indiana limestone. The high altar is of marble adorned with mosaic: the plans included a marble reredos, but this has not been erected. The pulpit is a replica of the pulpit of St Giles's, Edinburgh.

Most of the glass is by M. Meredith Williams and Mrs Williams, but the west windows, and those of the Lady chapel and north porch, are by W. E. Tower, of the firm of Kempe.

In 1926 H. O. Tarbolton made a survey of the fabric, and in 1926–7 the tiled roof was replaced by one of copper, under the direction of Laurence H. Smart, L.R.I.B.A. The new roof was damaged by a hurricane in 1948, and restored in the following year. Various works of repair, from 1947 to 1951, cost £24,529.

PRO-CATHEDRAL OF ST JOHN BAPTIST, BUENOS AIRES
[DIOCESE OF ARGENTINA AND E. SOUTH AMERICA WITH THE FALKLAND ISLANDS]

The site—part of the property of the suppressed Merced Church and Convent—was granted by the National Government: the church was built half at the cost of H.M. Government, and half at the cost of the British residents. It was opened on 6 March 1831—"the first example of Grecian architecture seen in the city".

Plans for a new cathedral were made in 1881 by J. Pitt Bayly, architect, of Fulham Place, Paddington. These remained on paper.

The bishop's throne and canons' stalls were erected after the formation of the diocese: war memorial reredos 1920.

CHRIST CHURCH CATHEDRAL, PORT STANLEY, FALKLAND ISLANDS

A temporary church was made unsafe by a peat-slide.

A design for a permanent cathedral was made in 1882 by J. O. Scott: it included a tower "to some extent founded on Killaloe". An appeal for £6,000 was made, but the scheme was considered to be too expensive, and a simpler design was made by Sir A. W. Blomfield. The foundation stone was laid on 6 March 1890. The materials had to be brought from England, and the boggy soil made strong foundations necessary: the eventual cost was over £10,000. It was consecrated on 21 February 1892: the tower was completed in 1903.

The style is 13th century. The chancel screen and bishop's chair were made of oak from Canterbury Cathedral. The east window (1928) is by A. K. Nicholson.

COLLEGIATE CHURCH OF ST GEORGE, JERUSALEM

ST ANDREW'S CATHEDRAL, SINGAPORE

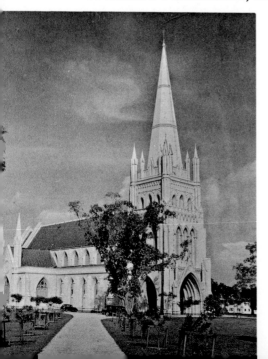

SS. MARY AND NICOLAS'
CATHEDRAL,
SEOUL, KOREA

ST THOMAS'S
CATHEDRAL,
KUCHING, BORNEO

ST THOMAS'S CATHEDRAL, KUCHING, BORNEO

HOLY TRINITY CATHEDRAL, GIBRALTAR

ST PAUL'S COLLEGIATE AND CATHEDRAL CHURCH, VALLETTA, MALTA

12

Europe

HOLY TRINITY CATHEDRAL, GIBRALTAR

The only Anglican place of worship in Gibraltar at the beginning of the 19th century was the Garrison Church, where civilians were allowed to be baptized or married, but where they could not worship owing to lack of space. In 1819 a committee of merchants approached the Lieutenant-Governor, General Sir George Don, asking his help towards building a church. Protracted negotiations about finance and a site ended after the Earl of Chatham became Governor, and the work was begun in June 1825.

Colonel Richard Pilkington, the commanding Royal Engineer, was instructed to prepare plans for the church. He used the Moorish style, giving as his reason the fact that the Moors entered Spain through Gibraltar, and so introduced this style into Europe. General Don, who had done so much towards getting the church built, died before it was completed, and was buried in the unfinished building before the place where the altar was to stand. The church was completed by 1830, except for the turrets at the west end. It was eventually consecrated in 1838, in the presence of the Dowager Queen Adelaide.

In 1842 the first Bishop was consecrated, and it became a cathedral.

The vestries on the north were added in 1950 from designs by Robert Atkinson, F.R.I.B.A.

The cathedral was almost unharmed throughout the two world wars, but when ammunition was being unloaded from the R.F.A. *Bedenham* on 27 April 1951, there was an explosion which shook Gibraltar. The roof of the cathedral was moved, and all the glass was shattered; but the walls withstood the blast, and it was possible to effect repairs. The restoration included a new mahogany reredos, with an east window above of Christ in glory.

ST PAUL'S COLLEGIATE AND CATHEDRAL CHURCH, VALLETTA, MALTA

Founded by Queen Adelaide in 1839. The architect was Richard Lankersheer, the English Director of Public Works. The building began to collapse, and the committee sought the professional advice of the Admiralty architects. Their report showed that the Ionic portico was in danger of falling, and that the whole building must be condemned as insecure. Lankersheer died in 1841 at the age of 38, and the committee applied to William Scamp to save the church. Scamp had been clerk of the works at Windsor Castle under Wyatville, and designed the first church of St Mary, Slough. He came to Malta in 1841 to report on the naval accommodation there. He rescued the church, and designed and built the tower and spire. When he returned to England in 1845, Queen Adelaide presented him with a silver candelabrum "in grateful remembrance of his services in completing the Collegiate Church of St Paul at Malta". (See H. M. Colvin, *A Biographical Dictionary of English Architects*, 1954, pp. 530–1.)

13

China

OUR SAVIOUR, CANTON, is the cathedral of the Diocese of South China. Kiangsu used to be called the Diocese of Shanghai. The chapel of the old St John's University serves as a pro-cathedral. HOLY TRINITY, SHANGHAI, was built for the English in 1868–70, designed by Sir Gilbert Scott—a good-sized cruciform church, with a detached tower and spire on the south. H. Lester of Shanghai left money to beautify it. This was carried out in 1928: mosaic paving for the chancel and sanctuary, carved stalls, and a memorial window in the south transept.

The building has been repaired by the Government, and is now the headquarters of the Chinese Church (Chung Hua Sheng Kung Hui).

ST JOHN'S (American) pro-cathedral was designed by W. P. Wentworth of Boston.

CATHEDRAL OF OUR SAVIOUR, PEKING
[DIOCESE OF NORTH CHINA]

After the destruction of the mission buildings in the Boxer rising, a congregation had grown up which was too large for the temporary church, and Bishop Scott decided to build a new church. Friends in England contributed, and S.P.G. and S.P.C.K. made grants, and the church was consecrated on 28 October 1907.

The design was suggested by Bishop Scott. He took the cross as the ground plan, and "built a superstructure which should incorporate as much as possible the advantages of Western construction and of Chinese decoration". The nave has subsidiary transepts for catechumens: at their intersection with the main roof is a pagoda-like lantern. A similar but larger lantern is at the intersection of the main transepts. Below this is the altar, with Chinese carving, with a screen of trellis work behind dividing it from the Lady chapel. The chapel is a memorial to

Deaconess Jessie Ransome. The windows in the apse are memorials to Bishop Wilkinson of Truro, and of St Andrews, Dunkeld, and Dunblane, and other benefactors of the Mission.

Ten years after the building of this cathedral, the Bishop wrote notes for the Bishop of Fukien, who was planning to build.

CHRIST CHURCH, NINGPO, is the pro-cathedral of the Diocese of Chekiang.

The Diocese of Ngo-Hsiang (Hankow), formerly supported by the American Church, has ST PAUL's, HANKOW.

ST MICHAEL'S CATHEDRAL, TAI-AN
[DIOCESE OF SHANTUNG]

The project of the cathedral took shape during the furlough of Bishop C. P. Scott in 1910. J. Francis Doyle of Liverpool provided the plans, and the work was taken in hand late in 1913. A. P. Dowglass went from England to take charge. The workmen were all Chinese: the master-carpenter was Wang Hsing-kuei. The cathedral was consecrated on the feast of St Michael and All Angels 1915: the eastern parts were finished, but only the east end of the nave. The style chosen was late 12th century. Unlike Peking Cathedral, it is deliberately *not* Chinese in style. The plan, aisled nave, transepts, central tower, porches, chancel, chapel, vestry, and organ chamber. The walls of granite, the roofs covered with dark red tiles, manufactured locally under the direction of the architect. Woodwork of *ch'iu-mu* wood. The main altar of rich brown stone.

The cathedral was blown up by the Communists in January 1947. Compensation is to be paid, and a new cathedral is to be built.

CHRIST CHURCH, FOOCHOW, is the cathedral of the Diocese of Fukien. It was built by the American Episcopal Church, and is brick E.E., with two western towers.

The cathedral of LINLIN, in Hunan, was bombed by the Japanese, and the Diocese of Kwei Hsiang is now without a cathedral.

HOLY TRINITY, KAIFENG, is the cathedral of the Diocese of Honan.

The Diocese of Wanken (formerly Anking) has HOLY SAVIOUR, ANKING, a Gothic cathedral built by the American Church.

The cathedral of the Diocese of Shensi is at SIAN.

In Szechuan is the pro-cathedral at PAONING, built by Bishop Cassels. It was in progress in 1912: work was suspended for a time owing to the unsettled state of the country, but it was completed and opened in 1914. George Rogers was the superintendent of the works.

It is of brick, Gothic, but with a Chinese-style roof; cruciform, with two low western towers.

ST JOHN'S CATHEDRAL, HONG KONG

The Reverend V. J. Stanton collected subscriptions for a church that would serve as a cathedral. By 1845 a site had been obtained, and he had collected £2,000. The Government promised to "tender effectual aid"; and S.P.C.K. gave help.

The foundation stone was laid on 11 March 1847, and the church was opened on 11 March 1849: it was consecrated in 1852.

The first stone of the chancel was laid by the Duke of Edinburgh on 16 November 1869. In 1870 Lavers, Barraud, and Westlake, of Endell Street, supplied glass for the east window, which "consists of five lights, surmounted by a rose, and most of its details are borrowed from the west window of Lincoln Cathedral". The chancel was not finished until 1872.

The bishop's throne was erected in 1899. In 1900 Lady Jackson gave eleven windows for the chancel, and in 1902 new stalls were provided.

14

Japan

St Paul's pro-Cathedral, Fukuoka (Diocese of Kyushu) was built by English missionaries.

Holy Trinity Cathedral, Tokyo, was built by the American Bishop Channing Moore Williams: a Gothic church with an apse. It was destroyed in the earthquake of 1923, and rebuilt on its present site in 1927: it was consecrated on 17 October. The chancel and altar were the gift of the Women's Auxiliary of the Diocese of New York. It was damaged in the Second World War, and repaired afterwards.

Holy Trinity Cathedral, Kyoto, was also an American church. It was built through the generosity of Holy Trinity, Philadelphia, and consecrated in 1901. Of dark red brick, Gothic, with an embattled tower.

PART II

The Protestant Episcopal Church
in the
United States of America

ALL SAINTS' CATHEDRAL, ALBANY, N.Y.

CATHEDRAL OF THE INCARNATION,
GARDEN CITY, LONG ISLAND

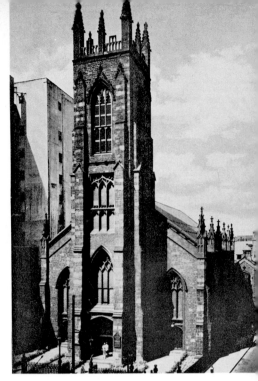

HOLY TRINITY CATHEDRAL,
PORT-AU-PRINCE, HAITI

CHRIST CHURCH CATHEDRAL,
HARTFORD, CONNECTICUT

TRINITY CATHEDRAL, NEWARK

ST LUKE'S CATHEDRAL, PORTLAND, MA

Introduction

MOST of the churches that were built in America in the 18th century were simple and unambitious; but there are, as is well known, some that are very good examples of the Wren-Gibbs type (chiefly Gibbs). They were, like so many similar churches in England, designed by their builders, or by some educated gentleman, with the aid of books such as Gibbs's *Book of Architecture*.

Thomas Jefferson (1743–1826) and Charles Bulfinch (1763–1844) were both amateurs: Benjamin Henry Latrobe (1764–1820) had a professional training. Jefferson looked to Roman models, Bulfinch followed the best English fashions, and Latrobe was a pioneer of the Greek Revival; all three are people of importance in the story of American architecture. But for many years the average church was built in the old fashion, and many that are said to be in the Colonial style are, in fact, post-Revolution in date.

Gothic made its appearance quite early: Latrobe made several designs for the Roman Catholic cathedral at Baltimore, from 1804 onwards, of which one was Gothic. The Reverend Henry Caswall, who left England for America in 1828, describes several Gothic churches in his *America and the American Church*, 1839. His favourite was Christ Church, Hartford, "the noblest specimen of Gothic architecture which I have seen in America". But the arrangement of the churches left a good deal to be desired. "The Communion-table seldom occupies its appropriate place, but is often little more than a narrow board placed in front of the reading desk. . . . In front of the table are the rails which divide what is called the chancel from the body of the church, and include the pulpit, the desk, and the table. This arrangement was, doubtless, introduced in order to save room, but it is contrary to the usage of primitive times, and shows little respect to the altar so far as outward appearances are concerned." The font was generally placed by the rails, and was never near the entrance: pews were almost all rented. But Caswall says that some better-arranged churches had been built.

The ecclesiological idea of correct arrangement was bound to come sooner or later: it was advocated by Bishop John Henry Hopkins, in his *Essay on Church Architecture*, as early as 1836.

The New York Ecclesiological Society was founded in 1848. It was closely united with the English society, and the *Ecclesiologist* remarked that the Americans had looked to England for their first lesson. But it warned them against adhering too rigorously to English types of church. Citizens of Michigan or Maine might seek inspiration from Sweden or Norway, while Georgia, Florida, and Texas might look to the cities of North Italy. An important architect who tried to carry out the new ideas was Richard Upjohn—another man who had had no special professional training. He was born at Shaftesbury in 1802, and came to America in 1829. He began as draughtsman to Samuel Leonard, builder and sperm oil merchant, and opened a school of drawing. Then he set up as an architect of New Bedford in 1833; he moved to Boston in 1835, and his first church—St John's, Bangor, Maine—was built in 1836. Then he moved to New York, and designed the rebuilding of Trinity Church, a competent piece of Perpendicular, which was begun in 1841 and consecrated in 1846. From then onward he produced many churches which, though not always up to the exacting standards of the *Ecclesiologist*, were generally satisfactory from the ecclesiological point of view. In 1857 he founded the American Institute of Architects, of which he was president for nineteen years. He died in 1878. His son Richard Michell (1828–1903) entered his office, and Hobart Upjohn, the grandson, succeeded to the practice. (See Everard M. Upjohn, *Richard Upjohn, Architect and Churchman*, 1939.)

Church building after the middle of the century continued much as in England; but a new element was introduced by Henry Hobson Richardson (1838–86) who had been trained in the École des Beaux-Arts, and who came to favour a Romanesque style (e.g. Trinity Church, Boston), derived from Southern France and Spain, which he considered particularly suitable to America.

But this was challenged by Ralph Adams Cram (1863–1942), who was in practice as an architect from 1889. It seemed to Cram that Richardson's Romanesque had "no relationship to national, racial, or historical Christianity in U.S.A.", and he determined to take up Gothic at the point which it had reached at the time of the Reformation in England. He was at first partner with Charles Francis Wentworth. Bertram Grosvenor Goodhue (1869–1924) entered the office of Renwick, Aspinwall, and Russell at the age of 15, and joined the firm of Cram and Wentworth as head draughtsman in 1889. At the age of 21 he entered the competition for New York Cathedral. He made the winning design for the cathedral at Dallas, and brought the commission to the firm—but this did not come to anything. The firm afterwards became Cram, Goodhue, and Ferguson: in 1914 Goodhue withdrew.

The Gothic works of the firm are very numerous: at a later period their scope was widened, and they used other styles. But it is with Gothic that one usually associates them. Cram was author of *Church Building* (1901), *Ruined Abbeys of Great Britain* (1905), *The Gothic Quest* (1907), *The Substance of Gothic* (1916), *My Life in Architecture* (1936), and other books. Gothic in America is not dead, and there are some quite recent large and handsome Gothic churches, such as have not been attempted in England since the Great War.

The first Bishop of the American Church, Samuel Seabury, was consecrated in 1784, but for a long time there were no cathedrals. A cathedral for New York was proposed in the 1820's, but nothing came of this. Twenty years later, when the Ecclesiological movement was beginning to influence American churchmen, some interest began to be taken in the subject of cathedrals. Frank Wills, the architect of Fredericton and Montreal cathedrals, was a leading member of the New York Ecclesiological Society, and read several papers at its meetings: one, on 23 May 1849, was on *The Arrangement of a Cathedral as differing from that of a Parish Church*. The (English) *Ecclesiologist* thought that it was too antiquarian, and that Wills had no theory of a modern Anglican cathedral.

When St Paul's, Buffalo, was reopened in 1851, after having been rebuilt from designs by Richard Upjohn, the *Morning Chronicle* asked why a really ecclesiastical system of episcopacy could not be restored: Bishop De Lancey should assume the title of Bishop of Buffalo, and place his seat in its church. The *Ecclesiologist* commented, "The American Church must come to cathedrals, sooner or later, therefore we say, let it be as soon as possible." St Paul's, Buffalo, was not what they could wish, but it was the best church in the Diocese of Western New York. Episcopacy was mutilated and ineffective without the *ecclesia cathedralis*. The opportunity was also favourable elsewhere: the original Diocese of New York was beginning to breathe again, and (Holy) Trinity would be suitable for a cathedral. "At the same time, were a cathedral to be built, *de novo*, as such, with the intention of its being worthy to be the Cathedral Church of the greatest capital of the new world, we should be still more rejoiced." The Roman Catholics were building cathedrals throughout the Union: the Anglicans should go and do likewise.

The New York Society in 1851 asked Bishop Medley of Fredericton to address them on cathedrals and the cathedral system: "he endeavoured to convince them (and he trusted not without success) that it was not the impracticable, or unreal thing, which many of them had been led to consider it."

The Transactions of the Society for 1855 contained two papers by the Reverend John H. Hopkins, jun., on *The Cathedral System in the City* and *The Cathedral System in Rural Dioceses*. He considered that the absence of cathedrals was "one of the many ill results of the Popish corruption and Erastian mal-practice that have so largely tainted the channel through which our historical Church has descended to us from the apostles of our LORD". The corruptions of the English Cathedral system were the greatest obstacle to the introduction of anything like it into the United States. What was needed was a return to the primitive idea of the system. The ideal cathedral church for New York would be cruciform, and large enough to hold eight or ten thousand worshippers, and a choir of five hundred. There must be neither pews nor pew rents. Choral service should be twice a day, and more often on Sundays and festivals. There should be a staff of from twelve to twenty-four clergy, forming a body of city missionaries, under a dean, precentor, treasurer, and chancellor. Round this centre should be grouped choristers' schools, seminaries for the priesthood, a church-hospital, a sisterhood-house, a dispensary, an asylum for aged clergy, and a library. The second paper, on the Cathedral System in Rural Dioceses, applied the same principles to the altered circumstances.

The Right Reverend G. W. Doane, Bishop of New Jersey, looked on St Mary's, Burlington, as his cathedral, and included a bishop's throne in the new church, consecrated in 1854. Bishop Whitehouse of Chicago made plans for a cathedral in 1853; being frustrated in his plans for a grand building, he began negotiations in 1861 for obtaining the Church of the Atonement, Washington Street, which was converted into the Cathedral of SS. Peter and Paul.

Bishop Kip in the 50's placed his episcopal chair in Grace Church, San Francisco, and called it his cathedral; but he did so in his right as rector, and when his incumbency ceased, the name of cathedral was dropped. But in 1863, after California had become a diocese, it again became Grace Cathedral.

About 1859, Bishop Nicholas Hamner Cobbs of Alabama outlined his vision of an American cathedral, and expressed his desire that the diocese should have one.

The foundation stone of Bishop Whipple's cathedral at Faribault was laid on 16 July 1862. The question of a cathedral for Wisconsin was suggested by Bishop Kemper in 1865. The diocesan council in 1868 asked the General Convention for authority to establish a cathedral at Milwaukee, but there was opposition to the scheme.

The temporary cathedral of Albany was opened in 1872. In the same year the Vestry of Christ Church, Reading, Pennsylvania, placed the church at the disposal of Bishop Howe, and it became known as the Cathedral of the Diocese of Central Pennsylvania.

Bishop Alexander C. Garrett of Dallas, at the consecration of Omaha Cathedral in 1883, spoke of the need of cathedrals.

And, since then, most dioceses have acquired a cathedral of some sort. Only New York and Washington are full cathedrals, with no parish life; the rest are parish churches as well, with a communicant list. In some, the Bishop is the rector, and the Dean is appointed: in others, the Dean is the rector.

America itself was, generally speaking, the mission field of the Episcopal Church during the 19th century; but there are some churches built by Americans abroad, particularly in China and Japan. The American mission in Africa was begun in 1835, and the first Bishop of West Africa (afterwards Liberia) was consecrated in 1851. In 1898 Puerto Rico and the Philippines were acquired by America. Cuba was given a nominal independence. The Hawaiian Islands were annexed in the same year, and the Virgin Islands were bought from Denmark in 1917.

I have included those churches that are listed as cathedrals in the *Episcopal Church Annual*. I am told that there are others that are commonly regarded as cathedrals; but the line had to be drawn somewhere.

The attentive reader may notice some slight differences of phraseology in this section. The English tend to build a church on a site, the Americans on a lot or a location. The English lay a foundation stone, the Americans a cornerstone. And when the time comes to demolish a church, the English pull it down, the Americans tear it down. The English found a diocese, the Americans organize it.

I have preferred to build my churches on sites, and to pull them down; but the influence of my sources has generally caused me to organize dioceses, and to lay cornerstones. I hope that this compromise will be acceptable both to English and to American readers.

15

First Province (New England)

CHRIST CHURCH CATHEDRAL, HARTFORD
[DIOCESE OF CONNECTICUT]

The parish was organized in 1762, and a site for a church was obtained. Stone was collected for a foundation, but the work was held up by the depression following the French and Indian War in 1763, and a few years later the land was illegally sold, and had to be recovered by law. At the end of the Revolutionary War the parish was practically extinct, but in 1786 a new organization was formed, and the collection of subscriptions began. The contract was let in March 1792, and the frame was raised in June. It was a large church for its time, and further subscriptions had to be collected in 1795 to complete it. The consecration was on 11 November 1801.

The present church was designed by Ithiel Town, whose plans were accepted in 1827. Suggestions were made by Bishop Thomas Church Brownell, and the Reverend Nathaniel Sheldon Wheaton, who had been in England in 1823–4, seeking help for the new Washington College (now Trinity College). The ground was broken during that summer. The cornerstone was laid by Bishop Brownell on 13 May 1828, and Bishop Hobart consecrated the church on 23 December 1829.

Ithiel Town was born in 1784, and attended Asher Benjamin's school of architecture in Boston between 1804 and 1810. He settled at New Haven, and built Center Church (1812–14), and Trinity (1814–15). He took Martin Euclid Thompson (1787–1875) into partnership between 1827 and 1829. Thomas Rust was employed as a draughtsman, and Alexander Jackson Davis was also a member of the firm. The erection of Christ Church was supervised by James Chamberlain.

The drawings survive, and derivations are noted on them: the exterior central doorhead panel was copied from St Saviour's, Southwark; the side windows from St Mary's, Oxford; the "groin joints" from York, etc. The Reverend Dr Wheaton modelled the plaster flowers and stone heads himself, and presented the west window—a transparency of the Transfiguration, after Raphael, painted by W. Bacon of London. The tower was incomplete at the time of the consecration, and a committee was appointed in 1833 to obtain a plan: the collection of subscriptions began in 1838, and the work was duly done. A chapel or lecture room was added at the back in 1835. A font and bishop's chair were given in 1840.

The east end terminated in a combination of altar, desk, and pulpit. In November 1878 Mrs Goodwin offered to give a chancel and a parish building, with a chapel and rooms for social and business meetings: these were added in 1879. The architect was Frederick Charles Withers (1828–1901), an Englishman, and brother of Robert Jewell Withers, who built and restored many churches in England, to the great satisfaction of the ecclesiologists. Both were in the office of T. H. Wyatt. Frederick emigrated to America in 1853, and practised first at Newburgh, N.Y. Then he moved to New York, and entered in 1864 into partnership with Vaux and Olmsted. He designed the reredos and chancel fittings at Trinity Church, New York. In 1866 the firm won the competition for a chapel at Yale, but this was not built. Withers was a link between the archaeological Gothic revivalists and the later Victorians: he used polychrome and bands of colour, but with restraint. He was the author of *Church Architecture: Plans, Elevations, and Views of Twenty-One Churches and Two School Houses*, 1873.

Choir stalls were given in 1887–8, and a reredos was erected in the chapel.

Pinnacles were added to the exterior in 1902. The Nativity chapel in the south-west corner was formed in 1908. In 1916 the chapel of 1879 was made into a choir room, and its altar and reredos were placed in the chapel of St Dorcas in the north-west corner.

Christ Church was made a cathedral in 1919. In that year a new altar of Caen stone was provided, and the reredos was enlarged; bishop's throne, dean's stall, altar rail, and choir parapet were erected.

Repairs and decorations were done in 1924, the foundation and roof trusses were reconditioned in 1932, and the interior was painted and decorated in 1938.

ST LUKE'S CATHEDRAL, PORTLAND
[Diocese of Maine]

Maine was part of Massachusetts until 1820, and was included in the Eastern Diocese, which was organized in 1810, and included all New England, except Connecticut. On the death of Bishop Griswold in 1843, the Eastern Diocese was divided into the Dioceses of Rhode Island, Maine, and Massachusetts.

The cornerstone of the cathedral was laid on 15 August 1867, by Bishop Neely; the first service was held in the church on Christmas Day 1868, and it was consecrated on 18 October 1877. The architect was Charles Coolidge Haight (1841–1917) of New York City.

It is built of blue Cape Elizabeth ledge stone: the buttresses and copings, doors and window sills, are of Nova Scotia freestone, alternating in red and grey. The style is 13th century, with coupled lancets in the aisles and triplets in the clerestory: there is a rose window in the sanctuary.

The wooden reredos was carved by Johann Kirchmeyer, under Ralph Adams Cram.

ST PAUL'S CATHEDRAL, BOSTON
[Diocese of Massachusetts]

The first bishop was consecrated in 1784.

The church was built in 1819–20 by Alexander Parris (1780–1852), and Solomon Willard (1783–1861), who carved the Ionic capitals. Parris, who had been apprenticed as a carpenter, was executive for Bulfinch in the Massachusetts General Hospital, and later built the Quincy Market: he and Willard were the planners of the Bunker Hill monument in Charlestown (1825–42), and the stone Temple in Quincy (1828). Willard carved the capitals of the steeple of Park Street Church.

The front of St Paul's is of Acquia Greek sandstone from Virginia.

The interior is severely plain. The pulpit was designed by Richard Upjohn.

In 1907 it was proposed to build a cathedral on an island in Charles River: some years before, a lady had made a bequest of a million dollars. Plans for developing the Charles River basin in 1906 included putting an island in the river: both A. A. Shurtleff and R. A. Cram made plans for a cathedral to stand at the west end of it.

ST JOHN'S CATHEDRAL, PROVIDENCE
[DIOCESE OF RHODE ISLAND]

The first church, known as King's Church, was begun on St Barnabas' Day 1722. Colonel Joseph Whipple gave £100, and victualled the labourers: the total cost was £770. It was called St John's from 1794.

On 19 March 1810, a committee was appointed to build a new church: the cornerstone was laid on 5 June 1810, and it was consecrated on 11 June.

The master builders were Smith and Asa Bosworth, and the carpenter was John Holden Greene (1777–1850), who made the design.

James De Wolf Perry was consecrated Bishop of Rhode Island in this church in 1911: he made it the cathedral of the diocese on 11 June 1929. In February 1957 parish and cathedral were separated.

It is plain Gothick, with rusticated angles: there is a low, pinnacled tower. A Renaissance chancel was added in the 1920's with altar piece in London City church style, by Cram, Goodhue, and Ferguson. The most striking feature of the interior is the shallow dome, 62 feet in diameter.

Henry-Russell Hitchcock points out (*Rhode Island Architecture*, 1939, p. 30) that the exterior mainly follows Bulfinch's Federal Street church, Boston, which was built in the previous year. "The interior, which has a shallow dome within a square plan like Bulfinch's Hollis Street church, has rather charming delicate clustered piers supporting the dome at the rear, although the piers at the other end are Doric; and once had balconies whose fronts were decorated with almost Venetian tracery, all in the manner of Batty Langley."

CHRIST CHURCH CATHEDRAL, SPRINGFIELD
[DIOCESE OF WESTERN MASSACHUSETTS]

The diocese was organized in 1901.

Christ Church was built in 1876.

The pulpit and lectern were carved by Kirchmeyer: glass by Heaton, Butler and Bayne, Kempe, and La Farge.

16

Second Province
(New York and New Jersey)

ALL SAINTS' CATHEDRAL, ALBANY

When William Croswell Doane was consecrated Bishop (in 1889), St Peter's, Albany, offered itself as his cathedral, and was accepted for the time being. But the Bishop had more ambitious plans.

A gift of $50,000 from Erastus Corning, sen., made possible the incorporation of the Corning Foundation for Christian work: a block on the north side of Elk Street was bought by this Corporation, and St Agnes' School was built on the site. The necessity for a chapel for the school brought forward the idea of a cathedral again.

On 8 June 1872, the standing committee of the diocese consented to the organization of a new parish. A building on the corner of Elk and Hawk Streets—the disused furnace of Townsend Brothers—was bought and furnished as a temporary cathedral: it was opened on All Saints' Day 1872. On 27 March 1873, the cathedral was incorporated by a special act of the legislature. In the summer of that year, the Bishop was in England studying the working of the English cathedrals: he gave the results of his researches to the Diocesan Convocation in 1874.

It was at first intended to build on the site of the cathedral chapel, but the ground could not support a heavy building. Mr Corning, jun., bought a strip of land on the south side of Elk Street, and gave it to the Chapter: the purchase was completed on 30 June 1882.

Two architects were asked to make plans: Henry Hobson Richardson of Boston (1838–86), and Robert Williams Gibson (1854–1927)—an English architect, who had come to New York in 1881. Richardson's design was for a large cathedral in his favourite Romanesque style, with three towers, an apsidal choir, and an eastern chevet. Gibson's design was in an elaborate and original Gothic style, with certain Spanish features: this was accepted.

On 3 April 1883, the Chapter decided not to begin until $100,000 had been secured. The ground was broken early in 1884, and the cornerstone was laid on 3 June. The foundations for the whole building were laid: when the funds came to an end, they were covered up, and the work stopped.

In 1885 work was resumed, and the walls of the choir were carried up a stage. The Bishop wrote: "The building of the cathedral was a slow and difficult process. It progressed in stages, sometimes quite far apart. But that gave time to Mr Gibson, the architect, who was then living in Albany, and I to discuss and decide all the little details of the arrangement for the inside and out, and the proposal was to put up a building which would hold a large congregation with a deep cathedral choir, and to put it up in such a way that it could not be enlarged but completed by building up, that is to say, we built what might be called the first floor of the nave, the two transepts, and the choir."

The building was ready for use by 1888. The choir and the nave had been completed as far as the triforium: the transepts, west front, and temporary clerestory were of brick, covered with a wooden roof. The completed portion was dedicated on 20 November 1888.

For 14 years nothing was added to the structure. Then in 1902 a gift of $200,000 from J. P. Morgan, sen., made it possible to resume work. The completed choir was consecrated on 15 November 1904. The towers have not been completed, and there is a flèche at the crossing, where a tower was planned.

On a trip to Europe, the Bishop was able to secure some 17th-century stalls from a dismantled church in Bruges. These were augmented by others made to harmonize with them, most of which were memorials, or gifts from parishes or missions in the diocese.

The High Altar was the gift of the Sisters of the Holy Child Jesus, founded in Albany in 1873. Under the bishop's throne is a stone from the Angel steeple of Canterbury Cathedral.

The large window at the west is by John La Farge: the rose window in the north transept is by Maitland Armstrong. Most of the rest of the glass is by English artists.

In St Michael's Chapel, or the State Chapel, on the north side, are all the flags that have flown over Albany, and the official flag of the Episcopal Church.

Bishop Doane, who died in 1913, is buried in the cathedral.

HOLY TRINITY CATHEDRAL, PORT-AU-PRINCE
[MISSIONARY DISTRICT OF HAITI]

In 1861 the Reverend James Theodore Holly, a negro priest, arrived from New Haven, Connecticut, with about 100 negro immigrants. Holy Trinity parish was organized in 1863. In 1874 an independent national church was set up—Église Orthodoxe Apostolique Haïtienne—and Fr Holly was consecrated Bishop. After his death in 1911, the Haitian Church asked to be made a missionary district of the American Church. This was done in 1913, but a bishop was not appointed until 1923. In the meantime the Bishops of Cuba, the Panama Canal Zone, and Puerto Rico administered the district, and the Reverend Albert Rupert Llwyd supervised the work. A site was bought in 1918, and the cornerstone of the new cathedral was laid on 8 November 1924, the year after the arrival of the first Bishop, the Right Reverend Harry R. Carson.

The plans were first drawn by Robert T. Walker of Cambridge, Massachusetts. Modifications were made by a local architect and an engineer—Adrien Scott and Léonce Maignan—under the superintendence of Lieut.-Commander R. L. Pettigrew. It is a "simple and traditional design, influenced by French architecture, but adapted to the Haitian climate". The builder was Daniel Brun of Port-au-Prince. The church was finished in 1928, and dedicated on the Feast of the Epiphany 1929. The old church, which had been consecrated in 1872, was used as a school from 1928 to 1932, and then taken down.

The cathedral is Romanesque in style, cemented and whitened externally; the roof was originally of tiles.

The interior was to begin with severely plain. In 1943 Mr Dewitt Peters came to Port-au-Prince, and the Centre d'Art was established under his direction. In 1947 he suggested to the Bishop, the Right Reverend Charles Alfred Voegeli, that Haitian artists might decorate the apse. The Bishop agreed, and the paintings were completed in March 1950. Under the direction of Mr Peters and Selden Rodman, of the Centre d'Art, the work was divided between Philomé Obin, Rigand Benoit, Castera Bazile, and Gabriel Levêque.

This aroused interest, and within a year enough money was subscribed for the work to be continued. It was decided to decorate the walls of the Lady chapel, the transepts, and the small chapel originally intended for a baptistery. Philomé Obin executed the painting in the small chapel, and Castera Bazile undertook the north transept; in the Lady chapel and the south transept the work was divided between Adam Lentus, F. Pierre, Toussaint Auguste, Wilson Bigaud, and Prefete Dufaut. These paintings were finished in April 1951.

Afterwards, Jason Seley, an American sculptor living in Haiti, offered to carve a crucifix, which was erected in 1953.

Then Jasmin Joseph, a Haitian sculptor, filled the three windows of the south porch with open carvings. A gallery was built above the aisle between the sacristy and the chancel, and Mr Joseph executed a front of sculptured bricks, each with an apostle as the central feature. The organ was moved from the chancel into the aisle, and for this he made another screen of sculptured bricks, in the form of angels. This work was completed in 1955.

Recently the floor has had to be repaired, and the tiles have been replaced by a metal roof.

CATHEDRAL OF THE INCARNATION, GARDEN CITY [DIOCESE OF LONG ISLAND]

The diocese was organized in 1868, and the first bishop was appointed in 1869. A short time before, a wealthy New York merchant, Alexander T. Stewart, had bought 10,000 acres of land in Hempstead Plains in order to establish "a village where people might lease pleasant homes for a reasonable sum". He planned a large church at the centre of the Garden City, but died before he could complete the project. His widow decided to build the church as his memorial, and, at the suggestion of Bishop Littlejohn, it was built as the cathedral of the Diocese of Long Island. The cornerstone was laid on 28 June 1877, and the cathedral was consecrated on 2 June 1885. Mrs Stewart also built the cathedral schools—St Paul's for boys and St Mary's for girls.

The cathedral is of brownstone, in an exuberant Gothic style. It consists of nave and aisles, with a gabled west tower and crocketed spire, rather German-looking; transepts, and choir with apsidal sanctuary. The octagonal baptistery is to the north of the choir. The height of the spire is 221 feet, the width of the transepts 109 feet. The nave was to have been longer, but Mr Stewart's executor "drew a blue pencil through two bays", and used the money that was saved for building the chancel.

Mr Stewart was a collector of marbles, many of which were used in the cathedral. The steps from the nave to the choir are of Italian dove and Bardiglio marble: the pavement of the choir is green and black Greek marble, and Siena. The sanctuary rail is Siena.

The carved oak pulpit is a memorial to Frederick Burgess, the second Bishop of Long Island (1902–25). The woodwork of the choir and sanctuary is of mahogany. The altar was made at Antwerp: the carved panels are of Italian statuary marble. The pontifical throne, behind the altar, and the sedilia and canopies, are of elaborately carved stone.

The baptistery is plentifully adorned with marble: the font is of white Italian marble, with a mahogany cover. The figure of the Good Shepherd is a copy of one made in solid gold by Rudolph Marchall of Vienna, for the Emperor Franz Joseph, who sent it as a gift to the Pope.

All the windows, which form a complete scheme, are by Clayton and Bell, who sent their own workmen to instal them.

An altar in the north transept was erected in 1950 as a war memorial. The design was made by Thomas M. Bell, who also carried out alterations in the chancel and sanctuary, and completely redecorated the interior: the work was done by John Hartell and Co. of New York.

"There is probably no other cathedral church in this country which is as complete in detail as this Gothic shrine: it may be alone, also, in being the only cathedral which was constructed by a single donor, and intended from its inception as a cathedral. It is a monument to the dream of one man, erected to God's glory, a worthy use of a fabulous fortune."

The bodies of Mr and Mrs Stewart lie in a small chapel beneath the nave.

DIOCESE OF NEW JERSEY

The Right Reverend George Washington Doane, Bishop from 1833 to 1859, was rector, during practically the whole of his episcopate, of ST MARY'S, BURLINGTON. The cornerstone of the original church was laid on 26 March 1703, and it was ready for use on 22 August. In 1708 Queen Anne gave pulpit and altar cloths and a silver chalice and salver. But the church took some time to complete. The first rector, John

Talbot, who died on 29 November 1727, is supposed to have been consecrated Bishop by the Nonjurors.

A new steeple was added to the church in 1748, and in 1763–8 it was extended to the west, the interior was rearranged, and a gallery was added. In 1810–11 there were further enlargements, and a new pulpit was erected: in 1820 a new organ was provided. Bishop Doane consecrated the church in 1834.

In 1838 a bishop's chair was presented, and the Bishop himself gave a font.

The church still stands, but a new one was built nearby, from plans by Richard Upjohn. The cornerstone was laid on 17 November 1846, and it was consecrated on 10 August 1854. It is cruciform, with a central tower and spire. The style is First-Pointed, "with a considerable sprinkling of Second-Pointed, in the tracery of the windows, and in the woodwork and decoration". The font, of Caen stone, was designed by Dudley and Condit, who also designed the bishop's throne. The chancel floor is paved with Minton's tiles, and the polychrome was the work of Mr Akeroyd. The woodwork is of black walnut.

After the division of the diocese in 1874, John Scarborough, the fourth Bishop, made his home at Trenton, without any parochial charge. In 1886, in his annual address to the Convention of the Diocese, he said that he wanted a Bishop's Church. Christ Church, Trenton, was in process of formation, and this should be the cathedral. But in 1891 it was admitted into union with the Convocation as a parish. However, it was made a pro-cathedral by his successor in 1916, and served until Trinity, Trenton, was accepted as a cathedral in 1931.

TRINITY CATHEDRAL, TRENTON

The beginning of the new cathedral was made possible by Ferdinand W. Roebling, who also rebuilt the Synod Hall.

The ground was broken on 6 May 1935, and work began in June: the cornerstone of the cathedral, on top of the crypt, was laid on 5 October. The first service was held in the crypt on 5 January 1938.

The crypt is in the Norman style, from designs by Samuel Mountford of the P. L. Fowler Co. of Trenton: the builders were Karno-Smith Co. Inc, also of Trenton.

Approximately 13 million pounds of material were used, chiefly con-

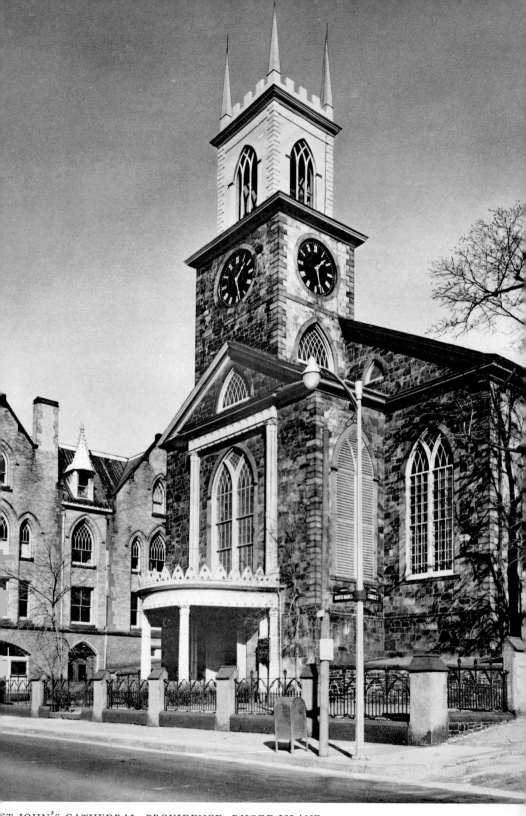

ST JOHN'S CATHEDRAL, PROVIDENCE, RHODE ISLAND

ST JOHN'S CATHEDRAL, PROVIDENCE, RHODE ISLAND

ST PAUL'S CATHEDRAL, BOSTON, MASSACHUSETTS

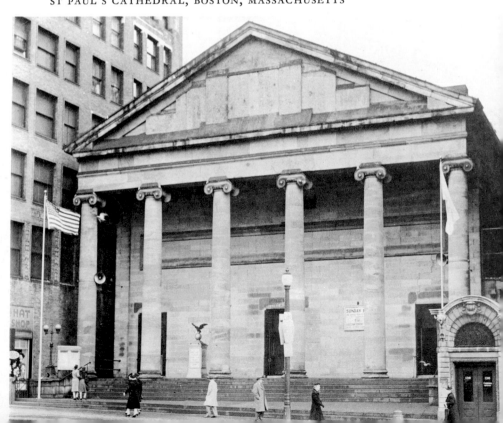

crete: the main columns were calculated for a load of 4,700 tons. The floor is of stone slabs.

The fittings are those of Trinity Church, Academy Street, founded in 1859. The stalls were designed by the architect, and executed by Cunningham and Hacker of Philadelphia. The glass is by Valentine F. D'Ogries of New Hope, Pa. The stones and windows of Trinity are stored in the crypt, and will be used in the fabric above ground. The chapel of the Blessed Virgin, known as the Lee memorial, has been removed from the original site, and will be reconstructed. There will also be a Caesarea or Jersey Chapel, a memorial to all former bishops of New Jersey. Stones from all the Colonial parishes will be set in the walls, and the names of all the congregations in the diocese will be perpetuated. As Caesarea is the name that was later pronounced as Jersey, memorials of the Caesareas of the Holy Land will be incorporated.

In the cathedral grounds is All Saints' chapel, built in 1927 to replace the older church.

The cathedral is to be 14th-century Gothic, of a rather Bodleian appearance, cruciform, with a central tower.

CATHEDRAL OF ST JOHN THE DIVINE, NEW YORK

The diocese was organized in 1785.

The first suggestion of a cathedral was made in 1828 by Bishop Hobart (1816–30), who said that the best place for it would be in the neighbourhood of Washington Square. In 1872 Bishop Horatio Potter (1861–87) referred to the subject in his Convention address. A charter was obtained in 1873. Bishop Henry Codman Potter (1887–1908) collected funds.

A competition was held, and four sets of plans were selected: the winning design was that of Messrs George L. Heins and C. Grant La Farge. George Lewis Heins was born at Philadelphia in 1860, graduated at the University of Philadelphia, and studied architecture at the Massachusetts Institute. He joined Christopher Grant La Farge (1862–1938) in 1884; both acted as architectural assistants to John La Farge, decorative artist. They entered into partnership in 1886. The New York design was "a bold and florid piece of eclecticism—more Byzantine than Romanesque within, more Gothic than Romanesque without. The

12

plan was very compact and un-Gothic". There was to have been a central dome, surmounted by a pyramidal tower.

The foundation stone was laid by Bishop Potter on 27 December 1892, and services were held in the crypt from 1899.

Heins died in September 1907, and La Farge continued until April 1911. By that time, the four granite arches and eight buttresses, that were to support the dome at the crossing, were built; but quicksands and springs had been discovered on the site, and it was clear that the design could not be carried out. Guastavino was called in to roof the crossing with a light terra cotta dome, and La Farge was superseded by Cram and Ferguson, who redesigned the cathedral: the Romanesque style was abandoned, and 13th-century French Gothic adopted instead. In that year, the first service was held in the unfinished choir and crossing.

The seven chapels at the east end were built between 1911 and 1918: each was the gift of some individual or family, who chose their own architect, subject to the approval of the architect to the cathedral. Two were designed by Heins and La Farge; Henry Vaughan of Boston, a pupil of Bodley, was the architect of three; Cram and Ferguson designed one, and Carrère and Hastings one. John Merven Carrère (1858–1911) studied at the École des Beaux-Arts under Victor Robert, Charles Laisne, and Léon Ginain. He entered the office of McKim, Mead and White in 1883, and then became partner with Thomas Hastings (1860–1929). They did work in the Spanish style, but came to like the French Renaissance. They designed the Century Theatre, New York City, and the New York Public Library.

In 1916 the ground was broken for the nave, and the foundations were laid. The baptistery was begun in 1924, and consecrated on 15 April 1928. The foundation stone of the nave and aisles was laid on 9 November 1925, and the fabric of this part of the church is complete. The transepts, begun in 1927, are not yet finished.

The building is entirely of stone—the core of the walls Maine granite, the outer facing Mohegan granite, from Peekskill, N.Y., the inner surfaces Bedford, Indiana, limestone, and Wisconsin dolomite. The only steel is in the ridge of the nave roof.

The plan is, nave with aisles and outer chapels, and narthex between the bases of the west towers; transepts (not completed); and apsidal choir with ambulatory and chapels. The baptistery is to the east of the north transept.

The total length is 601 feet; the width of the nave and aisles 146, of the transepts and crossing 330, and of the choir and ambulatory 70.

EXTERIOR

The completed cathedral is to have two similar pinnacled western towers, and a flèche over the crossing. Cram's original sketches showed twin towers with lofty spires at the north and south transepts, with a massive and rather low tower over the 100-foot-square crossing. Then the idea of transeptal towers was dropped, and a large central tower was planned. This was redesigned several times. In 1927 the problem was thought to have been solved by a new design, but this was given up in the 40's, and the flèche substituted.

The doors of the central portal of the west front are of bronze, by Henry Wilson: they were cast by M. Barbedienne of Paris. The figures in the doorway of the north tower—the Martyrs' Portal—are by John Angel, carved in Indiana limestone. The sculptures on three of the eastern chapels—St Saviour, St Columba, and St Boniface—are by Gutzon Borglum.

INTERIOR: NAVE AND AISLES

The glass in the west windows is by Charles J. Connick (1875–1945): the north and south windows of the narthex are by Ernest W. Lakeman.

The piers of the nave are alternately massive and slender: transverse ribs springing from the smaller intermediate columns make the vaulting sexpartite. The triforium and clerestory are erected on the outer arcades.

Bays of the nave have been built by special groups of contributors, and have special names: the subjects of the glass in the windows are chosen to correspond.

The Sports Bay (St Hubert's Chapel): window of chapel by D'Ascenzo Studios of Philadelphia (established in 1900 by Nicola D'Ascenzo, who was born in Italy, came to America in 1882, and died in his 84th year on 13 April 1954).

The Arts Bay: chapel and clerestory windows by Charles J. Connick.

The Crusaders' Bay: chapel and clerestory windows by Ernest W. Lakeman.

The Education Bay: clerestory window by Charles J. Connick.

The Lawyers' Bay (St Yves chapel) contains an altar and reredos to the memory of the Very Reverend William Mercer Grosvenor, the first Dean. The altar is of marble, the reredos is a triptych of carved walnut. The chapel and clerestory windows were made by Wilbur Herbert Burnham of Boston.

The Ecclesiastical Origins Bay: chapel and clerestory windows by W. H. Burnham.

The Historic and Patriotic Societies' Bay (St Alban's) is furnished as a memorial to William Thomas Manning, tenth Bishop of New York (1921–46). The tomb has a recumbent effigy of the Bishop, of Carrara marble, carved by Constantin Antonovici. The chapel window is by Ernest W. Lakeman.

The All Souls' Bay has an altar to the memory of Mabel Drury (died 1930): the painting of the reredos is by Leo Cartwright of Boston. The chapel window was designed and made by Otto W. Heinigke and Loris A. Withers, of the firm of Heinigke and Smith. Here is the Shrine of the Golden Book, designed by Cram and Ferguson, containing the Book of Remembrance, with the list of names of contributors to the building of the cathedral.

The Missionary Bay: chapel window by W. H. Burnham.

The Labour Bay: chapel and clerestory windows by Nicola D'Ascenzo.

The Press Bay: chapel and clerestory windows by Nicola D'Ascenzo.

The Medical Bay: the altar and reredos are a memorial to the Reverend Dr Starr, 1928. The clerestory and chapel windows are by Reynolds, Francis and Rohnstock.

The Religious Life Bay: chapel and clerestory windows by Reynolds, Francis and Rohnstock.

The Army and Navy Bay: chapel and clerestory windows by Ernest W. Lakeman.

The Motherhood Bay has a doorway in the lower part, instead of a chapel: the clerestory window is by D'Ascenzo.

The pavement of the nave and aisles was paid for largely by the offerings of visitors to the cathedral: it contains the names of places to which pilgrimages have been made in Christian history.

The twelve Barberini tapestries, in various parts of the cathedral, were made in the 17th century under the direction of Jacques della Riviera, from cartoons by Jean Francois Romanelli. They were originally designed for the Barberini Palace at Rome, were afterwards in the

Ffoulke collection at Washington, and were given by Elizabeth U. Coles.

The Mortlake tapestries, after cartoons by Raphael, were given by Margaret Louise Bruguiere in 1954: they are hung in various bays of the nave.

The carved pulpit (1916) is a memorial to Bishop Henry Codman Potter: it was designed by Henry Vaughan, and is made of marble from Knoxville, Tennessee.

CHOIR AND AMBULATORY

The lower part of the choir is of the original Romanesque design: the upper part is Gothic, by Cram and Ferguson.

The pavement is of varied marbles and tiles. The stalls, the design of which is based on those in Henry VII's Chapel, Westminster Abbey, are a memorial to Susan Watts Street (1818–93).

The Historical Parapet, enclosing the bishop's throne on the south, and a stall on the north, was dedicated on 1 November 1922: it was designed by Cram and Ferguson. The figures, modelled by Ferrari and carved by John Evans and Co. of Boston, represent outstanding figures in twenty centuries of Christian history.

The High Altar is of white Vermont marble, in memory of Anna Livingston Morton, 1918. Above it is a cross with a figure of the reigning Christ carved by Cornelia van Auken Chapin.

The Magna Carta pedestal, at the right of the altar, is supported by a shaft of three stones from the Abbey of Bury St Edmunds.

The eight great columns of the apse have shafts of light grey marble from Bear Island on the coast of Maine: they were all given as memorials.

The steel gateways leading to the ambulatory were given in memory of L. P. Morton (1824–1920), Vice-President, and Governor of the State of New York, and Anna his wife (1846–1918), "whose gifts made possible the building and furnishing of the choir of this cathedral".

The chandelier at the entrance to St Ansgarius' chapel is of hand-cut Bohemian glass, and was given by the Republic of Czechoslovakia in 1927.

Behind the High Altar is the tomb of Bishop Horatio Potter (died 1887): the architect was Thomas Nash of New York, and the sculptor of the figure was Isidore Konti.

The clerestory windows of the ambulatory are by James Powell.

THE EASTERN CHAPELS

The Chapel of St James. This was consecrated on 2 May 1916, and was given in memory of Bishop Henry Codman Potter (died 1908) by his wife. The windows were given to her memory by her children. The chapel was designed by Henry Vaughan in a Bodleian 14th-century style. The interior walls are of limestone from Bedford, Ind. The altar is of marble from Knoxville, Tenn., and there is a carved stone reredos. The glass is by Henry Wynd Young, and members of his firm, and Ernest Lakeman. In the south aisle, of three bays, is the recumbent figure of Bishop Potter, in Seravezza marble, by James E. Frazer. Three Italian paintings of the 17th century were given in 1935, and there is a Flemish tapestry presented by Mr Courtlandt Palmer.

The Chapel of St Ambrose. This chapel was erected by Sara Whiting Rives to the memory of members of the Whiting family: it was dedicated on 23 April 1914. It was designed by Messrs Carrère and Hastings in a Renaissance style. The floor is laid with grey Siena, red Verona, and cream Cenere marbles: the side walls are lined with Rosata marble. There is an elaborate altar piece of carved and gilded wood. The glass is by Henry Wynd Young, under Messrs Godwin and Sullivant, architects, of New York.

The Chapel of St Martin. This was consecrated in 1918, in memory of William F. Furniss, Sophia his wife, and their daughter Sophia R. C. Furniss, Cram and Ferguson were the architects, and the style is French 13th century. The interior walls are faced with Bedford, Ind., limestone, and there is a wall arcade under the windows. The pavement is of Knoxville, Tenn., pink marble, with a border of black Belgian. The glass is by Charles J. Connick. The statue of Joan of Arc, by Mrs Anna Hyatt Huntingdon, was placed here in 1922. The aumbry, dedicated on 18 April 1935, is a memorial to General Richard Delafield.

The Chapel of St Saviour was consecrated on 19 April 1911: it was built by August Belmont in memory of his wife Bessie Morgan Belmont. The architects were Heins and La Farge. The style is 14th century, though the east window has no period precedent. The interior walls are of Minnesota dolomite: the pavement is of stone from Hauteville, France, with a mosaic border: the steps to the altar are of pink Georgia marble: the lower part of the east wall is faced with red Siena marble, and the altar is of white Carrara. The statues in niches on each side of the east window were carved by Gutzon Borglum. The glass in the east window is by Hardman of Birmingham.

The Chapel of St Columba. Consecrated on 27 April 1911: the gift of Mary Augusta King, to the memory of Mary Leroy King. Designed by Heins and La Farge, in a Romanesque style, with windows of no period precedent. The walls are of Minnesota dolomite, the pavement is of stone from Illinois. The vaulting over the sanctuary is faced with mosaic. The grisaille glass above the altar is by Wilbur Herbert Burnham: the rest of the glass by Clayton and Bell.

The Chapel of St Boniface. Erected by George Sullivan Bowdoin and his wife Julia Grinnell Bowdoin, and their children, and consecrated on 29 February 1916. This is by Henry Vaughan, in pure Bodleian 14th-century style. The interior walls are of Indiana limestone; the pavement is of pink marble from Knoxville, with a border of Belgian marble. The altar is of grey Knoxville marble. There is a carved reredos: the glass is by C. E. Kempe.

The Chapel of St Ansgarius. (This is the St Anskar who makes so mysterious an appearance in the revised English calendar of 1928.) Another chapel by Henry Vaughan. It was consecrated on 3 April 1918, in memory of William Reed Huntington, for 25 years Rector of Grace Church. The walls are of Indiana limestone; the pavement is of pink Knoxville marble and mottled marble from Vermont. The carved stone reredos, and the altar, were given by Mrs Julia Grinnell Bowdoin. The glass is by C. E. Kempe. To the north of the sanctuary is a niche made of stones from Worcester and Ely cathedrals.

THE BAPTISTERY

This was begun in 1924, and consecrated in 1928; it was built by members of the Stuyvesant family in memory of their parents. The plan is octagonal, the style Southern European Gothic. The walls are of Indiana limestone. A coloured frieze of sculpture runs round the walls. The statues and the bust of Augustus Van Horne Stuyvesant were modelled by John Angel. The font is of Champville marble, carved by Albert H. Atkins: an octagonal panelled shaft rises from the centre.

OTHER BUILDINGS

The Cathedral House and Ogilvie House (the residence of the Bishop) are by Cram and Ferguson. The choir school (1913) is by Messrs Walter

Cook and Winthrop A. Welch. Heins and La Farge designed the Diocesan House, completed in 1912, and the Synod House (1912–13) is by Cram and Ferguson.

TRINITY CATHEDRAL, NEWARK

The diocese was organized in 1874, and was at first known as Northern New Jersey: the name was changed to Newark in 1886.

The original church was built in 1742–43: it was 63 × 45 feet, and 27 feet high, with a steeple 20 feet square and 95 feet high. The parish was incorporated by royal charter on 10 February 1746, and a missionary was sent by S.P.G. in that year.

The church was rebuilt in 1809–10, except for the lower part of the tower: the cornerstone was laid on 22 May 1809, and it was consecrated by Bishop Moore of New York on 21 May 1810. The architect was Captain Josiah James, a member of the parish and a vestryman. The *New York Gazette* (29 May 1810) wrote, "The church is in a style of simple elegance, and reflects much credit on the taste and skill of those by whom it was planned and executed."

A portico was added at the west end, and a steeple to the tower: the body of the church is of brown stone, with plain pointed windows; there was originally a triple pointed window at the east end. The ceiling is plain, with a cove.

A font was given in 1841. Chancel, vestries, and organ chamber, designed by Richard Upjohn, were completed in 1863. Pulpit, lectern, and furniture in the chancel, were given in 1896.

At the Convention of the Diocese in 1906, a committee was appointed to recommend a plan for the creation of a cathedral foundation. Christ Church was designated as a pro-cathedral. In 1914, Grace, St Paul's, and Trinity were considered, but no action was taken until 1918, when Trinity became a pro-cathedral. In 1931 a tract of land was bought as a site for a cathedral and other diocesan buildings, but Cedar Grove was too far off, and the project proved impracticable. Trinity was established as a full cathedral in 1944.

Plans have been made by William Hugh Thompson, A.I.A., for recasting the interior, dividing the body of the church into nave and aisles with a Doric colonnade, and enlarging the chancel.

CATHEDRAL OF ST JOHN THE DIVINE, NEW YORK. *The Sanctuary*

CATHEDRAL OF
ST JOHN THE
DIVINE, NEW YORK

The Chapel of St Columba

CHRIST CHURCH,
PHILADELPHIA,
PENNSYLVANIA

CATHEDRAL CHURCH
OF THE NATIVITY,
BETHLEHEM, PENNSYLVANIA

CATHEDRAL CHURCH OF
THE INCARNATION,
BALTIMORE, MARYLAND

ST LUKE'S CATHEDRAL, ANCÓN
[MISSIONARY DISTRICT OF PANAMA CANAL ZONE]

The Missionary District was constituted in 1919: it includes the Canal Zone, and the Republics of Panama, Colombia, Costa Rica, and Nicaragua.

The cathedral is Romanesque, with an Italian-looking porch.

It took the place of the Chapel of St Luke, a frame building, owned by the Government, and served by the Protestant chaplain of the Gorgas hospital.

ST JOHN'S CATHEDRAL, SANTURCE
[MISSIONARY DISTRICT OF PUERTO RICO]

The Missionary District was established in 1901.

The former St John's was in the city; the new one was built outside, with the money from the sale of the site, and $10,000 from a New York layman. In 1929 the church needed a further $8,000 to complete it.

ST PAUL'S CATHEDRAL, BUFFALO
[DIOCESE OF WESTERN NEW YORK]

The site was given by the Holland Land Co. to a congregation organized in 1817. The diocese was organized in 1838.

Richard Upjohn's first drawing for a new church was made on 6 March 1848: it is said to have been made while he was talking to the committee. His plans were considered too expensive; new plans were accepted on 28 March 1849. Work was begun in September, the foundation stone was laid on 12 June 1850, and the consecration was on 22 October 1851. The contractor was Thomas R. Williams of New York.

The church was made a cathedral in 1866: the tower and spire were built in 1870, and the bell turret, flanking the chancel, was completed in 1871.

The site is triangular, and the body of the church was placed parallel to the long side: this left room in one angle for the tower, and on the other side for a chapel.

The style is 13th century. This is how the Toronto *Church* described it at the time of the consecration: "The church is built of red sandstone with dressed rubble work, in the 'Early English' style, with a bell-turret at the north-east angle, and the tower and spire, which is not yet erected, at the south-west angle; in place of transepts there is on the north side a chapel, so that the church presents from every point from which it is viewed a different appearance, yet producing a harmonious effect as a whole. The roof is covered with green slate, which contrasts well with the dark sombre colour of the building.

"The interior is in strict keeping with the exterior, being finished with open timber roof with carved tracery, supported upon wooden columns rising from the ground. The pitch of the roof the aisles is somewhat less than that of the nave which is nearly equilateral, the timbers coloured as black walnut, and between the rafters the ceiling is painted azure blue. . . .

"The chancel is raised above the nave by three rather deep steps, and is 28 feet by 24 feet: it is lighted by a beautiful triplet window to the east filled with richly stained glass in medallions and intersecting circles and quatrefoils; the south side is lighted by two lancet windows and on the north is one of the faces of the organ. The altar-table is placed on a very richly-carved frame, and within the rails there is a credence table, sedilia for the officiating clergy, and a chair for the bishop; outside the rail but still within the chancel, there are stalls from any of which the prayers may be said, and a lectern for the lessons. . . . The whole of the furniture of the church is made of black walnut, which combined with the smallness of the windows, filled as they are with stained glass, if it is a fault, gives the church perhaps too much of a dim light, but certainly is it better than the opposite one of having too much light."

There was a fire 10 May, 1888—after which there was a restoration by R. W. Gibson, who altered the exterior slightly and the interior a good deal.

17

Third Province (Washington)

CATHEDRAL CHURCH OF THE NATIVITY, BETHLEHEM

The diocese was first organized in 1871 (under the name of Central Pennsylvania) and Mark Antony de Wolfe Howe was consecrated Bishop. In 1872 the Vestry of Christ Church, Reading, placed the church at his disposal. He accepted, and it became known as the cathedral of the diocese. Bishop Nelson Somerville Rulison (1895–7) came to live at Bethlehem, and designated the Nativity as his Cathedral Church.

It was founded in 1862, and is a stone Gothic building, with a detached north-west tower in English 14th-century style.

ST JOHN'S CATHEDRAL, WILMINGTON
[DIOCESE OF DELAWARE]

The parish was organized in 1855, in what was then known as Brandywine Village, and in 1856 the Vestry obtained part of the site of the Green Tree Inn. A school was built, which was used for worship. On 25 March 1857 full possession of the lot was obtained, and steps were immediately taken for pulling down the inn and building the church. The designs were made by John Notman of Philadelphia. The cornerstone was laid on 13 June.

The blue granite for the walls came from the Tatnall Quarry near-by: the building was ready for the roof by August. The founder, Alexis I. du Pont, died in this month: his will, in which he had left money for finishing the church, was found to be invalid, but his widow came to the rescue. In March 1858 the Vestry decided not to finish the spire in stone, as had been proposed. The church was consecrated by the Right Reverend Alfred Lee, Bishop of Delaware, on 3 November.

In 1886 the organ was moved from the north transept to an organ chamber, and the gallery in the south transept was taken down.

In 1917 the Vestry decided on improvements and additions, but these were not carried out until 1919. The chancel was lengthened by 11 feet. St Mary's chapel was built as a memorial to Mrs Natalie du Pont, the Parish House, built in 1885, was altered, and a new rectory was built.

In May 1935 Bishop Philip Cook designated St John's as the Cathedral Church; in 1946 the buildings were renovated; and on 14 May 1947, it was constituted a full cathedral, and a Chapter was formed.

There is glass by William Willet and Henry Lee Willet; the Lady chapel windows are by D'Ascenzo.

TRINITY CATHEDRAL, EASTON

The diocese was organized in 1868.

The cathedral is of stone, cruciform, with an incomplete south-west tower. The style is 13th century.

ST PAUL'S CATHEDRAL, ERIE

The parish was organized in 1827, and is the oldest in the district. Services were held in the Court House until a church was erected in 1832. The present church, Victorian Middle-Pointed, was built in 1866. The diocese was organized in 1910.

The redecoration and refurnishing of the interior of the cathedral was begun in the 1930's, resumed after the war, and completed in 1952: architect J. Ellsworth Potter of Cleveland, carving by the Theodore Kundtz Co. of Cleveland, glass by the Henry Lee Willet Studio of Philadelphia. There is much woodwork in English 15th-century style. The chapel to the right of the choir was the gift of Mrs James N. Thayer, in memory of William H. Warner. The screen to the baptistery on the other side, with gates of 17th-century Venetian ironwork, is a memorial to the Behrend family. An organ loft was built above the sacristy adjoining the chapel.

The All Saints' Memorial Chapel, a new addition, was dedicated on 7 July 1957.

The reredos of the high altar contains fragments of the *Lawrence* and the *Niagara*, Commodore Perry's flagships in the battle of Lake Erie in 1812. The altar rail of the chapel contains five bronze spikes from the *Wolverine*, the first all-steel ship in the U.S. Navy, which was made in Pittsburgh and brought on rails to Erie, and was the last warship to sail the Lakes.

ST STEPHEN'S CATHEDRAL, HARRISBURG

The parish was incorporated in 1827. The church is Gothic, with an embattled tower.

The diocese was organized in 1904, and the first bishop was appointed in 1905.

CATHEDRAL OF THE INCARNATION, BALTIMORE [DIOCESE OF MARYLAND]

In 1907 Bishop Paret (1885–1911) drove in a hansom cab to the corner of Charles Street and Merrymans Lane, now University Parkway. He stood for a few moments with the Reverend Dr Edwin B. Niver, rector of Christ Church, and then struck the ground with his cane. "This", he said, "is the site for the cathedral".

In May 1908 the diocese committed itself to building, and a group of Baltimore laymen provided the purchase money for the ground—about $50,000.

During the time of Bishop John Gardner Murray (1911–29) a most ambitious design was made by Cram, Goodhue, and Ferguson for a very large Gothic church consisting of aisled nave with two west towers and a west porch, central tower, transepts, choir with aisles and subsidiary transepts, and a projecting chapel at the north-east; also cloisters, choir school, synod hall, library, sacristies, and chapter house. This was an unfulfilled dream: only the apse was built.

The undercroft of the pro-cathedral was built in 1911, and the upper church was completed in 1932. The architect was Philip H. Frohman, architect to Washington Cathedral. It is a moderate-sized Middle-Pointed church, of clerestoried nave, aisles and chancel, with a flèche. It was established as a cathedral in 1955, and consecrated on 6 November.

There is glass by Sanborn: the east window is a memorial to Bishop Murray.

CHRIST CHURCH, PHILADELPHIA
[DIOCESE OF PENNSYLVANIA]

The cathedral of the Diocese of Pennsylvania is not yet built. Christ Church is not, strictly speaking, a cathedral, but it is the mother church of the diocese, and was for very nearly fifty years the bishop's church; and it has had so intimate a connection with the organization and development of the Episcopal Church, that it would hardly be possible to leave it out.

The first Christ Church was built in 1695; Governor Nicholson was a contributor. It was enlarged in 1711, and on 11 June 1717, the Vestry resolved that a subscription be prepared for building a steeple. (Extracts from the Vestry minutes are given in *A Historical Account of Christ Church, Philadelphia*, by the Reverend Benjamin Dorr, 1841.) Another proposal was made on 11 August 1720, that a subscription be made for enlarging the church, building a tower, and purchasing bells.

Dr Richard Welton who had been in charge of the church, and who had been consecrated a Bishop of the Nonjuring succession in 1723, was recalled to England in January 1726 (but went to Portugal instead, and died there): he was succeeded by the Reverend Archibald Cummings, in whose incumbency progress began to be made. In April, 1727, the Vestry resolved to make an addition of 33 feet at the west. The cornerstone was laid on 27th. On 2 May Dr John Kearsley reported to the Vestry that he had ordered the digging and laying of foundations for the addition to the church and for the steeple. Kearsley himself—"an eminent physician of Philadelphia"—made the design, and he and three others were appointed overseers of the work.

On 2 September 1728, the purchase of an organ was decided on. The glazing of the windows—the addition being nearly completed—was ordered on 20 September 1730. In 1731 measures were taken to remove the old building, and build the east end of the new church.

26 May 1732: the pulpit was too remote from the new part, and was to be moved further into the body of the church. A seat for the Governor to be made where the pulpit used to stand.

There are no minutes from October 1732 to April 1735, during which time the east end was built. On 25 May 1735, the Vestry agreed that money be applied to finishing the exterior. On 7 May 1739, another subscription paper was drawn up: the inside was still unfinished, and some pews and a gallery were to be added. On 16 April 1743, the Vestry agreed that the gallery at the west end be run out, and built entirely over the west aisle. On 27 August 1744, the wardens reported that the church was finished; the workmen had been agreed with, and materials had been purchased for rebuilding and regulating the seats, which were to be of the dimensions of those at St Martin-in-the-Fields. On 23 October the committee appointed to audit and settle the accounts passed a vote of thanks to Kearsley. A chandelier was bought during this year.

On 2 June 1746, the Vestry viewed several drafts of a tower and spire, and agreed that "the draft which Mr Harrison drew" should be followed. 11 March 1751: the steeple to be built, and bells to be purchased. 16 April: Kearsley and three others to be supervisors of the work. 19 October 1753: a ring of bells to be purchased. By August 1755 £3,162 9s. 11d. had already been spent on the steeple. It was probably completed soon afterwards. The builder was Robert Smith, head of the Carpenters' Company. 22 November 1763: an organ to be bought. On 15 April 1765, the Vestry ordered its erection: it was finished by January 1767. On 15 June Anthony Denormandie gave a quotation for whitewashing and repairing the church and repairing the windows, which was accepted.

On 14 August 1769, the Vestry was told that Mrs Mary Andrews had left £100 for a monument and a pulpit: the monument had been paid for, and it was resolved that the balance of the money should be used for the erection of the pulpit. At the next meeting John Folwell's plan was accepted.

On 4 June 1771, it was stated that Robert Smith had examined the steeple and found it dangerous: he was empowered to procure workmen and materials and repair it. The cost was £644 2s. 10d.

Kearsley died in January 1772. In that year William White, the future Bishop, became assistant minister.

On 4 July 1776, the Vestry decided to omit the prayers for the King.

On 23 May 1785, the first Convention of the Episcopal Church met in Christ Church: the constitution was framed, and the Prayer Book was drawn up. Of the first 29 Conventions, all but one were held here, and eleven bishops were consecrated here between 1795 and 1858. The Prayer Book was adopted at the Convention of 1789.

On 14 September 1786, White was elected Bishop at the Diocesan Convention. He sailed for England on 30 October, and was consecrated on 4 February 1787: on 28 May he held an ordination at Christ Church.

On 10 April 1788, a committee was appointed to plan an alteration in the chancel and reading desk. On 22 January 1789, thanks were given to Mr Gostelowe for presenting a mahogany Communion table and making a font. On 26 November 1790, a committee that had been appointed to provide a pew for the President reported that they had done so. Washington and his family occupied it for six years.

There were no more alterations in the church until the 1830's. On 7 April 1834, a committee was appointed to consider the alteration of the galleries, etc. On 7 May they submitted to the Vestry a letter from Thomas U. Walker, architect of Girard College, and of the dome and extensions to the Capitol at Washington. He proposed to alter the galleries by the introduction of slip pews, to move the organ back, to rebuild the galleries away from the columns, to reseat the church, to lay a new floor, etc. The proposals were accepted on 25 January 1836, and work began in June. A new organ was provided, but the old keyboard and case were kept. Bishop White died on 17 July, while the work was in progress, and was buried in the church on 20 July.

On 5 September 1838, the Vestry received a report on repairs to the steeple.

In 1881 the church was reseated. The spire was struck by lightning in 1908, and repaired afterwards.

The church is of brick: the walls of the tower are of stone, but with a brick facing. The side elevations are of two stages, with arched windows, pilasters, and a balustrade and urns: the east end has a Venetian window and an attic storey above the entablature. The interior clearly shows the influence of St Martin-in-the-Fields—which must have crossed the Atlantic very rapidly: there are Doric columns on plinths, each with its entablature. The steeple is certainly based on one of the alternative designs for St Martin's.

This admirable 18th-century church is preserved as a national shrine.

TRINITY CATHEDRAL, PITTSBURGH

In 1787 John Penn, jun. and John Penn conveyed the land on which the present cathedral stands to the "Trustees of the congregation of the

Episcopalian Church, commonly called the Church of England". The land had been used as a burial ground by the Indians, and also by the French before the fall of Fort Duquesne. No church was built, and no rector was called until 1797. The parish was incorporated in 1805, and a church was built in 1808—not on the site given by the Penns, which was used as a cemetery, but on a triangular piece of ground bounded by Liberty Avenue, Sixth Avenue, and Wood Street. It was of brick, octagonal in plan, with a lantern and dome in the centre.

During the rectorate of the Reverend William Thompson, who was appointed in 1821, but served for less than two years, a proposal was made to sell the church, and to build a new one on the ground given by the Penns. After Thompson had left, the parish was without a rector, and a young layman, John Henry Hopkins, volunteered to act as lay reader. He then decided to enter the ministry, and gave up his practice at the bar: he was ordained in 1824, and appointed rector of the parish. In 1830 he was called to be assistant minister at Trinity Church, Boston, and in 1832 he was consecrated Bishop of Vermont.

He made the design for the new church himself, having borrowed, it is said, engravings of some English cathedrals, and a volume of Britton. The result was a picturesque Gothic church, all embattled, with a pinnacled tower, and four lower towers at the angles. It was consecrated on 25 June 1825.

In 1865 the Diocese of Pittsburgh was organized—the first division of the Diocese of Pennsylvania; and Dr John Barrett Kerfoot, President of Trinity College, Hartford, was consecrated Bishop in Trinity Church on the Feast of the Conversion of St Paul 1866. This was the last time that Bishop Hopkins officiated in the church.

The last services were held in October 1869. The new church, designed by Upjohn and Lloyd, was consecrated in 1872, on the Feast of the Conversion of St Paul.

On 4 January 1928, a meeting of the congregation authorized the rector, wardens, and vestrymen to offer the church to the Bishop as a cathedral: the offer was accepted at the Convention of the Diocese which met on 25 January.

The cathedral is of sandstone and granite, in 14th-century style, cruciform, with a tall south-west tower with crocketed spire. The chancel is apsidal. The decorations were suggested by those of the Sainte Chapelle, Paris.

13

CATHEDRAL SHRINE OF THE
TRANSFIGURATION, ORKNEY SPRINGS
[DIOCESE OF VIRGINIA]

This historic diocese, organized in 1785, has no cathedral. The "Shrine" is a summer conference centre.

CATHEDRAL OF SS. PETER AND PAUL,
WASHINGTON

In 1792 Thomas John Claggett was appointed Bishop of Maryland, and in 1793, at the first convention over which he presided, he appointed a committee to consider the establishment of a church in the new Federal City. At the same time, Washington employed Major Pierre L'Enfant to lay out plans for the city: among the public buildings, a church was proposed, to be used for national purposes, equally open to all denominations. Nothing came of this, but the idea was not entirely forgotten.

The first registrar of the Treasury, Joseph Nourse, had his house on Mount Alban: this house eventually became St John's church school for boys, and an upper room was used as a chapel. Here the great-granddaughter of Joseph Nourse taught in Sunday school; and when she died, she left some money for the building of a free church on Alban Hill. The church was built a few years afterwards.

Later in the century there was talk of establishing a Diocese of Washington. The Reverend Charles Hall, Rector of the Church of the Epiphany, said, "When it does come, this must be the site of the cathedral".

A meeting to discuss the cathedral project was held in 1892 at the house of Charles C. Glover: on 6 January 1893, the Protestant Episcopal Cathedral Foundation of the District of Columbia was incorporated by Act of Congress, the corporation being "empowered to establish and maintain within the district of Columbia a cathedral and institutions of learning for the promotion of religion and education and charity".

The new Diocese of Washington held its first convention early in 1895, and Dr Henry Yates Satterlee was elected Bishop. He first chose St Mark's, Washington, as his pro-cathedral, and later the Church of the Ascension.

Soon afterwards, the Mount St Alban land came on to the market: an appeal was made, and friends subscribed the sum that was needed for the original payment. On 7 September 1898, the Cathedral Chapter became owners of the property, and a large mortgage.

In 1901 the National school for girls was erected at the north-west of the property. In 1901 the first open-air service was held, and in 1902 the Little Sanctuary was erected. As the plans for the cathedral became known, many gifts were received: the Jerusalem altar was erected in the Little Sanctuary, and so was the pulpit made of stone from Canterbury Cathedral, given by Archbishop Davidson.

In 1905 a gift of $50,000 from Mrs Julian James of Washington paid off the debt for the land, and made it possible to concentrate on plans for the building. The Cathedral Landmark was given by Mrs James, and set up on Ascension Day 1906.

In the summer of 1906, the question of the choice of an architect came up. The Bishop was to see architects in Europe, and the rest of the committee were to correspond with American architects. The Bishop conferred with various English bishops, and saw one or two architects; but having met G. F. Bodley, he decided to go no further. On 10 October the Chapter agreed to the appointment of Henry Vaughan of Boston, and Bodley. Bodley came for a short visit, with Hare, his chief assistant.

Extracts from the Bishop's correspondence with the architects are given in Appendix 1 of *A Master Builder, Life and Letters of Henry Yates Satterlee, Bishop of Washington*, by Charles H. Brent. Bodley, one of the last of the convinced Gothic architects of the 19th century, was of course delighted with the scheme. "The opportunity that your coming cathedral will afford is *vast*, for good. It would be grand if your newer world in America should show the world that the ancient dignity and beauty of religious architecture can be achieved in these days. It *could* be so. Gothic art with all its acceptance of the beauty of nature, as its basis, and its added spiritual, aspiring, fervour could do all this. I know that the limitations of possibilities must be fully taken into account and that a certain amount of modern character must be made to play its part. But that need not be to the detriment of real grandeur and beauty and religious feeling." (6 July 1906.)

"I do not think that excess of richness is desirable, but rather much dignity and even solemn grandeur. They were more joyous in the Middle Ages than we are now. There must be beauty as well as dignity

—but it may be chastened beauty. I do not think too ornate a character is desirable. To give a religious, solemn aspect may be more teaching, may it not, in these days? So please do not expect too ornate a building. But it shall be one as dignified and religious looking as one can make it." (31 January 1907.) "This wonderful Gothic art, neglected, dying, nearly dead, has such an opportunity given it in the building of your cathedral that the love and enthusiasm for it may be revived, and the Old World may be recalled to its early love." (28 April 1907.)

The plans arrived in June 1907, and were accepted almost immediately by the Chapter. Their only criticisms were, that the west towers were too low, that the choir ought to be raised more than one step above the nave, and that the proposed red stone was too dark. Bodley did not agree about the towers (31 July), but on 13 September he promised a new elevation of the west end, enriched, and with the towers a little higher. In October he died.

The foundation stone—a granite block, enclosing stones from Bethlehem—was laid on 29 September, when addresses were given by President Roosevelt and the Bishop of London.

Bishop Satterlee died in February 1908.

The ground was broken in 1908. Vaughan continued as architect after the death of Bodley; and after Vaughan's death, nine years later, Philip Hubert Frohman, of the firm of Frohman, Robb and Little, of Boston and Washington, took over, making some revision of the design. "While there was neither need nor desire to depart radically from the original plans which had been roughly laid down, he refined and restudied them to such an extent that the existing building is essentially his creation. . . . The cathedral's axis was tilted just enough to give the impression of maximum length. The great central pillars leaned out by exactly the right amount to counteract the impression produced of bending inward by foreshortening. . . . The columns at the intersection of transept walls with nave and choir always involve difficult architectural problems; the medievalists were seldom successful in finding a completely satisfactory solution. Mr Frohman devised four entirely different treatments for the four corners, none of them exactly like anything that had been done before." Western aisles were added to the transepts.

The cathedral when complete will consist of a nave of eight bays with double aisles, and west towers with narthex between; transepts with east and west aisles and porches; central tower; choir with chapels, and small additional chapels in the angles between the chapel walls and the eastern aisles of the transepts; and apsidal sanctuary.

The Bethlehem Chapel, under the apse, was finished first, and has been used for daily service since 1912.

The apse was the second portion completed: the building and furnishing of it were made possible by a gift of $500,000 from Mr and Mrs Archibald D. Russell. In 1924 work was begun on three bays of the choir aisles, which had reached clerestory level by the autumn. Early in 1927 the central piers were well advanced, and the two crypt Chapels of the Resurrection and St Joseph of Arimathea were structurally complete. In that year the Bishop appealed for funds for building the vaulting over the choir and crossing. Funds for the purchase of a large quantity of the stone were given, and the Chapter underwrote the amount needed for the rest; but there remained the cost of the working of the stone and the actual construction. In October a nation-wide appeal was made. In the spring of 1928 an anonymous donor gave $500,000 to construct the north choir aisle, and to furnish the Chapel of St Mary. By the spring of 1929 the vaulting of the choir was well advanced, and contracts had been placed for the construction of the crypts under the nave and the nave floor.

In this year the Washington Cathedral Stained Glass Studio was established, under the charge of Lawrence Saint. A gift of $200,000 from Frederick Prince enabled plans to be made for the Chapel of St John in the south choir aisle. The monument of Bishop Harding was dedicated in this year. By midsummer it was possible to let a contract for 50,000 cubic feet of stone for the transepts. The Pilgrim Steps were also undertaken, to lead to the future south transept. The architect revised the drawings for the transept, enlarging the portal, and framing it with turrets.

In 1930 the contract for the building of the north transept was made, at a cost of $1,147,000: a large part of the funds was the gift of George F. Baker.

In 1931 the crypts below the nave and Pilgrim Steps were dedicated. The choir was opened in 1932. The Chapel of the Holy Spirit, between the Chapel of St Mary and the north transept, was completed in 1936.

The north transept is complete, and part of the north cloister has been built, which will connect the cathedral with the future chapter house and administration building. The south transept has been completed to the top of the triforium. Work on the nave was begun again in 1950;

three bays have been completed, and one more bay of the outer aisle on the south.

EXTERIOR

The whole cathedral is built of Indiana limestone. The central tower will be the Gloria in Excelsis tower. This was the idea both of Bishop Satterlee and of Bodley, who wrote (5 March 1907): "It is a little remarkable that when at sea, going out, a design came into my head of the central tower having large figures of angels below the belfry stage each holding a scroll with the 'Gloria in excelsis Deo', one word on each scroll. I say rather remarkable for the same idea struck you, too."

The North Transept was opened in 1932, but with the sculpture left unfinished. The Women's Porch was dedicated in 1942: the figures are by Italo Fanfani, who also carved the three figures below the east window of the apse. The south transept is still unfinished. The doorway will be a memorial to Charlotte Root Pepper.

INTERIOR

Choir and Sanctuary

The stalls are of carved oak: at the east on the north is the seat of the Presiding Bishop (1941), the gift of the Right Reverend Paul Matthews, Bishop of New Jersey 1915–37: on the south is the stall of the Bishop of Washington, a memorial to the Right Reverend William C. Doane, Bishop of Albany. The clerestory windows are by Wilbur H. Burnham and Earl Edward Sanborn, and Lawrence B. Saint.

The altar rail was given in 1942. The altar, of stones from Jerusalem, was the gift of 70 dioceses, missionary jurisdictions, and congregations of the Episcopal Church: it was consecrated in 1902, before building was begun. Altar cross, vases, and candlesticks, to the memory of the Right Reverend James De Wolf Perry, were dedicated on 21 October 1956: the cross was designed by Frohman, and the vases and candlesticks by J. Francis Coote. The carved stone reredos has figures by Angelo Lualdi of Boston, who set up a studio in Florence in 1935, where many skilled craftsmen helped with the work. The bishop's chair, on the north of the sanctuary, is made of stones from Glastonbury.

The two windows of the sanctuary are by E. E. Sanborn: the three-light windows of the apse are by Wilbur H. Burnham and Joseph Reynolds.

CHAPELS

The Chapel of St Mary, to the north of the choir, was the gift of Larz Anderson, whose tomb is here: it was opened for worship on Ascension Day 1932. The wooden reredos was carved by Ernest Pellegrini of the Irving Casson-A. H. Davenport Co., of Cambridge, Massachusetts. Three windows on the north are by Lawrence B. Saint. On the walls are six large 16th-century tapestries from Brussels.

To the west of this is *The Chapel of the Holy Spirit*. The ironwork screen at the entrance was the work of Samuel Yellin of Philadelphia, who also designed the grilles in St Mary's Chapel, the Children's Chapel, and the crypt corridor south of the Bethlehem Chapel. The painting of the reredos is by N. C. Wyeth of Chadds Ford, Pa.; the window by Nicola D'Ascenzo.

The Chapel of St John is south of the choir. The two eastern bays are a memorial to Norman Prince, whose tomb, by Paul Landowski, is here. The third and fourth bays commemorate the Reverend W. M. Jones and his brother Lucian; and the fifth, Francis T. A. Junkin. There is a carved stone reredos, and the wall above is filled with panelling and blind tracery. The glass is by Lawrence B. Saint.

To the west of this is *The Children's Chapel*, a memorial to Roland Leslie Taylor. It has a fan vault and a carved and painted wooden reredos. The window is by Henry Lee Willet.

CROSSING

The choir screen was executed in the studios of Irving Casson-A. H. Davenport Co. The pulpit, of stones from Canterbury Cathedral, was designed by W. D. Caröe. The lectern, of Indiana limestone, was given as a memorial to the Right Reverend Alexander Mackay-Smith, Bishop of Pennsylvania.

NORTH TRANSEPT

The glass in the rose window, given by Rose J. Coleman, was made in the cathedral studios under Lawrence B. Saint. Other glass is by Wilbur H. Burnham, Joseph Reynolds, and Reynolds, Francis and Rohnstock.

In the western aisle, for the time being, is the statue of George

Washington, carved in white Vermont marble by Lee Lawrie, and given in 1943. Here is also the tomb of the Right Reverend James E. Freeman, third Bishop of Washington, who died in 1943, with an effigy of Tennessee marble designed and executed by Bryant Baker of New York City.

The stone screen in front of the stairway to the crypt was carved by Italo Fanfani. The kneeling figure of Abraham Lincoln was executed by Herbert Houck. This part of the cathedral—the screen, the two windows, and the stairway—was dedicated on 20 November 1936, and was the gift of Mrs Florence N. Hildrup.

SOUTH TRANSEPT

The three two-light windows in the south wall were filled with glass by Reynolds, Francis and Rohnstock in 1955: the glass of the rose window must wait for the completion of this part of the cathedral.

The eastern aisle is a war memorial: the three windows here were made by Reynolds, Francis and Rohnstock. The baptistery in the western aisle was dedicated on 11 May 1954: the font, of Tennessee marble, was designed by the cathedral architect and carved by Joseph Ratti. The two windows are by Wilbur H. Burnham.

The window in the second bay is by Evie Hone (1953).

In 1955 designs were made for the screen to the inner doorway of the Pepper memorial portal, and screen on the west side of the War Memorial Chapel, by Herbert Read of Exeter. Two small windows were placed in the south-west turret, designed and executed by Rowan le Compte, the gift of the Manning family.

NAVE AND AISLES

The east bay of the outer aisle on the north is the memorial of the Honourable Frank Billings Kellogg, dedicated on 30 September 1940: it includes a small window by Reynolds, Francis and Rohnstock.

The opposite bay on the south is the memorial to the Honourable Andrew W. Mellon. The second bay on the south is a memorial to Generals Robert E. Lee and Stonewall Jackson. Two windows here are by Wilbur H. Burnham.

In the third bay is the Woodrow Wilson memorial. The bay and the tomb were dedicated on 11 November 1956. The sculpture was modelled by Carl L. Bush, and the carving was done by Messrs Del Frate, Lugiani, Morigi and Ratti, stone carvers to the cathedral.

HEDRAL OF
ETER AND PAUL,
HINGTON

*Architect's conception
e completed structure*

CATHEDRAL OF SS. PETER AND PAUL, WASHINGTON

CHRIST CHURCH CATHEDRAL,
INDIANAPOLIS, INDIANA

ST LUKE'S CATHEDRAL,
ORLANDO, FLORIDA

JOHN'S CATHEDRAL,
CKSONVILLE, FLORIDA

CHRIST CHURCH CATHEDRAL, LOUISVILLE, KENTUCKY

CHRIST CHURCH CATHEDRAL, EAU CLAIRE, WISCONSIN

CRYPT CHAPELS

Bethlehem Chapel. The altar and reredos are of Indiana limestone: the central panel of the screen was carved from one block of stone by John Evans of Boston. The lectern is by Angelo Lualdi. The glass in the aisle to the south is by C. E. Kempe, and that in the ambulatory by Walter Tower. Here is the alabaster tomb of Bishop Satterlee, designed by W. D. Caröe.

The Chapel of St Joseph of Arimathea, under the crossing, has a painting behind the altar by Jan Hendrik de Rosen. The silver cross and candlesticks were the gift of King George VI.

The Chapel of the Resurrection, under the south transept, is in the Norman style: it is a memorial to the Right Reverend Alfred Harding, second Bishop of Washington. His monument was designed by W. D. Caröe, and carved by N. Hitch. The Venetian glass mosaic was placed in the semi-dome of the apse in 1951: it was designed by Hildreth Meiere and executed by the Ravenna Co. of St Louis, Missouri. The altar cross and candlesticks are from the Samuel Yellin studio. In 1954 three windows by Reynolds, Francis and Rohnstock were placed in the ante-chapel.

The contractors for the building are the George A. Fuller Co. About $10 million has been spent on the cathedral so far, and it is estimated that another $18 million will be needed to complete it. It is hoped that it will be finished "in our generation". It is planned as a national, as well as a diocesan centre; besides Woodrow Wilson and F. B. Kellogg, Admiral George Dewey and Cordell Hull are buried there.

18

Fourth Province (Sewanee)

ST PHILIP'S CATHEDRAL, ATLANTA

The diocese was organized in 1907.

A Union church was built in 1845, from which the Episcopalians withdrew in 1849, and built St Philip's: a frame church, with a tower and vestry room. It was occupied by Federal troops in 1864. The Federal Government reimbursed the Church for war damage, and $5,000 was raised by a Northern communicant, General George Meade.

A new brick Gothic church was built in 1880–2 on a lot adjoining the frame church. In 1918 the old building was given to the negroes of the parish, who moved it to Irwin and Fort Streets.

The second church was demolished in 1935, and the seats, chancel rail, windows, and Communion service were transferred to the new cathedral.

ST JOHN'S CATHEDRAL, JACKSONVILLE
[DIOCESE OF FLORIDA]

The first Anglican service was held in Jacksonville in 1829, and a parish was organized in 1834. The cornerstone of a church was laid on 24 April 1842, by the Bishop of South Carolina. The building was ready for services within a short time, but was not completed until 1851, when it was consecrated by the Bishop of Georgia. This church was destroyed when the town was burned by Federal troops on 29 March 1863: a temporary church was built afterwards.

In 1870 steps were taken to build a permanent church, to seat 800 and cost $25,000. Edward T. Potter of New York was engaged as architect. Work was begun in 1873, the cornerstone was laid on 7 April 1874, the first services were held on Easter Sunday 1877, and the consecration was on 7 May 1882. It was of brick, in an early Gothic style: the transepts, chancel, and tower were never completed.

The church, and all the other parish buildings, were destroyed by fire on 3 May 1901.

A committee for building a new church and rectory was appointed in July. The rectory was built first, from designs by Messrs Snelling and Potter; on 18 February 1902, the committee met Mr Snelling, and Mr Hawes, the chief clerk of the firm; the plans and elevations for the new church were considered and approved, and Snelling and Potter were appointed architects. The cornerstone was laid on 18 February 1903, the church was opened on Easter Sunday 1906, and the consecration was on 15 May 1911.

It is cruciform, with a low tower in the angle between the chancel and the south transept. The style is Perp., with some curiously out-of-scale features (e.g. the parapet of the tower), and some features that recall the designs of E. B. Lamb. There are hammer-beam roofs with pendants: the east and west windows are large traceried spherical triangles. There is glass by Payne.

The Diocese of Florida was organized in 1838, but the first bishop was not consecrated until 1851. St John's became the cathedral of the diocese one hundred years later.

CHRIST CHURCH CATHEDRAL, LOUISVILLE
[DIOCESE OF KENTUCKY]

Built in 1822 from designs by Graham and Ferguson.

The diocese was organized in 1829.

The church was originally almost square, with two tiers of windows. In 1872 it was extended, and a new Gothic front was built with two towers, one with a spire. "Richard Barnes was treasurer for the construction. . . . It was his practice to proceed with the erection of the walls as fast as the money came in. As soon as the sum he had in hand was spent, he dismissed the workmen and held up construction in real pay-as-you-go style." (Isabel McLennan McMeekin, *Louisville the Gateway City*, 1946, p. 187.)

It became the cathedral in 1892.

CATHEDRAL SHRINE OF ST GEORGE THE MARTYR, LEE COUNTY
[DIOCESE OF LEXINGTON]

The diocese was organized in 1895.

A mission station under the name of the Cathedral Shrine of St George the Martyr was established in 1948. The charter, revised in 1957, provides for a centre for conference, education, evangelism, retreat, etc.; a cathedral church will be built in the future.

CHRIST CHURCH CATHEDRAL, NEW ORLEANS
[DIOCESE OF LOUISIANA]

The congregation was organized in January 1805. The non-Roman population was so small, and so many denominations were represented, that separate churches were impossible. A meeting was held, to decide on the denomination of the common church: it decided that it should be Episcopal. A church was built on the corner of Canal and Bourbon Streets. It was demolished in 1835, and a new church was built on the opposite corner.

The architect was James Gallier. He was born in Ireland in 1798, studied at the Art Schools in Dublin, and later in England, and came to New York in 1832. He worked there for two years, then left for the Gulf Coast in 1834, and won the competition for Mobile City Hall. Then he came to New Orleans, bringing Charles Dakin as his partner. Charles' brother James H. Dakin (a pupil of Town and Davis of New York) joined them a year later. After 1836, Charles left for Mobile, and Gallier and James Dakin separated, each to found a firm. Christ Church (1835–7) was by Gallier with James Dakin. It cost $48,000, and had an Ionic portico—now the front of the Knights of Columbus building.

The first Bishop of the diocese (1841) was Leonidas Polk, who was killed in 1864 leading his troops to battle.

The site of the church was sold in 1845, and a new and larger church was built on the corner of Canal and Dauphine Streets at a cost of $50,000.

This was sold in 1886, and the congregation moved to another new church, on St Charles Avenue: it was made a pro-cathedral in 1891.

In 1890 Mrs Harris gave the bishop's house and rectory, communicating with the church by a vine-covered cloister.

The window at the west, and the font, are from the old Canal Street church.

ST LUKE'S CATHEDRAL, ORLANDO
[Diocese of South Florida]

A site was offered in 1881. On 30 December the Bishop of Florida met the Church people, and promised help if they would help themselves. They secured the site in January 1882, and a contract for building was made. The church was finished by 1884, with "exceptionally fine windows" and "beautiful church furniture made in New York". The building is now part of the Cathedral Parish House: it was consecrated in 1892.

In that year the Missionary Jurisdiction of South Florida was set apart by General Convention, and the Reverend William Crane Gray was elected Bishop. St Luke's was designated as a cathedral in March 1902.

In 1922—the year in which the diocese was constituted—the old building was moved to make room for a larger church. Plans were made by Frohman, Robb and Little of Boston, the architects for Washington Cathedral, and the cornerstone was laid by Bishop Cameron Mann in 1925.

The cathedral, which is not yet completed, is in 14th-century style, traditional in design, but with a low-pitched tiled roof with projecting eaves. The glass is by Henry Lee Willet of Philadelphia. The rood above the high altar, and the dossal, are a recent gift. The war memorial altar was designed and executed by Mrs Helen Woodman.

ST MARY'S CATHEDRAL (GAILOR MEMORIAL),
MEMPHIS [Diocese of Tennessee]

Tennessee became the sixteenth State of the United States in 1796. By 1829 four parishes had been formed, and the first episcopal convention was held. The first three conventions were presided over by bishops from North Carolina: in June 1833 the fourth convention elected the Reverend James Hervey Otey as the first Bishop of Tennessee. Towards the end of his life he moved to Memphis, next door to St Mary's, a small

Gothic mission church of wood, which had been built in 1857 and consecrated in 1858. He died in 1863.

His successor, Charles Todd Quintard, who was elected in 1865, after the Civil War, persuaded St Mary's to offer itself as the Bishop's Church. From January 1871 it was known as St Mary's Cathedral. It was enlarged afterwards.

Bishop Quintard seems to have planned to divide the diocese into three, with a bishop and a cathedral church in a central city in each section; but the General Convention did not agree to this. He invited the Sisters of St Mary, in New York, to open a girls' school and a home for orphans in Memphis. In 1878 four sisters and two priests died in the yellow fever epidemic, and an altar was erected to the memory of the sisters in 1879.

In 1892 the Bishop asked for a coadjutor, and the Reverend Thomas Frank Gailor was elected: he became the diocesan in 1898. In 1896 he began a movement for building a new cathedral of stone: work was begun in 1898, but funds were only sufficient to construct the crypt. In 1906 part of the superstructure was added—the stone front, and side walls of wood.

In 1919 Bishop Gailor was elected president of the National Council. While he was away from Memphis, his admirers, under the leadership of the Dean, decided to complete the cathedral, and the finished building was dedicated on 19 January 1926. Bishop Gailor died in 1935.

The cathedral is of white stone, in a "modified type of Early English": it is cruciform with a central tower. The altar (the memorial to the Sisters of St Mary), reredos (a memorial to Sister Hughetta), altar rail, chancel rail, and pulpit are of marble, carved in Italy. The glass is by Len Howard, of Kent, Connecticut.

The Gothic Bishop's House, built in 1902 on the site of Bishop Otey's home, was converted into a Diocesan House after Bishop Gailor's death. The Sisters of St Mary left Memphis in 1910, and the Bishop bought their buildings: these were pulled down in 1952—except for the chapel, built in 1888, which is now part of the cathedral. A parish hall and Sunday School rooms, in the same style as the cathedral, were built on the site.

19

Fifth Province (Mid-West)

ST JAMES'S CATHEDRAL, CHICAGO

The Diocese of Illinois was organized in 1835. The Dioceses of Quincy and Springfield were divided off in 1877, and the name was changed in Chicago in 1884.

Bishop Whitehouse made plans for a cathedral in 1853, and secured some land; but there was opposition to the scheme.

"We are glad to see that the unhappy dispute which threatened to put a stop to the erection of the 'Bishop's Church' (i.e. cathedral, the first formal one in the United States) in the most important and growing city of Chicago have happily come to an end, and Bishop Whitehouse and his convention are uniting in pursuing the good work." (*Ecclesiologist*, No. cxi, December 1855, p. 400.) But this was premature: the site had become unsuitable, and the contract for its purchase was cancelled. The Bishop's plans for building an imposing church were frustrated, and in 1861 he began negotiations for buying the Church of the Atonement, Washington Street, which he converted into the Cathedral of SS. Peter and Paul. This was destroyed by fire in 1920.

St Luke's, Evanston, served for a while as a pro-cathedral, but St James's, Chicago, was the cathedral to all intents and purposes, and on 4 June 1955, was constituted as such.

It was begun in July 1835: the basement was occupied first, and the church itself on 26 March 1837. It was rebuilt by Edward Burling in 1857, and destroyed in the great fire of Chicago, and rebuilt in 1875.

The architects were Clarke and Faulkner.

Some alterations are being planned, particularly the enlargement of the sanctuary.

CHRIST CHURCH CATHEDRAL, EAU CLAIRE

The parish began in 1858, though it was served at first only by itinerant clergy. In 1873 a frame church was erected, which lasted until 1912, when the present church, of limestone, in early 14th-century style, took its place.

The diocese was constituted in 1929, from parts of the Dioceses of Milwaukee and Fond du Lac, and Christ Church became the cathedral.

An educational centre was built in 1954 as an addition to the parish house, and in 1956 the church building was completed in every respect.

The architects for the church and parish house were Purcell, Feick and Elmslie of Minneapolis.

ST PAUL'S CATHEDRAL, FOND DU LAC

Regular church services were held from 1849, and the first St Paul's was built in 1851. A new church was built on the present site in 1865. The diocese was founded in 1875, and the first Bishop, John Henry Hobart Brown, took steps to change the organization of St Paul's from that of a parish to that of a cathedral.

The church was burned down on 25 January 1884. In the rebuilding the transepts and chancel were added, St Augustine's Chapel, the choir room, and the sacristies. The first services were held in the rebuilt cathedral on Easter Sunday 1887. The architect was Richard Michell Upjohn.

It is cruciform with a tower at the (ritual) south-west: the cathedral is, in fact, built north and south.

The font is of marble, under a French Gothic canopy of Bedford stone. The angels in the roof were carved in the Black Forest region of Germany, and were obtained by Bishop Grafton (1889–1912: one of the original members of S.S.J.E.—the Cowley Fathers). Then he ordered the statues of the Apostles; and afterwards invited the family of wood-carvers to Fond du Lac. They established themselves there, and were responsible for most of the woodwork of the cathedral, except for that in the Chapel of St Augustine. For more than 20 years they worked for the churches of the diocese: after Bishop Grafton's death they were merged with a larger firm of church furnishers, and the descendants of the original family no longer live in the city. The paint-

TRINITY CATHEDRAL, CLEVELAND, OHIO

TRINITY CATHEDRAL, CLEVELAND, OHIO

ST MARK'S CATHEDRAL,
GRAND RAPIDS, MICHIGAN

ST MARK'S CATHEDRAL, MINNEAPOLIS, MINNESOTA

ings in the nave and chancel are the work of Miss Anna Milo Upjohn, a niece of Bishop Brown.

The Chapel of St Michael contains a stone from Westminster Abbey, a bust of Bishop Brown, a relief of Jackson Kemper, the first Bishop of the Church in Wisconsin, and the effigy of Bishop Grafton.

The altar of the Chapel of St Ambrose was carved by a Fond du Lac workman: the cross was on the high altar before the fire.

The pulpit was also carved by a local man. The cross on the high altar was given to Bishop Grafton in 1903 by Mrs Meynell Ingram: it is of Spanish workmanship.

In the "north" transept are a figure of St Margaret, by an English sculptress, and the remains of the original font of the cathedral, recovered in 1940.

The Chapel of St Augustine to the left of the chancel was built by Bishop Brown's sister in memory of their parents: it was used as the chapel of the Order of St Monica, a community of widows founded by the Bishop. The woodwork was executed by a local carver. The marble plaque on the front of the altar was the work of a priest, who died soon after executing it: there is a similar one at St Mary's, Kansas City. The paintings of the reredos are said to have come from Italy.

CHRIST CHURCH CATHEDRAL, INDIANAPOLIS

The diocese was constituted in 1838, under the name of Indiana: Michigan City (now Northern Indiana) was set apart in 1895. The name of the diocese was altered to Indianapolis in 1902.

The parish of Christ Church was formed in 1837, and the cornerstone of the first church was laid on 7 May 1838. The church was of wood—"a beautiful Gothic edifice": it was consecrated on 16 December. The present church was designed by William Tinsley (1804–85), who was born and trained in Ireland and practised there, and came to Indianapolis in 1852.[1] It was begun in 1857, and opened in 1859; the bells were placed in the tower in 1860, and the spire was built in 1869. The cost was about $20,000. The Rector, the Reverend J. C. Talbot, afterwards Bishop of the Diocese, wrote: "For architectural beauty and strict truthfulness of construction it is not surpassed by any church edifice in the West, perhaps by few anywhere." It is 13th century in style, with an

[1] For a complete account of Tinsley see J. D. Forbes, *Victorian Architect, the Life and Work of William Tinsley*, 1953.

14

aisleless nave with hammer-beam roof, transepts of very slight projection, and an apsidal chancel.

The Parish House was dedicated in 1928. In 1953–4 the church was restored and redecorated. The architect was George R. West, and the work was done by Rambusch of New York. "The existing marble and mosaic-decorated altar was simplified.... A Crucis Gemma is suspended above the altar and is made precious by the addition of lapis lazuli and malachite. The bishop's throne of carved, fine oak has the added dignity of a simple velvet tester. Choir stalls, likewise of oak, have carved and gilded finials symbolic of the Human and Divine natures of Christ. Three overly prominent apse windows were removed and the entire chancel wall was painted heraldic red, enlivened with pure gold and medieval motifs."

On 10 October 1954, Christ Church was dedicated as the cathedral of the diocese.

ST PAUL'S CATHEDRAL, DETROIT
[DIOCESE OF MICHIGAN]

Detroit was founded by the French, and was under French rule until 1760. After it became part of Upper Canada, the Anglicans were ministered to by British military chaplains and by missionaries of S.P.G. It came under the U.S. flag in 1796, but was visited by the Reverend Richard Pollard, a missionary stationed at Sandwich, Ontario.

The parish was organized in 1824, and in 1827 Bishop John Henry Hobart of New York laid the cornerstone of the first church, which was consecrated in 1828. It was Gothic, with a pinnacled tower. The diocese was organized in 1832, and the first Bishop, Samuel Allen McCoskry, was consecrated in 1836.

The second St Paul's was consecrated in December 1852. "It is built of stone in the Early English style, and is 133 feet long and 70 feet broad. The tower, placed on the south-west corner, is 22 feet square at the base, and has an octagon spire, the top of which is 181 feet from the ground.... The side walls are divided into seven bays by buttresses, doubling at the corners. There is no division, externally or internally, into nave and aisles—one large hall with an open roof. The chancel is a mere recess only 13 feet deep, 27 feet wide. The side windows are divided by slender mullions with tracery in the heads...." (*The*

Register—a Philadelphia Church paper.) This church was moved to Indian Village, Detroit, in 1901, and renamed the Church of the Messiah.

The present cathedral was designed in the Boston office of Cram, Goodhue and Ferguson: George G. Mason of Detroit was the associated architect. The cornerstone was laid by Bishop Williams in 1908, and the church was completed—apart from the tower—and dedicated in 1911: it was consecrated in 1919. The material is grey limestone, and the style is 13th century. Cram was well satisfied with it: "Certainly a Gothic church", he wrote, "and certainly a cathedral, yet it follows no recognized model. I never go inside without a certain feeling of grateful satisfaction and a renewed belief that here something was actually accomplished towards the revitalizing of Christian architecture." It consists of nave with passage aisles, west narthex, and north and south porches; transepts, chancel with chapels and sacristies on each side, and sanctuary without aisles. There is a chapel under the sanctuary, in which the last three bishops of Michigan are buried.

There is much wood-carving by Johann Kirchmeyer—"the last representative", wrote Cram, "of the great medieval schools of wood-carving, though throughout all his work appears a vitality which gives it a modern quality and removes it from the category of mere archaeology". The glass is by Heaton, Butler and Bayne, Mayer, Powell, Willet, and Charles J. Connick (north transept, aisle, and clerestory windows, Connick; aisle windows, Heaton, Butler and Bayne, and Powell; south transept window, Willet). The tile flooring of the chancel, aisles, and narthex was made by the Pewabic Pottery. The altar is of carved Caen stone: the mensa incorporates a stone from Canterbury.

Grace Chapel keeps the name of Grace Church, which was amalgamated with St Paul's in 1909: the altar is a memorial to the first rector and his wife. Two windows by Mayer of Munich were brought from Grace Church, and the lectern came from the old St Paul's. Here are two tapestries woven by Van Aelst of Brussels from designs by Raphael. The tablet given by the Essex Scottish Regiment, as a record of friendship between the United States and Canada, was designed by Cram and Ferguson.

Nativity Chapel has above the altar a painting by Leo Cartwright of the visit of the Magi. The font is here, and also a small font of the early 19th century, in which Indian converts were baptized.

ALL SAINTS' CATHEDRAL, MILWAUKEE

The first Bishop, Jackson Kemper (1854–70) raised the question of a cathedral at his diocesan council in 1865. The council in 1868 asked the General Convention for legislature to give the diocese authority to establish a cathedral at Milwaukee. This was given, but there was opposition to the scheme.

In 1873 a building was purchased from the Congregationalists, and opened as All Saints' Cathedral on Whitsunday 1873.

The Bishop (Welles) at the council of 1879 described the need and purpose of a cathedral; and in 1882 he reviewed the subject from 1865 onwards. Then the Committee on Constitution and Canons presented legislature regarding the cathedral, which was acceptable to the Bishop; and this was adopted.

GRACE CATHEDRAL, MENOMINEE
[Diocese of Northern Michigan]

The Missionary Jurisdiction of Northern Michigan was organized in 1893: it became the Diocese of Marquette in 1895, and the name was changed back to Northern Michigan in 1937.

Grace parish was organized in 1887. A frame church, dedicated in 1886, was moved to a new site in 1899.

In 1926 the land opposite the County Court House was bought, with a house and barn: the ground floor of the house was converted into a chapel and parish rooms, and the upper floor into a residence for the rector. The surrounding land was to be divided up and sold, and a new church was to be built on the property.

The depression caused difficulties and delay, and the church was not built until 1950. In 1955 it became the cathedral of the diocese. It is very simple Gothic, faced with light tan brick, and furnished in oak. The marble font came from the previous church.

TRINITY CATHEDRAL, CLEVELAND
[Diocese of Ohio]

The original church was founded in 1816, by a congregation meeting in the home of Phineas Shephard of Brooklyn Village. The diocese was organized in 1818, with Philander Chase as its first Bishop.

The present cathedral, of Indiana limestone, was finished in 1907.

The architect was Charles Frederick Schweinfurth, who was born at Auburn, New York, in 1856. He graduated in 1872, travelled in England, France, Italy, and Spain, and studied architecture at New York, Boston, and Philadelphia. He practised at New York from 1880 until 1883, when he moved to Cleveland. His work was chiefly domestic, and church and collegiate buildings. Julius Adolph Schweinfurth (1858–1931) was his partner. He died in 1919.

The cathedral is 15th century in style, cruciform, with a central tower.

The Mather memorial window is by William Willet; side chapel window by Young; chancel aisle window by Connick; chancel window by Hardman.

There is an oak boss from Southwark Cathedral.

ST JOHN'S CATHEDRAL, QUINCY

The Diocese of Illinois, including the entire State, was organized in 1835, and Philander Chase was appointed Bishop. The parish of Quincy was founded in 1837, and is the fourth oldest in the State. The diocese was organized in 1877, and St John's was designated the cathedral church.

The nave was built about 1850, and the transepts and chancel were added some five years later. It is of stone, in the plainest Lancet style, with an embattled tower: there is a plaster ceiling.

The altar and the carved and painted reredos, by Ralph Adams Cram, were erected in 1901: the altar in the north transept is about ten years later.

In 1956 the interior was completely restored, replastered, and re-decorated.

ST PAUL'S WAYSIDE CATHEDRAL, CINCINATTI [Diocese of Southern Ohio]

The diocese was organized in 1875.

St Paul's Cathedral, completed in 1852, was taken down in 1937, and the Bishop decided not to rebuild immediately. He conceived the idea of a mobile cathedral—a large trailer fitted as a chapel, with a movable end. This is sent round to do mission work in the diocese.

ST PAUL'S CATHEDRAL, SPRINGFIELD

The first service was held by Bishop Philander Chase in June 1835, and the parish was organized immediately afterwards. The first church, a frame building, was begun in the summer of 1838, and first used on 1 September.

The permanent church was begun in 1846, and consecrated on 25 June 1848: the architect was Henry Dresser, a brother of the rector. It was simple Gothic, rather old-fashioned for its date, with long, unadorned two-light windows and a pinnacled and battlemented tower. The *Illinois Daily Journal* wrote: "Having been designed by a western architect, as well as executed by our own workmen, and with funds collected mostly on the spot, it may be considered highly creditable to all who have been engaged in its erection and decoration."

The screen was erected, and the church was reseated and otherwise adorned, towards the end of the century.

The diocese was organized in 1877.

In 1911 the parish decided to build a new church on a different site. In 1912 the congregation moved into the parish hall, and the old church was pulled down. Much of the stone—Sangamon sandstone—and many of the furnishings were re-used in the new building, which was ready by 1913. The church, with sacristies, choir room and offices, guild rooms and hall, cost rather over $66,000.

The plans were made by John Sutcliff of Chicago, diocesan architect, and approved by Ralph Adams Cram.

The style is Perp., with a Yorkshire-looking tower. The pillars are of concrete, wainscoted, and the arches of red brick: the roof is a hammer-beam. William Ridgely, who died in 1918, left a legacy, which was used for a new organ, altar, reredos, and sanctuary floor. The altar is of Caen stone; the oak reredos was carved by Alois Lang. The American Seating Co. had the contract for the whole work. There is glass by the Willet Co. of Philadelphia: the Hereford-Moore window is by Jacoby of St Louis, Mo.

ST MARK'S CATHEDRAL, GRAND RAPIDS
[DIOCESE OF WESTERN MICHIGAN]

The diocese was organized in 1874, and the first bishop was consecrated in 1875.

St Mark's Church was founded in 1836, and the building was completed and opened in 1841. It is of local limestone, in a very simple Gothic style, with two small octagonal towers at the west end. The transepts were completed about 1868, and the chapel, of brick, was erected in 1873. The towers were remodelled about 1888. They have most original Gothic tops, which might remind Londoners of the tower of St Mary Magdalene's, Bermondsey. The stucco has recently been moved from the walls.

20

Sixth Province (North West)

ST JOHN'S CATHEDRAL, DENVER
[DIOCESE OF COLORADO]

The first services were held in 1860. Soon afterwards a parish—St John's Church in the Wilderness—was organized, and a small church was built. In September 1879 the Reverend H. M. Hart came from England to take charge of the parish, where he remained for 41 years. On St Matthew's Day 1880, the cornerstone of a new and much larger church was laid, which was to become the first cathedral of the diocese.

The Missionary District of Colorado and parts adjacent was constituted in 1865; the diocese was organized in 1887. Western Colorado was made a Missionary District in 1892: in 1898 it was made part of the Missionary District of Salt Lake: in 1907 it became a Missionary District again: and in 1919 it was merged with the Diocese of Colorado.

In May 1903 the church was almost entirely destroyed by fire, and the congregation worshipped for a time in Temple Emanuel. The site of the present cathedral was bought, and the chapter house was built; it was used for worship from 1904 to 1911 during the building of the nave of the cathedral. The first services were held in the new building on 5 November 1911.

The architects were Tracy, Swartwout and Lichfield of New York. Evarts Tracy was born in New York in 1868. He took his B.A. at Yale in 1890, and was at the École des Beaux-Arts from 1892 to 1894. He was with McKim, Mead and White from 1890 to 1895, and alone from 1895 to 1901: in 1901 he entered into partnership with Egerton Swartwout (1870–1943). He died in 1922.

The body of the church, of Indiana limestone, is in the 15th-century style, and consists of vaulted nave with passage aisles and a tall clerestory, with two towers: the apsidal choir is of brick, and was designed in Romanesque style to contain the 11 windows saved from the old cathedral.

The reredos is the work of Josef Mayr and Peter Rendl of Ober-ammergau: there are 17 figures, carved in oak, of the principal men responsible for the English Bible: in the centre is a figure of Christ. The carving of the pillars and of the stalls is by Rendl, who also executed Geibert's Last Supper for the front of the altar.

Eight aisle windows, and the large window over the gallery, are by Edward Frampton of London; clerestory glass is by Phipps, Ball and Burnham; two aisle and two clerestory windows are by C. J. Connick; and there is a small window by Tiffany over the north doors. The windows in St Martin's Chapel are by D'Ascenzo.

TRINITY CATHEDRAL, DAVENPORT
[DIOCESE OF IOWA]

The diocese was organized in 1853. Henry Washington Lee, the first Bishop, was responsible for the building of the cathedral, which was consecrated on 18 June 1873. The architect was Edward T. Potter of New York. John David Wolfe of New York, with his daughter, gave $25,000, and David J. Ely of Chicago and New York gave $15,000 as a memorial to his daughter Mrs Sarah Ely Parsons.

It is French Gothic in style, of stone, with a roof of variegated tiles, and consists of nave of four bays with aisles, and apsidal chancel. There is the base of a tower at the south-east: it was to have been surmounted with a short French-looking spire.

Deanery, Parish House, Diocesan House, and Bishop's residence are grouped round the cathedral.

DIOCESE OF MINNESOTA

1. CATHEDRAL OF OUR MERCIFUL SAVIOUR, FARIBAULT

This was the first church in America to be built as a cathedral. It was founded by Henry Benjamin Whipple, the Apostle of the Indians, who was appointed Bishop of Minnesota in 1859. When he came to Faribault, he found a flourishing Episcopal community under the Reverend James Lloyd Breck, one of the pioneers of this area, and a worker among the Indians. He and his colleague, the Reverend David P. Sanford, had built a Church of the Good Shepherd. Breck raised

$4,000 among the people, and Alexander Faribault, a French-Canadian fur-trader and a Roman Catholic, gave seven acres of land for the use of the Bishop—who therefore decided to make Faribault his see city, and began the cathedral in 1862: the cornerstone was laid on 16 July. The dedication was suggested by the Right Reverend A. C. Coxe, Bishop of Western New York. Work went on rather slowly: "When we had means we worked, when we had none we waited on God in prayer." The church was completed, except for the tower, in 1869, when Bishop Jackson Kemper of Wisconsin consecrated it. The cost was about $100,000.

Dr Breck had established a school, which developed into Shattuck Grammar School; and a school of divinity. Bishop Whipple and his wife began St Mary's Hall. Bishop Machray of Rupertsland paid a visit in 1868, and was shown the cathedral and the other institutions. "Bishop Whipple, with the accents of profound regret, said that their organization had come somewhat late into the field": Machray resolved that his organization in Rupertsland would be in time.

The cathedral is 13th century in style, cruciform, with an aisleless nave and apsidal chancel: the material is blue limestone from the east bank of the Straight River. Glass by George Morgan and brothers of New York. One window was the gift of the Reverend Ezekiel Gilbert Gear, the first missionary of the Church in Minnesota; two were given by Indians, and others by parishes, or friends of the Bishop.

The architect was James Renwick (1818–95) of New York, who designed St Patrick's (R.C.) Cathedral, New York; Grace Church, Calvary Church, etc.

Bishop Whipple died on 16 September 1901, and was buried under the altar. The tower—Somerset Perp. in appearance, except for its height—was completed to his memory, and dedicated on All Saints' Day 1902.

The bishop's throne was erected in the 1930's: some of the carving was done by Anton Lang. In 1934 the old Bishop's Residence was pulled down, and the chapel was removed to the cathedral. The plaques and the triptych were made for the Whipples during a stay in Italy. The chair belonged to William White, first Bishop of Pennsylvania (1787–1836).

In the same year the chapel under the chancel was constructed. The wooden cross on Bishop Whipple's tomb is from the old Church of the Good Shepherd.

Minneapolis is now the see city of the diocese, but Faribault still has the title of cathedral.

2. ST MARK'S CATHEDRAL, MINNEAPOLIS

St Mark's began as a mission established in 1858, and the first building was a small wooden chapel, consecrated on 22 June 1859. On 26 February 1863, it was moved to another site. The parish was incorporated in 1868. A new church of stone was then built on Sixth Street, and consecrated on 21 September 1871. This was used until 1908, by which time plans had been made for a large new church on a different site.

The architect was Edwin Hawley Hewitt (1874–1939), who had worked during his time at the University in the office of Cass Gilbert, the architect of Minnesota's Capitol. After graduating, he studied at Boston, and entered the office of a firm of Boston architects. He then studied for four years at the École des Beaux-Arts at Paris, under Jean Louis Pascal, and travelled in England, Spain, Switzerland, and Italy: he returned to America in 1904. He wrote: "I was brought up in the Church. My father (Dr Charles Nathaniel Hewitt) served on the building committee of one of the most beautiful little churches in the Northwest, namely, Christ Church of Red Wing.... I got my earliest impressions there. I believe that this laid the basis of any development I have made along the line of church architecture."

The cornerstone of St Mark's was laid on 15 November 1908, and the church was opened on 29 September 1910: it was consecrated, after the debt on the building had been paid off, on 13 May 1920. In 1941 it became the new cathedral for the Diocese of Minnesota.

It is 15th century in style, and consists of nave, aisles, and chancel, with a (ritual) south-west tower. The exterior is of Bedford Indiana limestone; the stonework of the interior is of Kasota stone, and the walls are of brick. The window tracery and vaulting ribs are of manufactured stone, and the filling of the vaulting is of hard-burned tiles. The floor is paved with Ruabon tiles, except in the chancel and sanctuary, which have tiles made by the Grueby Co., of Perth Amboy, N.J.

In May 1949 the figure of Christ was placed on the façade—a memorial to Bishop Whipple. It was carved by John Rood, who afterwards executed the rest of the sculpture on the front, completed in 1952, in memory of Frederick Grant Atkinson.

The glass of the large five-light window is by Charles J. Connick; the aisle windows are by Connick, and Weston and Leighton of Minneapolis. The font, of Knoxville marble, is the work of John Evans of Boston. The pulpit was carved by Isaac Kirchmeyer of Oberammergau, in the workshop of William F. Ross and Co., of East Cambridge, Mass.

The high altar is of Kasota stone: the wooden reredos was carved in the studios of Irving and Casson of Boston. The glass in the window above (1911) was designed by William Bladen, and made by the Gorham Company of New York. Four clerestory windows are by Charles J. Connick. Capitals in the choir were carved by James Earl Fraser of New York, Arnold Flaten (two), and Alonzo Hauser, from designs by John Rood (two).

The Hewitt Memorial Chapel, to the right of the chancel, was dedicated in 1920 in memory of Helen Hewitt, daughter of the architect of the church, who himself painted the picture in the reredos. The painting over the altar was executed by Harry Winfield Rubins, who was also responsible for the woodwork. The glass is by Charles J. Connick.

The Jaffray Chapel, in the Parish House, contains the altar from the old St Mark's, and the glass from the north transept window, by John La Farge.

TRINITY CATHEDRAL, DULUTH

When the General Convention met at Minneapolis in 1895, the Diocese of Minnesota petitioned the Church to take over the northern two-thirds of the diocese, and constitute it a Missionary District. In October 1896 a Bishop of Duluth was elected, and he was consecrated on 2 February 1897. He was anxious that the Missionary District should become a diocese as soon as the endowment could be raised: this was achieved in 1907.

Trinity Cathedral began with the opening of a Sunday school in 1901 in a disused car-barn. In 1905 a priest took charge, and in October the mission was reorganized as Trinity Parish. About this time, the building was bought, together with the land around it. Plans for a church to serve as a cathedral were made by John Sutcliff of Chicago, with the help of a local architect. It was decided to build on the east of the site, to allow for enlargement, or for the erection of other buildings: if more accommodation had been needed, the church would have been used as a chapter house or convention hall.

The cornerstone was laid on 29 September 1906, and the first service

was held in the lower chapel on 2 February 1907. The completed building was dedicated on Trinity Sunday.

In 1909 the constitution and statutes of the cathedral were adopted,
and in 1915 the legislature passed an act of incorporation. When the
debt was paid off, the cathedral was consecrated on 15 September 1918.
Many of the furnishings were gifts.

When the diocese was reunited with Minnesota in 1944, it was
decided to retain Trinity as a cathedral for the time being; but there
were difficulties, and, as another church existed nearby, it was decided
in 1955 to close it. The building and its real estate were sold in November to a Lutheran Church. Since then, plans have been made for building a new church at the east end of Duluth—St Edward the Confessor
—with the proceeds from the sale.

ST PETER'S PRO-CATHEDRAL, HELENA
[DIOCESE OF MONTANA]

The Missionary District was constituted in 1880, and the diocese was
organized in 1904.

The church was built in 1880, of stone, at a cost of about $11,000.
New building by Whitehouse and Price: glass by Charles J. Connick.

TRINITY CATHEDRAL, OMAHA
[DIOCESE OF NEBRASKA]

Jackson Kemper, Missionary Bishop of Indiana and Missouri, and
Bishop Lee of Iowa, held the first Episcopal service in Omaha on 13 July
1856, and Trinity Church was organized afterwards. It was a mission
attached to the Diocese of Iowa, and shared a priest with Council Bluffs,
Iowa. A church was begun, but the panic of 1857 held up the work.
An appeal was made in 1859, and eventually a very modest, chapel-like
building was put up on a site leased for ten years from Jesse Lowe, the
first mayor of Omaha, who gave the bricks. The mission became a
parish in 1864.

Robert Harper Clarkson was appointed Missionary Bishop of
Nebraska in 1865, and the diocese was organized in 1868. A new site
for Trinity was purchased in 1866, and a larger church was built at a
cost of about $15,000, which was considered to be too much. It became
a pro-cathedral in 1868, but was destroyed by fire in 1869. A temporary
wooden church was built, which was ready by the end of the year, and

plans for a permanent cathedral were made by C. C. Haight of New York. There was considerable delay in beginning to build; meanwhile, in 1872, Trinity was made the cathedral church of the diocese.

Under Frank Millspaugh, who was appointed Dean in 1876, a renewed effort was made, and in 1880 plans made by Mr Harrison were adopted, and a contract was made for the erection of the present building. The design had to be reduced, and spire and chapter house were left out. The crypt was first opened for worship, and the completed building was consecrated in 1883. The rectory was begun in 1886: it was adapted as a parish house in 1920. In the 40's the church was entirely renovated, and the Nativity Chapel was constructed. A new parish house was built in 1956–7.

The cathedral is of stone, and consists of aisled nave with north-west tower, aisled transepts, and chancel with apsidal sanctuary. The style is Victorian Gothic, with slender pillars, stiff-leaf foliage, single-light windows with tracery in the heads, and larger traceried windows in the fronts of the nave and transepts.

The western part of the State was set apart as the Missionary Jurisdiction of the Platte in 1889. It was later called Laramie and Kearney, and was constituted the Missionary District of Western Nebraska in 1913. It was reunited with Nebraska in 1946. The pro-cathedral was St Mark's, Hastings, by R. A. Cram—"perhaps the most classic piece of church architecture in the Middle West".

GETHSEMANE CATHEDRAL, FARGO
[Missionary District of North Dakota]

North Dakota was included in the North-West Diocese in 1859, and in the Missionary Jurisdiction of Nebraska and Dakota in 1865. The Missionary Jurisdiction of Dakota was organized in 1868, and North Dakota was divided off in 1883.

The first service in Fargo was held in 1872, and a church was built in 1874. The Bishop said in his report for 1884: "The church, although a frame building, is a handsome structure. Especially does its interior decoration—which is rich, chaste, and devotional—give dignity to the House of God."

In 1890 he "ordered from the Pullman Palace Car Company a Gospel Car with a seating capacity of 80 and supplied with a robing room, pulpit, and font": it was labelled The Cathedral Car of North Dakota.

A new church was begun at the end of the century, and first used on 11 February 1900. The basement is of red sandstone, and it was hoped to build the whole church of the same material; but funds were insufficient, and it had to be of wood. The cost was $14,000. It was made a cathedral in September 1900, and consecrated, after the debt had been paid off, in December 1913.

In 1918 the Hunter Memorial Chapel was constructed in the basement. The reredos, the work of Mrs Hallenburg, was erected in 1938. In 1941 the chancel was furnished with a new bishop's chair, choir stalls, altar rails, and wainscot, and the nave was improved. The rebuilding of the basement was completed in 1946 at a cost of $27,000.

CALVARY CATHEDRAL, SIOUX FALLS
[MISSIONARY DISTRICT OF SOUTH DAKOTA]

South Dakota was part of the old North-West Diocese. In 1871 the western part was included in the Missionary Jurisdiction of Niobrara—which was combined with the rest of the State in the Missionary District of South Dakota in 1883. The first Bishop was William Hobart Hare.

The first church at Sioux Falls dated from 1872. In 1887 John Jacob Astor gave money to the Bishop for building "a church of permanent character, not so expensive as to be a burden for its support in a new country", as a memorial to his wife Charlotte Augusta Astor. The cornerstone was laid on 5 December 1888, and the completed church was consecrated on 18 December 1889.

It is of local stone, in a simple Victorian French Gothic style, with aisled nave and apsidal chancel of the same height.

In 1946 the interior was redecorated, and given new seating, lighting, reredos, choir stalls, etc., under the cathedral architect, Harold Spitznagel of Sioux Falls. Four new windows were inserted, by Robert M. Berg of St Paul, who also designed the redecoration. The chancel screen was taken down, and the baptistery remodelled.

ST MATTHEW'S CATHEDRAL, LARAMIE
[MISSIONARY DISTRICT OF WYOMING]

The first church here was consecrated on 21 September 1869: it was of wood, with an open roof. The cost was about $5,000, of which $1,000 was given by Bishop George Maxwell Randall, Bishop of Colorado and the parts adjacent from 1865 to 1873. Wyoming finally became a separate Missionary District in 1907.

The cathedral was established during the episcopate of the Right Reverend Ethelbert Talbot (1887–98).

The cornerstone was laid in 1892, and the cathedral, while still incomplete, was opened on 17 December 1896.

The architect was William Halsey Wood.

It consists of nave and aisles, with an engaged west tower surmounted by a broach spire; transepts, and chancel with small flanking towers towards the east.

There is a basement beneath for Sunday schools and guilds.

Laramie was the first community to offer the Bishop a home; and since it was on the railway, and was the site of the State University, and 50 miles nearer the centre of the State than the capital, Cheyenne, he seems to have considered it a good place to settle in. The centre of population is no longer near Laramie, but the cathedral remains.

TRINITY CATHEDRAL, DAVENPORT, IOWA

TRINITY CATHEDRAL, DULUTH, MINNESOTA

ST JOHN'S CATHEDRAL, ALBUQUERQUE, NEW MEXICO

GRACE CATHEDRAL, TOPEKA, KANSAS (BEFORE THE COMPLETION OF THE TOWERS)

21

Seventh Province (South West)

TRINITY CATHEDRAL, LITTLE ROCK, ARKANSAS

The diocese was organized in 1871, and Trinity parish in 1873.

The Bishop said in his report for 1878–9 that he wished to build a cathedral at Little Rock: a church to hold 800 could be erected for $6,000 or less. In 1884 he reported that the west end had been built—nave, aisles, tower, and baptistery—and a temporary chancel. He wanted to add one more bay before building the transept and permanent chancel. The entire cost of what had been so far erected, with windows, seats, etc., was only $4,500: the cathedral could be completed for $6,000 more.

The architect was his son, the Reverend A. W. Pierce, who superintended the work, and the contractor was Ambrose Pettifer of Little Rock. The chancel was begun in 1888.

The cathedral is of brick, in plain 13th-century style, with a low tower.

ST MATTHEW'S CATHEDRAL, DALLAS

The first St Matthew's, a wooden building, was first occupied in the summer of 1870. In 1874 the Reverend Alexander Charles Garrett was elected as the first Missionary Bishop of North Texas, and chose St Matthew's as his cathedral. The Missionary District became the Diocese of Dallas in 1895.

In 1876 another site was bought, and on 4 May the Bishop laid the foundation stone of a new church, which was first used on 3 June 1877,

15

though it was not yet complete. It was cruciform, 13th century in style, with a low-south-west tower, added somewhat later.

But the site was too near the railway station, so it was sold in 1889, and a new site bought on Ervay Street. The foundation stone of the third St Matthew's was laid on 22 December 1893. This ambitious stone church, which cost $100,000, was opened in 1895: after the debt was paid off, it was consecrated on 20 December 1899.

In 1927 the Vestry decided that another move must be made: the population had shifted, and St Matthew's had become a down-town church. On 22 June 1929, the congregation moved to the Chapel of St Mary's College, built in 1900, which was enlarged. A new cathedral was planned, but, with the depression, the scheme had to be abandoned.

GRACE CATHEDRAL, TOPEKA, KANSAS

Work was begun at Topeka in January 1857, and the Diocese of Kansas was organized in 1859.

On 9 September 1860, Grace Mission was incorporated as Grace Church, and on 15th of the same month plans were completed for building a church. It was begun in 1861, but was not ready for worship until 1865. It was a humble, lancet-lit building, with no chancel, and the base of a tower at the south-west. In 1873 an extension of 25 feet was made, including a chancel, the tower was completed, and a spire was built. On 5 June 1879, Grace Church was made the cathedral of the diocese.

Plans were then made for building a new cathedral, and a Guild Hall which could be used for worship until the cathedral was ready. The cornerstone of the Guild Hall was laid in 1888. But a period of financial depression followed; the hall, used as a pro-cathedral, was completed, but with a debt on it, and there was no chance of building the cathedral.

Early in the 20th century the scheme was revived under Bishop Millspaugh. A site was obtained, and a considerable sum of money was raised; the ground was broken in 1909, and the foundation stone was laid on 3 May 1910.

The exterior of the building was completed in 1912, after which work stopped for four years. In January 1916 a new campaign for funds was begun, which raised $50,000. Bishop Millspaugh, who had taken the greatest interest in the building and furnishing of the cathedral, died in that year. The cathedral—complete except for the top stage of the towers—was consecrated on 4 March 1917, by the Right Reverend James Wise, fourth Bishop of Kansas.

The architects were Root and Siemens of Kansas City.

The cathedral—which stands south and north—consists of nave with narthex and twin towers, aisles of three bays, and chancel with an internal apse: to the left is a chapel, and to the right are a sacristy and choir rooms. The arcades are low, with four-centred arches, and the nave has a hammer-beam roof. The completed towers were dedicated on 24 April 1955: they were to have been surmounted with spires, but the design was altered: the top stage of each tower now has octagonal angle turrets with pinnacles, and smaller pinnacles rising from shafts between the windows.

The glass is by the Van Gerichten Art Glass Studios, Columbus, Ohio, except for the clerestory windows in the chancel, which are the work of Giannini and Hilgart of Chicago. The glass in the rose window of the east transept is dated 1722. It consists of fragments of the glass made for the rose window in the north transept of Westminster Abbey, designed by Thornhill and executed by Joshua Price, which was inserted after the reconstruction of the window, and of Solomon's Porch, by William Dickinson, under Wren, in 1719–22. When Bishop Millspaugh was in London for the Lambeth Conference of 1907, he noticed the glass, in boxes in the cloister of the Abbey, and asked for some of it for his new cathedral. The Dean agreed, and a pattern of the window was sent to England, and the glass was fitted into it.

The carving of the altar, reredos, sanctuary panelling, lectern, and pulpit is by Alois Lang of Oberammergau. The screen, erected in 1954, is the work of the Ossit Church Furniture Company of Janseville, Wisconsin.

The painting of the Ascension on the wall of the apse above the altar is by Martin Hennings of Chicago.

The chapel to the left of the chancel was the gift of Dr J. C. McClinton and his wife, in memory of his father and mother. The altar and the wainscot of the sanctuary are made from pews from the original church, which were afterwards in the Guild Hall: the font, of Carrara marble, was in the Bethany College Chapel. The painting of the Transfiguration above the altar is the work of George M. Stone.

The cathedral possesses a baptismal spoon made for King Olaf of

Norway in 1571. There are two stones brought from England by Bishop Millspaugh: one from St Martin's, Canterbury, and one from Lindisfarne.

CHRIST CHURCH CATHEDRAL, ST LOUIS
[DIOCESE OF MISSOURI]

A site was secured in 1826, and building was begun. The congregation contributed $2,000, and Mr Horrell collected $700 in New York and Philadelphia. The church was opened on 10 November 1829. "A neat little building... but looking more like an academy than a church". It had a rusticated basement, four square-headed windows at the sides, and a lantern in the middle. It was designed by George Morton and Laveille.

The Missionary Jurisdiction of Missouri and Indiana was organized in 1835, and the Diocese of Missouri in 1840.

The plans for a new church were drawn and accepted in 1859.

The foundations were completed by 1860, but the Civil War divided the city, and prevented building for four years. The first service was held on Christmas Day 1867, though the building was not complete. It was admired by Charles Kingsley when he visited St Louis.

The architect was Leopold Eidlitz, who was born in Prague in 1823, and came to New York in 1843, where he became draughtsman to Richard Upjohn, with whom he built St George's, New York. He died in 1908. "Without doubt it is its author's masterpiece in the stricter kind of church architecture, a piece of skillful and scholarly Gothic in which the scholarliness by no means excludes individuality."

It consists of aisled nave with a north-west tower, transepts, and apsidal chancel. The Mary E. Bofinger Chapel was designed by J. B. Legg, and consecrated on 17 May 1894.

The cathedral was completed, and the north-west tower with octagonal lantern built, in 1912: the architect was Kivas Tully (1820–1905). The reredos of Caen stone was erected: it was copied from the altar screen at Winchester, changed slightly in proportion and detail, with a carving of the Nativity instead of a row of saints immediately above the altar. It was carved by Harry Hems.

The original glass was by Owen Doremus.

ST JOHN'S CATHEDRAL, ALBUQUERQUE
[DIOCESE OF NEW MEXICO AND
SOUTH-WEST TEXAS]

New Mexico was organized as a missionary jurisdiction in 1893, in which South-west Texas was included in 1895. It became a diocese in 1952.

The first Episcopal service in Albuquerque was held in 1879. A room in the old Court House was fitted up as a chapel. The first St John's—"a substantial stone church"—was opened in November 1882: in 1900 the mission became a parish, and subscriptions were taken to complete the building. It was made a pro-cathedral in 1920, and a cathedral in 1927. In 1930 the Cathedral House was built, with a cloister and vestibule, and the tower was heightened and a spire was added.

The new cathedral was opened on 11 November 1952: the cost has been more than $300,000. The furnishings are not yet complete. It is of brick, in a simple 13th-century style, with aisled nave and chancel, sanctuary, a western porch, and incomplete south-west tower.

ST PAUL'S CATHEDRAL, OKLAHOMA CITY

The first church, of wood, was built by the Reverend D. G. Gunn in 1893, and a new church was consecrated on 1 December 1901. In 1903 it was decided to build a permanent church at the corner of Seventh Street and Robinson Avenue, and the cornerstone was laid during the summer. It was completed in 1904.

In 1907 the territory of Oklahoma became the 46th State of the Union, and the capital was moved from Guthrie to Oklahoma City. It was thought that it should also be the See city of the Missionary District, and St Paul's was accepted by the Bishop as a pro-cathedral in 1908. It was consecrated on 28 August 1927. The Missionary District was made a diocese in 1938.

In 1947 an appeal was made for $300,000 to restore the cathedral and parish house, and to build a cathedral centre.

The cathedral is of grey brick with stone dressings, in a kind of Jacobean style, with dormer windows and a low tower. A new west doorway was added as part of the restoration. The altar and reredos are a memorial to Margaret Lee Culbertson.

CHRIST CHURCH CATHEDRAL, SALINA
[MISSIONARY DISTRICT]

The Missionary District was organized in 1903.

The cathedral was built as a memorial to Hermon Griswold Batterson, by Mrs H. G. Batterson of New York City. It was consecrated in 1907. The architects were Henry Macomb and Charles M. Burns of Philadelphia. It is built of native limestone, in 15th-century style; the altar is of Carthage marble, and the reredos of Silverdale limestone. There is a central tower with 11 bells. The interior woodwork, of black oak, was carved by the Lang family of Oberammergau.

CHRIST CHURCH CATHEDRAL, HOUSTON
[DIOCESE OF TEXAS]

The parish was organized in 1839, and during a visit by Bishop Leonidas Polk, four or five thousand dollars was raised for the building of a church. In 1841 there were only 17 communicants: Texas was still considered a foreign country, since independence had only recently been won at San Jacinto; Houston was remote and undeveloped, and yellow fever was common. But by 1845 the number of communicants in Houston had risen to 80.

Texas was administered first by Bishop Polk of Louisiana, and later by Bishop George W. Freeman of Arkansas, through the Foreign Committee of the Board of Missions. The diocese was organized in 1849. The congregation worshipped first in the Capitol Building. Then a brick church was built in 1846. The second church was completed in 1860 at a cost of $16,000. The cornerstone of the present church was laid on 31 March 1893. The architect was J. A. Tempest. It is of brick— some taken from the church of 1860—cruciform in plan and Gothic in style, with a somewhat elaborate roof. Damage was done by a fire in 1938.

Latham Building, with Sunday school classrooms, hall, library, and church offices, was opened in 1951.

GRACE AND HOLY TRINITY CATHEDRAL,
KANSAS CITY [DIOCESE OF WEST MISSOURI]

The first Episcopal services were held at Kansas City in September 1857 by the Right Reverend Cicero Stephens Hawks, first Bishop of

Missouri. The first parish to be organized was St Luke's, for which a church was opened in 1867. In July 1870 St Paul's Parish was organized: three years later the name was altered to Grace. A site for a church was bought in 1872, and the building was completed in 1874.

A new church was begun in June 1893. The parish decided that no debt should be incurred, but that work should only be undertaken when it could be paid for. The new church was first used for worship on 16 December 1894. The Reverend Cameron Mann, the Rector, afterwards Missionary Bishop of North Dakota and Bishop of South Florida, was the moving spirit. The tower was left incomplete. From 1911–17 the Rector was the Right Reverend Sidney C. Partridge, Bishop of the Diocese, to whom the Vestry had given the property as a Bishop's Church.

Trinity Parish was organized in 1883. In 1917 it was decided to merge the two churches, and Grace was kept as the place of worship.

At the meeting of the Diocesan Convention at Christ Church, Boonville, on 14–15 May 1935, Grace and Holy Trinity Church was offered as the cathedral church of the diocese. The offer was accepted, and the church was inaugurated as the cathedral on 29 October 1935.

It is of stone, with an apsidal chancel, and an elaborate ironwork screen.

ST MARK'S PRO-CATHEDRAL, SAN ANTONIO
[DIOCESE OF WEST TEXAS]

A Missionary District was constituted in 1874, and it was organized as a diocese in 1904.

The church was begun in 1860, but building was delayed by the Civil War: it was first used on 28 March 1875, and consecrated on St Mark's Day 1881. The architect was Richard Upjohn. It is built of cream-coloured limestone, and consists of nave and aisles of five bays, and an apsidal chancel. (No cathedral is mentioned for this diocese in the Episcopal Church Annual.)

22

Eighth Province (The Pacific)

HOLY TRINITY CATHEDRAL, JUNEAU
[MISSIONARY DISTRICT OF ALASKA]

When Bishop Rowe went to the Missionary District (in 1895) he made Sitka his See city, and St Peter's the cathedral. When Juneau was made the capital, he went there, and adopted Holy Trinity—a wooden building on a stone basement—as the cathedral. (But no cathedral is mentioned in the *Episcopal Church Annual*.)

TRINITY CATHEDRAL, PHOENIX
[MISSIONARY DISTRICT OF ARIZONA]

At the General Convention in 1874, the territories of New Mexico and Arizona were constituted a single Missionary Jurisdiction, and the first Missionary Bishop was consecrated in 1875. In 1892 Arizona and New Mexico both became Districts rather than Jurisdictions, but were under the same Bishop until 1911.

The first Episcopal service at Phoenix seems to have been held in 1885. The cornerstone of the first Trinity Church was laid on Trinity Sunday 1888: the building was completed at a cost of $5,500, and the first service was held on the Feast of the Epiphany 1889. It was of brick —a poor effort at Gothic, with two porches, one carried up into a low tower with a slate spire. The mission became a parish in 1908, and Trinity was later made a pro-cathedral.

On 31 October 1915, the cornerstone was laid for new buildings on the present site. The parish house was built first, services being held on the ground floor: the bishop's house was completed in 1918. The architects were Shepley, Rutan and Coolidge of Boston. George Foster Shepley was born at St Louis, Mo., in 1860, and studied at Washington

GRACE CATHEDRAL, SAN FRANCISCO, CALIFORNIA

GRACE CATHEDRAL, SAN FRANCISCO, CALIFORNIA

ST PAUL'S CATHEDRAL,
LOS ANGELES

ST MARK'S CATHEDRAL,
SALT LAKE CITY, UTAH

CATHEDRAL OF ST JOHN THE EVANGELIST, SPOKANE, WASHINGTON

TRINITY CATHEDRAL, PHOENIX, ARIZONA

HOLY TRINITY
CATHEDRAL,
HAVANA, CUBA

PRO-CATHEDRAL OF
THE HOLY TRINITY,
PARIS

University and Massachusetts Technical Institute: the firm succeeded to the practice of H. H. Richardson.

In 1920 the building of the cathedral began: it was consecrated on 1 April 1921. It is in Spanish Mission style, based on a church in Majorca. The walls are of brick, faced with white tufa from the Arizona hills: the woodwork is of California redwood.

GRACE CATHEDRAL, SAN FRANCISCO
[DIOCESE OF CALIFORNIA]

The original Grace Church was founded in 1849, and in September 1863, the Right Reverend William Ingraham Kip—Missionary Bishop from 1853, and Diocesan Bishop from 1857 to 1893—placed his episcopal chair there. This church was destroyed in the 1906 fire. Bishop Nichols and the Vestry decided to dissolve the parish and institute Grace Cathedral: the new site was given by the Crocker family.

The first drawings for the new cathedral were made by G. F. Bodley. The plans were revised and adapted to local conditions by Lewis Parsons Hobart—who was born in 1873, studied at the École des Beaux-Arts from 1900 to 1902, and was in practice at San Francisco from 1906. Afterwards, Cram and Ferguson were associated with him. Nothing really remains of Bodley.

On 27 January 1914, the Founder's crypt was opened. Work was halted by the Great War, and resumed at the end of the 20's: it was delayed again by the economic depression, but by 1940 the sanctuary, choir, transepts, Chapel of Grace, three bays of the nave, and one of the towers were completed. A carillon of 43 bells, by Gillett and Johnson, has been placed in the tower.

The style is French 13th century, and the material is reinforced concrete.

In the aisles are wall paintings by Jan De Rosen, who also painted the panels of the High Altar.

In the Chapel of Grace are a 15th-century altar and wooden reredos from the Continent. The Chapel of the Nativity has a painting by Jan De Rosen.

The organ, the gift of Mrs Harriet Crocker Alexander, was built in 1934 by the Aeolian-Skinner Company.

The windows were designed and made by Charles J. Connick of Boston, and completed by his associates after his death in 1945. His introduction to the cathedral was through the windows of the Chapel of Grace in 1929 and 1930. The three great chancel windows were undertaken next, and completed in February 1931. The south transept window was completed near the end of 1931, and another window of the choir was completed in 1932. In the spring of 1933, two clerestory windows in the east wall of the south transept: the window in the west wall of the north transept in 1934. The window in the Chapel of the Intercession was completed in 1936, and the one in the lower east wall of the south transept in 1941. Two aisle windows were inserted in 1946.

ST ANDREW'S CATHEDRAL, HONOLULU
[MISSIONARY DISTRICT]

T. N. Staley was consecrated Bishop, and came from England, with two other missionaries, in 1862, at the request of Queen Emma and King Kamehameha IV. The King had visited England before his accession, and attended services in Westminster Abbey and elsewhere; he had naturally decided that he wanted his kingdom to be Church of England.

The Bishop brought with him the plans for a cathedral by William Slater. The design was reviewed in the *Ecclesiologist* (No. CXL, June 1862): "The nave proper is three bays in length, while the western, or fourth bay, forming a species of narthex, is differently roofed from the rest of the church, and raised upon four steps. The reason for this arrangement is, that it is in fact the baptistery. . . . The internal combination of the bold single arch of the triforium and clerestory is capitally managed. The west door has a central trumeau with a flat lintel, and is entered by a stone Galilee porch. The transepts project but slightly, and are destitute of aisles. The choir terminates in a three-sided apse, with an ambulatory; and an external cloister runs round the nave. As suits the climate, the windows are few and narrow. At the west end is a small rose, while narrow couplets, widely parted, stand in each bay of the nave and aisle, and the clerestory is similarly treated, each bay being capped with a hipped dormer. The transept windows are composed of a rose and discontinuous couplet, and another discontinuous triplet stands at the east end. The choir aisles are lofty, and there is no clerestory, but a couplet in each aisle bay. The tower rises over the west end of the south aisle, and has two broad spire lights in the belfry storey. The broach is four-sided, with dormers at the base in the centre of each face, *vice* angle turrets. . . . As to the materials, from information furnished by the government surveyor, it is found that the islands afford a very good rough stone (a sort of coral rock) for general purposes, and that there are many natives who are accustomed to the working of it; but there is no stone which can be used for carving, mouldings, tracery, or ashlar walling. Accordingly, a severe early type has been chosen, which will depend for its decoration on painting. Timber is procured from Vancouver's Island. With these conditions it is obvious that the church must depend for its effect upon proportion and colour. . . ."

A pro-cathedral was built in 1866, and funds were raised for building the permanent cathedral as the result of Queen Emma's appeal to the English Royal Family and the Archbishop of Canterbury. Cut stone was sent as ballast round the Horn, and arrived late in 1865: the corner-stone was laid on 6 March 1867 by King Kamehameha V.

No more work was done until the early 80's, when Alfred Willis was Bishop. His building scheme was opposed by certain laymen, who thought the plans too ambitious, and wanted to sell the stone from England. But he had his way, and the erection of the chancel began in 1882. Queen Emma died in April 1885. By the autumn of 1886 the work had progressed so far that the Bishop and the congregation determined to worship in the new building on Christmas Day: this they were able to accomplish. Two bays of the nave were then built, and opened on 3 June 1888.

After the Hawaiian Islands had become a territory of the United States, Bishop Willis decided that the diocese should be handed over to the Episcopal Church. This was done in April 1902; the cathedral had been consecrated on 9 March. Two more bays were added in 1906–8.

In the same year, the marble high altar was erected, with money raised by Mrs Restarick, the wife of the first American Bishop. The tower was dedicated in 1912, as a memorial to Alice Macintosh, a devoted local churchwoman. The pulpit (1913) was also a memorial to her: she had been struck by the pulpit in St John's, Dresden, and wished to have it reproduced in the cathedral.

The font was a much earlier gift—from Lady Jane Franklin, who had visited Honolulu in the 50's, hoping to hear news of her husband, Sir John, the Arctic explorer, of whom nothing had been heard since 1845.

In 1954 a new floor was laid down, and the seating was renewed.

The cathedral is now (1957) being completed from plans by Carlton Winslow, A.I.A., of Beverley Hills, California. Two bays are being added, in the original style, with vestibules and a narthex of contemporary design: the entire west end, except for the doorway, will be of glass with bronze mullions: the glass is the work of the Wallis-Wiley Studio, Pasadena, California.

At the same time a steel and plaster roof is being constructed over the whole cathedral, and a new organ chamber is being made.

The general lines of Slater's design have been followed in the older parts, but with many alterations of detail, and some change of plan: the transepts and baptistery have been eliminated, and the tower has been built on the north.

The style is French Gothic, with square abaci and a minimum of mouldings.

ST MICHAEL'S CATHEDRAL, BOISE
[MISSIONARY DISTRICT OF IDAHO]

The Reverend St Michael Fackler arrived at Boise in the summer of 1864: a wooden church was completed in September 1866, and the parish was organized in August 1867. The Right Reverend Daniel S. Tuttle, first Missionary Bishop of Utah, paid a visit in October.

In 1899 the Reverend James B. Funsten was consecrated Bishop of the Missionary District of Boise (known as Idaho since 1907): he chose Boise as his residence, and St Michael's became the cathedral. Preparations for a new church had been made some years before. The ground was broken in September 1899, and the basement was completed in the winter. The contract for the superstructure was let in August 1900, and work on the interior began in 1901. The church was dedicated on 25 May 1902. The cost was $25,000, including $5,000 for the Deanery. The old wooden church was moved to a new site during that year, and renamed Christ Church.

St Michael's is of sandstone, in a simple Gothic style, cruciform, with an apsidal chancel. There are several memorial windows.

ST PAUL'S CATHEDRAL, LOS ANGELES

The diocese was organized in 1895.

The foundation stone of the present cathedral was laid on 20 May

1923, by Joseph Horsfall Johnson, Bishop from 1896 to 1928. The architects were Johnson, Kaufmann, and Coate. It is in the Italian Romanesque style, and consists of nave with a narthex and aisles, choir, and apsidal sanctuary. There are no windows on the south side, to allow for office buildings on the adjoining ground. It is constructed on a steel frame and built of manufactured stone made in Los Angeles: no natural stone is used. The floor of the nave is of Batchelder tile, made in Los Angeles; that of the sanctuary is of Escalette marble. The pillars are of marble from Minnesota; the altar is of Siena and Alabama marble. The choir stalls were made in Chicago.

The glass is the work of the Los Angeles Art Glass Company: the clerestory windows are a series of scenes in the history of the English and American Churches, ending with the laying of the foundation stone of the cathedral: the aisle windows have the arms of the first seven American dioceses.

The panels of the bishop's throne are the work of Oberammergau carvers.

There are various fragments collected by Bishop Johnson: a Roman brick from the nave of St Martin's, Canterbury; stones from St Lawrence's, Bradford-on-Avon, Westminster Abbey, Salisbury Cathedral, Hursley, Stratford-on-Avon, St Giles's, Cripplegate, St Paul's Cathedral, and St Martin-in-the-Fields; and a brick from the old church at Jamestown, Virginia. The bishop's throne contains wood from Winchester Cathedral.

TRINITY CATHEDRAL, RENO
[MISSIONARY DISTRICT OF NEVADA]

Bishop George Coolidge Hunting made plans in 1924 for building a parish church that would also be a cathedral: he died in that year. The ground was broken on 22 September 1929, and a beginning was made on the undercroft. A chapel to commemorate Bishop Hunting; the font, Joseph Cruickshank Talbot (Missionary Bishop of the North-West Diocese, 1860–5); the tower and spire, Ozi William Whitaker (Missionary Bishop of Nevada, Arizona, etc., 1869–74); the altar, Henry Douglas Robinson (Missionary Bishop of Nevada 1908–13).

(This is not listed as a cathedral in the *Episcopal Church Annual*.)

ST MARK'S CATHEDRAL, SEATTLE
[DIOCESE OF OLYMPIA]

The Jurisdiction of Olympia was formed in 1892, and it was organized as a diocese in 1910.

The building of a cathedral was first suggested by the Reverend E. V. Shayler, Rector of St Mark's, after the 1914–18 war: plans were made, and exhibited in the vestibule of the church. But in 1919 he left to be Bishop of Nebraska, and Bishop Keator died in 1924. In 1927 an attempt was made to raise funds, and to make a beginning, but the making of the plans and the preparation of the site took time, and building did not begin until 1930. The first part was ready for use by Easter 1931.

The architect was Arthur Brown of San Francisco. The original plan was for a church to consist almost entirely of the base of a large lantern tower, with a shallow nave and apse, and a suggestion of transepts. Funds ran short, owing to the depression, and all that was completed was the great central block of concrete, which was covered with a temporary roof. The parish had great difficulty in paying the interest on the mortgage, and in 1942 the bank foreclosed. The congregation moved out, the doors were boarded up, and for a while during the war the building was used by an anti-aircraft battery. In 1945 the Bishop persuaded the bank to allow the parish to reopen, and the mortgage was paid.

Steps are now being taken to complete the cathedral. New plans have been made by Young, Richardson and Carleton, and it is hoped that a beginning will soon be made on the apse.

ST STEPHEN'S CATHEDRAL, PORTLAND
[DIOCESE OF OREGON]

The diocese was organized in 1889. The cathedral is a wooden building. The previous church was destroyed by fire in 1926.

CATHEDRAL OF SS. MARY AND JOHN, MANILA [MISSIONARY DISTRICT OF THE PHILIPPINES]

The Missionary District was constituted in 1901.

The foundation stone of the cathedral was laid by Bishop Brent on

25 January 1905, and it was consecrated on 3 February 1907. The cathedral was destroyed in the Second World War.

The architect was R. Clipston Sturgis of New York. The material was reinforced concrete, and the design was based on the Mission architecture of South California. It was cruciform, with a low central dome, surmounted by a cross from the Convent of the Holy Trinity, Granada: there were two low western towers. The font, of white marble, was given by St Anne's Chapter of Domestic Missions, Church of the Heavenly Rest, New York. The pulpit was a memorial to Major John A. Logan. There were at first no stained-glass windows; all the windows were filled with mussel-shells. Bishop Brent worked out a scheme. A window, of Christ in glory, was put up over the altar, by Clayton and Bell: in 1930 two more were put up beside it, by the same firm—one a memorial to Bishop Brent, and the other to General Wood.

There are plans for building a new cathedral.

TRINITY PRO-CATHEDRAL, SACRAMENTO

The Missionary District of Northern California was organized in 1875: the name was changed to Sacramento in 1898. It was organized as a diocese in 1910.

ST JAMES'S CATHEDRAL, FRESNO
[Missionary District of San Joaquin]

St James's Mission was organized in Fresno in 1879, and a brick church was consecrated on 7 December 1884: the parish was organized in 1888. A new church was built in 1901. In 1910 Fresno became the See city of the new Missionary District of San Joaquin: St James's was made a pro-cathedral in 1911, and a cathedral in 1925. The building has recently (in 1957) been condemned, and is to be pulled down. The new cathedral will be built on a site near Fresno State College, about 6 miles away.

CATHEDRAL OF ST JOHN THE EVANGELIST, SPOKANE [Missionary District]

The Missionary District was organized in 1892. All Saints' Church was used as the cathedral—a wooden building erected in the 80's.

The site of the new cathedral was dedicated on 20 September 1925, and on 7 November the ground was broken for the first section to be built—the crypt, nave, aisles and narthex, and crossing. The foundation stone was laid on 10 June 1928: it is of local granite, inset with stones from the Mount of Olives, Glastonbury, and All Saints' Cathedral, Spokane, and a brick from the church of Jamestown, Virginia. The first portion was dedicated on 20 October 1929, when the congregations of St Peter's and St James's missions, and of All Saints', combined to form the congregation of the new cathedral. The first portion was conse- crated on 26 September 1943, and on 21 September 1948, ground was broken for the building of the eastern parts—choir, aisles, chapels, and sacristy. These were dedicated on 26 October 1952.

The tower was begun on 8 February 1951, the south transept on 24 June 1952, and the north transept in May 1953. The tower was com- pleted, and the south transept was first used, in February 1954, and the north transept was finished in September.

The architect is Harold C. Whitehouse, of the firm of Whitehouse and Price, Spokane. Fred Phair was the contractor for the first portion, and Henry George and Sons built the rest.

The exterior is of stone quaried near Tacoma, Washington, and cut by the Walker Cut Stone Co.: the interior of the nave is of sandstone from Boise, Idaho; the rest of the interior is of Indiana limestone. The carving is the work of Bernard Carrier.

The style is, generally speaking, English 15th century, but there are French flamboyant features—for instance, the western turrets, rose win- dow, and porch; and the tower, which is Perp., in outline, but with flamboyant detail.

The arcades are rather low: there is a small triforium stage, a tall clerestory (the tracery not yet complete), and a high-pitched arch-braced roof.

The glass is the work of Charles J. Connick Associates, Boston. The wood carving in the choir is by Ole Sunde of Seattle. The reredos is of Indian limestone: the five sculptured figures were carved by Archangelo Casceri of Boston.

To have built a Gothic cathedral of such size and elaboration in the 20th century is a considerable achievement, of which the Church people of Spokane are justifiably proud.

ST MARK'S CATHEDRAL, SALT LAKE CITY
[MISSIONARY DISTRICT OF UTAH]

Salt Lake City, the headquarters of the Mormons, was visited in 1864 by John Sheepshanks, then Rector of New Westminster, and afterwards Bishop of Norwich. He was asked by Brigham Young to preach at the Tabernacle, and did so. It was thought that his visit prepared the way for the sending of a bishop. In 1867 Daniel Silvester Tuttle was consecrated Missionary Bishop of Montana, Idaho, and Utah, and work began at Salt Lake City in that year. The District of Salt Lake was formed at the General Convention of 1898, and the District of Utah in 1907.

Richard Upjohn made the plans for the church, and the cornerstone was laid on 30 July 1870. The congregation moved into the basement in May 1871, and into the church in September. It was consecrated on in May 1871, and into the church in September. It was consecrated on added later. The building is of granite from the Wasatch mountains; the style is late 13th century.

The Bishop Spalding Memorial Hall was built in 1936. At present it is being completely remodelled, and joined to the cathedral by a cloister and porch. The architect is Ashley T. Carpenter of Salt Lake City.

23

Overseas Missionary Districts

BRAZIL

The Church of Southern Brazil was established in 1899 as an independent Anglican organization. In 1907 it was received into the American Church as the Missionary District of Southern Brazil. In 1949 the House of Bishops divided it into three districts: Central Brazil, Southern Brazil, and South-western Brazil.

TRINITY, PORTO ALEGRE, is the cathedral of the Missionary District of Southern Brazil.

MEDIATOR CATHEDRAL, SANTA MARIA
[MISSIONARY DISTRICT OF SOUTH-WESTERN BRAZIL]

Work began in Santa Maria—the fourth town in the State of Rio Grande do Sul—in 1900. The church was built by the efforts of the Rector, Mr Sergel: it is Gothic, and consists of nave and chancel, with a western tower. The first Bishop, the Right Reverend Egmont Machado Krischke, was consecrated in 1950, and the church became the cathedral.

HOLY TRINITY CATHEDRAL, HAVANA
[MISSIONARY DISTRICT OF CUBA]

The first recorded Anglican service was in 1762, when the English occupied Cuba for one year. In 1871 Bishop Whipple of Minnesota paid a visit, and a small mission was begun afterwards; but it had almost disappeared by the time of the Cuban War of Independence in 1895. The Missionary District was established by the General Convention in 1901, a year after Cuba became an independent republic. The first

Bishop, Albion Williamson Knight, was appointed in 1904, and the first cathedral was built by the efforts of himself and Dean Colmore. The designs were made in 1905 in the New York office of Cram, Goodhue and Ferguson: the foundation stone was laid on 10 January 1907, and it was opened on Palm Sunday 1908. The Spanish Colonial style was chosen, and the material was reinforced concrete: all was severely plain except for the front of the nave and the upper part of the tower, where "churrigueresco work was massed with great effect". Azulejos, or coloured tiles, were inserted in the cement work of the upper part of the tower.

In 1945 the site was sold: it was too noisy, and there was not enough room. The cathedral was taken down, and a new cathedral was built in the residential part of the town, together with a cathedral school and houses for the Bishop and the Dean. The old cathedral was sold for $210,000, the Bishop's House for $50,000, and the Dean's house and grounds for $54,000. $200,000 was raised from the friends of the cathedral in Havana, and a gift of $20,000 was given by the Overseas Department of the National Council in the United States. The new cathedral was consecrated on 30 November 1947.

The cathedral is the centre of missionary work in Cuba, and also a parish church serving a number of nationalities. Services are held in English and in Spanish.

TRINITY PRO-CATHEDRAL, MONROVIA
[MISSIONARY DISTRICT OF LIBERIA]

The district was established by the General Convention in 1850, and the first bishop was appointed in 1851.

The cornerstone was laid on 30 October 1853, and the church was consecrated on 22 February 1863, by Bishop Payne. The entire cost was met by the offerings of the Sunday school of St George's, New York.

This church was burned in 1874 and rebuilt afterwards, in the plainest Gothic.

SAN JOSE DE GRACIA CATHEDRAL, MEXICO
CITY [MISSIONARY DISTRICT OF MEXICO]

A small group of Christians, who had left the Roman Church, asked for a bishop in 1866. About the same time, another group of reformers

organized *La Iglesia de Jesus*. The Reverend Henry C. Riley was conse-
crated Bishop of the Valley of Mexico in 1879, and resigned in 1884.
Finally, Mexico became a Mission, the first Bishop, the Right Reverend
Henry D. Aves, being consecrated in 1904.

The old Spanish church of San Jose de Gracia was secured by Bishop
Doane in 1901: the Convent had been suppressed, and the buildings had
been turned into barracks.

It was built in 1660.

The two western bays of the nave were adapted as a school.

PRO-CATHEDRAL OF THE HOLY TRINITY, PARIS [CONVOCATION OF AMERICAN CHURCHES IN EUROPE]

The register of the Marbœuf Chapel in 1847 mentions an American
Episcopal church belonging to Colonel Thorn. In 1857 the worshippers
joined with other Americans in founding a community church in the
Rue de Berri. The first parish of the American Episcopal Church in
Paris was formed in 1858, and services were held in the Chapelle Tait-
bourt, Rue de Provence. On 24 February 1859, the congregation decided
to raise money to build a church; enough had been collected by 1863,
and the formation stone of a church in the Rue Bayard was laid on
12 September.

The Reverend John Brainerd, who became Rector in 1873, and
remained for 40 years, found that the church was becoming too small
for the congregation, and in 1880 he acquired the present site in the
new Chaillot district, just off the Champs Elysées. The church in the
Rue Bayard was sold to the Church of Scotland. Plans for the new
church were made by G. E. Street.

"Anyone who was ever in my father's office can bear witness to his
rapidity in designing; but I think a particularly good instance of his
power of conception is afforded by the American church in Paris, lately
opened. My father had been with the rector to see the site which it was
then proposed to buy, and had found it sufficiently suitable to decide in
favour of it. On his return to the rector's house, the latter asked him
whether he would be able to let them have a sketch of his design when
he had thought it out, so that intending subscribers might know to what
their money would be devoted. My father in return asked for paper,
and without further consideration made a detailed sketch to a scale of

about a twelfth of an inch to the foot. I don't remember how long he took to do it, but he was described as putting his pencil to paper with apparently no pause at all for reflection, and as fast as his hand could work. Now this sketch is, like Nasmyth's, not a mere suggestion of what might possibly be, but it practically represents the church as it stands there now. It is true that one large window has taken the place of two smaller ones in the west front, and that the tower and spire have been shifted from the south side to the north, but these are the only important modifications. Every proportion is exactly similar. The height of the church in relation to its width, the design and proportions of the tower and spire, the proportion of the whole to the site on which it stands. The artistic qualities of the sketch and the beauty of the design are obvious to the most unskilled eye; but the great point is the wonderful power of imagination which is implied in such a *tour de force* as this, and the immense self-reliance which could enable a man to bind himself, definitely, once for all, and at a moment's notice, to a design for a church, which was about the most costly parish church which he had ever to build, and was to stand in a great and splendid foreign capital as a monument of what the boasted English school of church architects could accomplish." (A. E. Street, *Memoir of George Edmund Street, R.A.*, 1888, pp. 133–4.)

The foundation stone was laid in 1881 by Bishop Littlejohn, and the church was consecrated on Thanksgiving Day 1886 by the Right Reverend T. B. Lyman, Bishop of North Carolina. The tower and spire were built in 1896, and the deanery in 1913, by A. E. Street.

Holy Trinity became a pro-cathedral in 1922, for the Convocation of American Churches in Europe. The cloisters were dedicated in 1923, as a memorial to Americans who served in the First World War.

This is an example of Street's work in its latest phase—the period of the Law Courts—when his churches no longer had "an excess of boldness or bluntness, a tinge of eccentricity, a truthfulness in displaying construction, which is too much like that of a candid friend". It is straightforward 13th century in style, with stone vaults to the aisles and chancel, and a wooden vault to the nave.

The altar piece was painted by Edwin Abbey.

1. GENERAL INDEX

2. INDEX OF ARCHITECTS, ARTISTS, CRAFTSMEN, CONTRACTORS, AND WORKMEN